IT'S GETTING
BETTER
ALL THE TIME

IT'S GETTING
BETTER
ALL THE TIME

100 Greatest Trends of the Last 100 Years

Stephen Moore and Julian Simon

CATO
INSTITUTE
Washington, D.C.

Library of Congress Cataloging-in-Publication Data

Moore, Stephen, 1960–
    It's getting better all the time: 100 greatest trends of the last 100
    years/by Stephen Moore and Julian Simon.
        p. cm.
    Includes bibliographical references and index.
    ISBN 1-882577-96-5 (cloth)–ISBN 1-882577-97-3
      1. United States—Social conditions—Statistics. 2. United States—Economic
    conditions–Statistics. I. Simon, Julian Lincoln, 1932– II. Title.

    HN60 .M665 2000
    306'.0973–dc21

                                                        00-063852

Printed in the United States of America.

Cato Institute
1000 Massachusetts Ave., N.W.
Washington, D.C. 20001
www.cato.org

Contents

List of Figures

Foreword

My children and I are very grateful to Steve Moore and the Cato Institute for pulling together one of the last of Julian's unfinished manuscripts and preparing it for publication. Since Julian died on February 8, 1998, this represents the sixth book or monograph that has already been, or will be, published after his death.

Reading this manuscript was a more complicated experience than working on or reading the other pieces, mostly because the topics discussed in this one bring back memories of the many conversations Julian and I had on these issues. Steve captures very clearly Julian's views about the 20th century, especially about the United States

Looking over the data that they have accumulated on such important indices as life expectancy, income, health care, infant mortality, and literacy, one sees that all of the trends are in a positive direction. Life expectancy, even in poor countries, increased enormously. Illiteracy fell by more than two-thirds, again even in the poor countries of the world. As recently as the 19th century, one of four children died before the age of 14. Per capita income has increased more than fivefold in the past hundred years. The 20th century was one of enormous improvements in the human condition.

I clearly recognize the soundness of the data that Steve and Julian bring to bear on their central thesis: that there was more improvement in the human condition in the 20th century than in all previous centuries, but I am still somewhat uncomfortable with the overall conclusion. I would tell Julian, you cannot ignore the fact that the 20th century was also the century that witnessed the rise of Nazism, Stalinism, and Maoism. It was the century that witnessed the death of at least 170 million people by their own governments. Nazi Germany killed more than 16 million people between 1933 and 1945, the Soviet Union killed 54.7 million between 1917 and 1987, and China killed 35.6 million between 1949 and 1987. In the 20th century at least four times as many people were killed by their own governments as were killed in wars. The accompanying table shows the number of people murdered by governments as a percentage of its total population for the 13th, 17th, 19th, and 20th centuries.

These figures, I used to argue with Julian, cannot be ignored. They are very much part of the overall 20th-century experience, and Julian would not disagree, but he would go on to emphasize that it is important to separate the United States from that experience. I would

Percentage of World Population Murdered by Governments (not including wars)	
Century	Percentage
13th	8.9
17th	4.7
19th	3.7
20th	7.3

SOURCE: Gerald W. Scully, "Murder by the State," National Center for Policy Analysis no. 211, September 1997, p. 7, http://www.ncpa.org/studies/s211/s211html.

mostly agree with that, but I would also argue that some groups and whole communities of people, including those living in the United States, cannot think about the 20th century without strong negative feelings, deep apprehensions, and a good deal of pain. For example, even American Jews, who certainly by the last quarter of the 20th century had come to recognize that the age in which they were living was the "Golden Age" of Jews, overshadowing 13th-century Spain, the earlier golden age in Jewish history, would have trouble acknowledging the 20th century in the positive terms with which it is characterized in the following pages. So would Gypsies, Armenians, and others. So, Julian, please, please exercise some moderation.

Having said that, I must also emphasize that, of all the people I have known in my professional life, no one had more respect for data than did Julian. No one emphasized the importance of ferreting out sound and reliable data from bogus data and junk science. No one recognized the difference, and the importance of the difference, between a "blip" and a long-term trend.

Over dinner, when the children were between six and eight years old, they would ask such questions as, How many people live in New York City? Julian would respond with a series of questions such as, What do you mean by live in New York? For example, do you include people who work in New York but don't live there? What do you mean by New York City, the five boroughs, or other areas? From such conversations our children came to understand the concept of the operational definition.

In his autobiography (another manuscript waiting to be published) Julian writes about an issue that I think is also pertinent here, because it again emphasizes his respect for data. When Julian decided, in about 1965, to venture forth into new areas of research, he thought about what were major problems facing the world and how he might contribute to resolving them. Several topics came to mind, but Julian opted to begin reading about human population, with the aim of contributing to the growing literature on the problems of overpopulation. He assumed that the pundits who were warning about the dangers of overpopulation—using such phrases as "the population bomb," "the population explosion," and "the likelihood of mass starvation," especially in the less economically developed countries of the world—were right and knew what they were talking about. He assumed that they had done sound scientific studies and were reporting conclusions based on those studies. He assumed that, when Paul Ehrlich, a biologist at Stanford, advocated putting something into our water system that would prevent women from getting pregnant, he was doing so because he had accumulated solid, valid data. Julian read and studied the population literature for more than two years. When he finished he concluded that there was no population bomb and that human beings are our "ultimate resource." There are no sound data that show that population growth or density explains poverty. Indeed, Julian came to see that, if you compare countries of similar ethnic communities and population density, it is not those factors, but the type of government, that explains why, for example, South Korea is much more prosperous than North Korea, West Germany was more prosperous than East Germany, and Taiwan is more prosperous than the People's Republic of China. More and more analyses led Julian to conclude that population growth does not account for economic development but that a country's political and economic structures do influence it heavily. As Julian continued to analyze studies of many different countries, he found a consistent lack of correlation between the country's rate of population growth and its rate of economic development.

So, even though I have reservations about describing the 20th century in the positive terms used in this book and believe it is crucial to emphasize over and over again that the data describe primarily the United States, I also recognize the validity and the importance of bringing together this enormous collection of long-term trends that do show significant improvements in the human material condition. It is important to have readily and conveniently available sound data on important long-term social trends.

RITA J. SIMON

Preface

In February 1998 Julian Simon died of a heart attack at the age of 65. Julian had been my mentor from the time we met at the University of Illinois in 1980—where he taught economics and I was an undergraduate student and then his research assistant. In 1983 we came to Washington together and I worked as his research assistant for the next several years. He was my mentor. After that we worked on and off together on projects for the next decade. At the time of his death, he and I had been well under way in collaborating on writing this book. In fact, he had just finished editing a preliminary first draft.

I'll take credit for the idea. I had gone to Julian and told him to take all his great material over the years (he wrote dozens of books and hundreds of scholarly articles) and construct a kind of index of human progress in the form of a book of charts that are easy to read and digest. I thought it might be particularly marketable if it were timed with the start of the new millennium. He said, great idea, let's do it together. (You can imagine how flattering that was.) Julian was a fanatic about collecting some of the most unusual data and statistics, and so his files that we plowed through together were a treasure chest of information on long-term trends on everything from life expectancy to the speed of the microchip. Julian was a fervent believer that the best predictor of the future was the past and that the best way to measure the past was to get the longest-term data possible to detect the real trend lines.

After Julian died the project went into hibernation for more than a year. Without Julian prodding me along and without his input, it languished. In late 1999 Cato published a preliminary version of the book in the form of a study titled "The 25 Greatest Trends of the 20th Century." That study received such an enthusiastic response that I was inspired to complete the book. (Julian's family was very supportive of finishing it too.) The book will serve as a handy and abbreviated compilation of many of his best ideas. The tragedy is that this book could have been so much better if Julian had lived.

Acknowledgments

I would like to thank the following people for helping produce this book. Many of them work at the Cato Institute. Stephen Slivinski and Phil Kerpen contributed countless hours creating all of the charts and tables. Jason Ziegler and Dave Miller provided assistance with the endnotes. David Boaz, Cato's executive vice president, reviewed the manuscript and provided invaluable editorial advice. Cato's president Ed Crane gave us an enthusiastic go-ahead to the project and agreed to publish it as a Cato book. The administrative assistance of Terri LaBonte, who put in long hours during the production process, is gratefully appreciated. I am grateful to Ed Hudgins for his advice on the section on transportation and communications.

Rita Simon offered valuable suggestions on the first drafts of the manuscript. Rita, along with David, Judith, and Daniel Simon, offered crucial moral encouragement to complete the book during stages when it seemed to be floundering. Allison Moore also provided sanity in the Moore household during the chaotic last stages of the book. Helen Demarest helped organize of all of Julian's writings and files.

I drew heavily on the work of several scholars, who deserve special mention. The sections on the American economy include incredibly valuable material first collected by economist Michael Cox of the Dallas Federal Reserve Bank and journalist Richard Alm. I highly recommend to readers their 1998 book titled *Myths of Rich and Poor*, which is a treasure trove of astonishing statistics on the U.S. economy and workforce.

I obtained many of our facts and data on race in America from the book by Stephan and Abigail Thernstrom, *America in Black and White*. The book, too, is chock full of data on and analysis of racial differences in America.

Another invaluable book is *Women's Figures*, by Diana Furchtgott-Roth and Christine Stolba, both of the American Enterprise Institute. The section of the present book on sexual equality was heavily influenced by that work.

The section on the environment was influenced by the Pacific Research Institute's *Index of Leading Environmental Indicators*, a monograph by Steven Hayward, Erin Schiller, and Elizabeth Fowler.

Those closely familiar with Julian's writings will find many of the graphs in this book familiar. In particular, Julian's 1995 book, *The State of Humanity*, is a much longer and more scholarly version of this book. For those who wish to do further reading on the improvement in the human condition over the centuries, we also recommend Julian's book *The Ultimate Resource II.* Wherever possible I have updated the statistics through 1999. (In almost all cases the updated numbers show continued progress.)

STEPHEN MOORE

2000

Introduction

"We step upon the threshold of 1900 . . . facing a brighter
dawn of civilization."
—*New York Times*, January 1, 1900

"If you had to describe the century's geopolitics in one
sentence, it could be a short one: Freedom won. Free minds and
free markets prevailed over fascism and communism."
—Walter Isaacson, *Time*, December 31, 1999

The Greatest Moment on Earth

The central premise of this book is that there has been more
improvement in the human condition in the past 100 years than in
all of the previous centuries combined since man first appeared on
the earth. This premise no doubt seems highly doubtful to many
readers. After all, every day we are bombarded with bad news:
AIDS, toxic waste, school shootings, homelessness, declining test
scores, global warming, a widening wealth gap between the rich
and poor, and so on. Yet over the course of the 20th century, almost
every measure of material human welfare—ranging from health,
wealth, nutrition, education, speed of transportation and communications, leisure time, gains for women, minorities, and children to
the proliferation of computers and the Internet—has shown wondrous
gains for Americans. Although the rest of the world lags behind the
United States in most measures of material well-being, almost
everywhere the same trend of improvement is evident. In fact, the
objective long-term trend of improved living standards for all of
humanity, but particularly for those living in the United States
since 1900, has no precedent.

In his best-selling book on the new global economy, *The Lexus
and the Olive Tree*, Pulitzer prize–winning journalist Thomas
Friedman describes the driving force behind human action at this
stage of history. He writes that people around the globe are pretty
much all pursuing the same goal: "the basic human desire for a better
life: a life with more choices as to what to eat, what to wear, where
to live, where to travel, how to work, what to read, what to write,
and what to learn." The United States in the 20th century became
the first nation on earth to achieve these choices for the vast majority

1

of her citizens. What is exciting about life on earth today is that with each passing year these same choices are now being offered to a more prosperous world citizenry.

We are particularly heartened by the spread of freedom and democracy across the globe over the past several decades. Although huge progress in this area is still yet to be achieved, human beings in most parts of the world are more liberated from government tyranny than ever before in history and thus freer to reach their full human potential.

Most Americans do not fully appreciate how truly fortunate they are to live in the midst of this most amazing time. As the work on this book was being completed, two newspaper stories underscored how good life is at this particular moment on earth. The first was the story of thousands of young people protesting in Washington, D.C., against the World Bank and the International Monetary Fund. It was a stark reminder of how affluent and relatively crisis-free our lives are today. The only thing that young and restless students could find to protest against was two relatively inconsequential organizations. The source of their anger was "globalization." Never mind that globalization is raising living standards around the world. The point is that today (less than ever before) humanity is not plagued with the horrible forces of the past that our ancestors lived in constant terror of: war, genocide, starvation, slavery, or disease. These are good times indeed, when the young feel that their greatest threat in life is the World Bank.

The second story appeared over the Associated Press newswire. It noted that one of the hottest selling grocery items in the United States today is gourmet pet food. The story also noted that one of the challenging nutritional problems in our country today is obesity—not in people, but in our pets. "Our dogs and cats are eating themselves to death," a veterinarian was quoted as saying. These are nice things to worry about. It was not always like this. Throughout most of human history the main challenge in life was getting enough to eat—for ourselves and our families, not our pets.

In 1933 the Chicago World's Fair was aptly titled "The Century of Progress." More has been invented in the past 100 years than the previous 1,000. In fact, most of human history has been one prolonged era of non-progress. From the time man first walked on the earth through about 1700, the improvements in human life were minute. Yes, there were periodic major discoveries: fire, agriculture, water power, and the wheel. Yet from generation to generation the gains

2

in living standards were imperceptible. Human population grew slowly because death rates often exceeded birth rates. (The population growth that so many worry about today is mostly a sign of our increasing effectiveness at conquering death.) "It is not uncommon," wrote Adam Smith in *The Wealth of Nations*, "in the highlands of Scotland for a mother who has borne 20 children not to have 2 alive."

Anthropologists inform us that for thousands of years the average human being could expect to live about 25 to 30 years. Although there has been great variability in the economic rates of growth among nations, historians tell us that the average global per capita income in today's dollars was a bit more than $200 a year. Queen Elizabeth once famously described England as containing "paupers, paupers, everywhere." The average speed of movement and communications throughout the ages was about 3 to 5 miles per hour and top speeds (on horseback) were no more than 30 miles per hour. In Europe doing the Middle Ages it could take months for word to spread that the Pope had died. (Now news travels instantaneously around the world because of the Internet and CNN.) Literacy rates were far below 10 percent. For the vast majority of the world's residents, life on earth truly was, as Thomas Hobbes depressingly described it, "nasty, brutish and short."

But starting in the mid-18th century with the dawning of the industrial age, the first flickers of real sustainable progress emerged. (The worst forecast of all time was made in 1798 by Thomas Malthus when he predicted unending misery for the mass of humankind forever.) The gains were even more momentous throughout the 19th century, following efficiency-rendering inventions such as the steam engine, electricity, the automobile, rubber production, the rotary printing press, the sewing machine, and the stove, to name a few. But even by 1900 and even in the richer nations such as the United States, most people were very poor by today's standards, and most still faced death at an early age. If the 19th century recorded impressive strides in the march toward greater prosperity, production, and health, the 20th century produced majestic quantum leaps in the quality of life.

The following figures attempt to dramatize the extent of these quantum-leap improvements in human well-being. We choose three measures that indicate this advancement: life expectancy, per capita income, and speed of communications. Notice that the gains have been almost vertical since the late 19th century. What readers will discover later in these pages is that almost all other objective measures of living standards show almost precisely the same J-shaped curve. We believe that the most impressive accomplishment of all has been the increase in human life spans. Consider that in the United States (and other industrialized nations) life expectancy is now about 75, or triple the historical rate. Life expectancy has increased so rapidly that *San Francisco Chronicle* columnist Jon Carroll recently quipped that "Americans have come to view death as optional."

Measures of Progress during the Millennium, 1000–2000 (stylized)

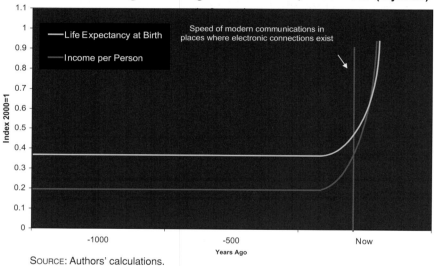

SOURCE: Authors' calculations.

Even in poor countries life expectancy has risen at an astonishing pace. In China, people in 1750 on average could expect to live to their late twenties; by 1985 Chinese people typically were living to their sixties. Now, most of humanity enjoy better health and longevity than the richest people in the richest countries did just 100 years ago.

Still unconvinced? Let us try to draw a mental picture of what life was like as recently as 100 years ago. The 19th century that was just ending was an era of tuberculosis, typhoid, sanitariums, child labor, child death, horses, horse manure, candles (still), 12-hour workdays, Jim Crow laws, tenements, slaughter houses, and outhouses.

4

Lynchings were common occurrences back then, and not just of blacks. (In the South, 11 Italians were lynched in the span of a month.) To live to 50 was to count one's blessings. For a mother to have all four of her children live to adulthood was to dramatically beat the odds of nature. About one in four American children in the 19th century perished before the age of 14. One hundred years ago parents lived in fear of their child's dying; nowadays, middle-class suburban parents live in fear of their child's not making the county select soccer team.

Industrial cities typically were enveloped in clouds of black soot and smoke. At this stage of the industrial revolution, factories belched poisons into the air—and this was proudly regarded as a sign of prosperity and progress. Streets were smelly and garbage-filled before the era of modern sewage systems and plumbing. (The automobile was hailed as one of the greatest pro-environment inventions in history because of the improvements over the filth associated with horses.) In 1918–19 the great influenza pandemic killed more than 700,000 Americans and between 20 million and 100 million more around the globe. In the first two decades of the 20th century, before the era of acid rain and global warming, pollution killed people—lots and lots of people. Deadly diseases were carried by milk and what then qualified as "drinking water." Cancer was not the primary cause of death as it is today because most Americans were doomed by infectious diseases and occasional epidemics before they lived long enough for their bodies to contract this degenerative disease.

Medical care was astonishingly primitive by today's standards. Abraham Flexner, writing in the famous Flexner report on medical education in 1910, commented that up until then, a random patient consulting a random physician only had a 50–50 chance of benefiting from the encounter. Health historian Dr. Theodore Dalrymple notes that up until the late 19th century it was often considered "beneath a physician's dignity to actually examine a patient." Most of the drugs used throughout the ages—including arsenic, which was still used up through the early 1900s—were useless and in many cases poisonous. Oliver Wendell Holmes supposedly once declared that if all of the drugs in his time were tossed into the ocean it would be better for mankind and worse for the fish.

The modern and ubiquitous amenities that make life more livable today were just gleams in the imaginations of forward-looking 19th century Americans. In 1900 H. G. Wells was writing prophetic futuristic prose about life 100 years hence in which he envisioned washing machines, electric ovens, and "miracle kitchens." In the early decades of the century wonder inventions began to appear for the first time in American homes: telephones, phonographs, canned foods, ice boxes. Edison's light bulb was just starting to become a basic household fixture, notwithstanding the *New York Times*'s warning that electric light could cause blindness. In 1903 the Wright Brothers' plane sputtered off the ground for less than 30 seconds and the modern transportation age was officially launched. Ford's model T (in any color that you wanted as long as it was black) began to roll off assembly lines, though for the wealthy who owned one there were less than a few hundred miles of paved roads to drive on. And even up through the 1920s, there were more horses than cars for transportation.

More than two-thirds of blacks and senior citizens lived in poverty. Most Americans who are considered "poor" today have routine access to a quality of housing, food, health care, consumer products, entertainment, communications, and transportation that even the Vanderbilts, the Carnegies, the Rockefellers, and the 19th century European princes, with all their wealth, could not have afforded. No mountain of gold 100 years ago could have purchased the basics of everyday life that middle-income Americans take for granted in 1999: a television set, vaccination against polio, a Haagen Dazs ice-cream bar, a sinus tablet, contact lenses (to say nothing of laser surgery), or the thrill of seeing Michael Jordan majestically soar through the air as if defying gravity while dunking a basketball. Today, almost all Americans can afford these things.

So why is it that after so many centuries of almost imperceptible human advancement has so much progress been compressed into the historical nanosecond of the 20th century? We believe that three relatively modern inventions have revolutionized human life. The first is electric power. Invented in 1873, electricity only started to become widely available in homes and factories in the early decades of this century. The magic of electric power not only brought us literally out of the darkness but also launched thousands of inventions, all of which have enabled humankind to begin to harness the forces of nature and thus improve nearly every aspect of our daily lives.

The second engine of progress has been modern drugs and vaccines. Just one of these wonder drugs alone, penicillin, has saved more lives in the past 50 years than all of the medical treatment and medicines before 1900. As Henry Sigerist wrote in *Civilization and Disease* in 1942, "Bacteria, our chief enemies once they were firmly entrenched in the body, seemed resistant against chemicals—until Nobel prize-winning bacteriologist Gerhard Domagk discovered the action of the drug prontosil, later to be developed and known as sulfanilamide. This was . . . only yesterday, and in the last few years dozens of highly effective sulfa drugs have been prepared."

Progress in the fight against the AIDS virus in recent years is but the latest demonstration of the awesome intellectual power that humanity can now muster against threats to our well-being. Or consider diabetes: If your child had diabetes 100 years ago, you had to watch helplessly as the child went blind and died early. Now injections, even pills, can give the child almost as long and healthy a life as other children.

The final transforming invention was the microchip. As the brains of the computer, the semiconductor has been mankind's passport to a whole new universe of knowledge. The average American worker with a Pentium-chip laptop computer has more computing power at his fingertips than was contained in all of the computers in the entire world during World War II. One hundred years ago, all of the greatest mathematicians in the world together did not have the problem-solving skills of a fourth-grader with a $39.99 Texas Instruments pocket calculator.

In this book we attempt to chronicle the improvements in human life in those and other areas over the past 100 years (or longer in cases where reliable comparative data exist). Below we briefly summarize some of the most glorious indicators of human progress.

Health: Throughout the centuries human existence has been primarily a struggle against early death. In the past 100 years that struggle has been largely won. The death rate of children under the age of 15 has fallen by 95 percent since 1900 in the United States. Parents should reflect long and hard on that statistic whenever they think life isn't treating them well these days. The child death rates in just the past 20 years have incredibly been halved in India, Egypt, Indonesia, Brazil, Mexico, Chile, South Korea, Israel, and scores of other nations. Almost all of the major killer diseases before 1900—tuberculosis, typhoid, smallpox, whooping cough, polio, malaria, to name a few—have been all but eradicated.

Nutrition: Nutrition and diets have been improving the world over. D. Gale Johnson, an agricultural economist at the University of Chicago, has discovered that fewer people worldwide died from famine in the 20 century than in the 19th century—not just as a percentage of the population, but in *absolute* numbers. That is a spectacular achievement in our ability to feed the planet, given that the world population is some four times higher today than 100 years ago. Malthus and his doomsday disciples suffered a terrible century. The price of food relative to our wages is now about 10 to 20 percent what it was in the 19th century. After spending 100,000 years trying to get enough calories, mankind is now trying to consume fewer. Even in China, where hunger and starvation has been a routine of life for centuries, the fastest growing nutritional problem is now obesity. In the United States, American agriculture is so extraordinarily productive that the agricultural policy challenge in Washington, D.C., is to try to get farmers to grow less food.

Children: The plight of children in the 19th century would make any modern social worker wince. About half of all children lived in poverty versus about 20 percent today; death before the age of five was not uncommon; and childhood ended at a very young age. Almost all teen-agers were in factories or fields, not in school. Child labor, though on the decline, was still generally considered necessary in factories and fields. According to a 19th century story retold recently by newspaper columnist Robert Samuelson, a boy of 19 earned a promotion to supervisor because he had already worked at the textile factory for 11 years.

Incomes: We live in the wealthiest society in the history of the planet. Throughout most of the past millennium, real incomes in Europe and North America were virtually stagnant, according to renowned economic historian Angus Maddison. In the 19th century, economic growth rates began to trend upward due to the industrial revolution. But the real steep gains in incomes were recorded over the course of the 20th century. Since 1900 real per capita incomes in the United States have grown at roughly a 2 percent annual rate, which may not sound too impressive until one realizes that this growth rate translated into a quadrupling in real per capita living standards in just 100 years. Many third-world nations—although still quite poor by U.S. standards—have increased their per capita incomes more than fivefold since 1900.

Poverty: Economic historians estimate that by today's standards, about half of the U.S. population lived in poverty up through the early 19th century. For blacks about three out of four households were poor versus about one in four today. The overall poverty rate is about 15 percent. The biggest reduction in poverty has been for blacks, women, children, and the elderly. A family living at the U.S. poverty level today has an income that is about three times higher than the average per capita income for the world. Most poor families today own a car, a colored television set, a VCR, and a microwave oven. They also consume more calories than those in wealthy families.

Work: Before 1900 almost all work was pure drudgery. Women often faced 70 hours a week of housework. (One of the most ludicrous fictions of the past is that mothers stayed home with children and thus "didn't have to work.") Factory work 100 years ago was low paying (by today's standards), dangerous (the job-related accident and death rates were many multiples higher than today), physically exhausting, and monotonous. The average factory wage back then was only about half of what is regarded as a poverty wage today. Almost two-thirds of all black women worked as household servants. On the farm, workweeks were even longer and the toil was even greater. In the middle of the 19th century, American farmers were still using spade and hoe. At the beginning of the 20th century, agriculture was not propelled by John Deere or Caterpillar tractors but by horse and mule. A farmer in the 19th century could produce in an hour of work just one one-hundredth of what his counterpart is capable of growing and harvesting today.

Recreation and Leisure: An affluent society has disposable income for recreation, sports, eating out, and other nonessentials that make life fun and entertaining. The single fastest major expenditure for Americans (other than taxes) has been for recreation. Today, the average U.S. household spends about 10 times as much on recreation as it did in 1900 and about 3 times as much as it did in 1950. Americans have 3 times more leisure time over the course of their lifetimes than their great-grandparents did.

Housing: In 1900 less than one in five homes had running water, flush toilets, a vacuum cleaner, or gas or electric heat. As of 1950 fewer than 20 percent of homes had air conditioning, a dishwasher, a dryer, or a microwave oven. Now between 80 and 100 percent have all of these conveniences. The homeownership rate has soared from 40 percent in the first half of the 20th century to more than 85 percent today.

9

Transportation: In 1900 there were more horses than cars for transportation and only a few hundred miles of paved roads. Today, 90 percent of American households own a car and motor some 2.6 trillion miles a year—which is the equivalent of driving to the moon 10 million times. In addition, safety has improved with increased travel. Many Americans have a phobia about air travel. However, based on the past decade's safety performance, if you flew one commercial flight per day, on average you could fly 21,000 years before dying in a crash, according to *Consumers' Research Magazine*.

The Computer Age: According to Hewlett-Packard's R. Stanley Williams, "The first computer, the ENIAC, was commissioned in 1946. ENIAC contained 14,786 vacuum tubes, weighed 60,000 pounds, and occupied 16,000 cubic feet. The amount of energy ENIAC expended to compute a single-shell trajectory was comparable to the explosive discharge to actually fire the shell." In 1949 *Popular Mechanics* magazine proudly announced that someday a computer would exist that would require just 1,500 vacuum tubes and would weigh just more than a ton. Today, a $999 laptop computer has more computing power than was available to all nations during World War II. A high school student can perform calculations in a few minutes that once would have taken a whole mathematics faculty weeks to solve. Twenty-five years ago almost no homes had computers; today more than half do.

Education: In 1900 only about 1 in 10 children went to high school. That is a figure so low that it would be an embarrassment even to a poor country today. Now in the United States more than 9 in 10 do. Illiteracy has fallen by more than two-thirds in the United States and even by a greater percentage in poor nations.

Environment: American cities are far healthier today—in terms of both water and air. Smog levels have declined by about 40 percent, and carbon monoxide is down nearly one-third since the 1960s even though there are nearly twice as many cars. Some of the most impressive advances in reducing air pollution have been recorded in the dirtiest cities, including Los Angeles, Pittsburgh, and Chicago. Airborne lead is down more than 90 percent from 40 years ago. Contaminated drinking water caused hundreds of thousands of deaths annually 100 years ago versus very few deaths today.

Natural Resources: By any measure, natural resources have become more available rather than scarcer. Consider copper, which is representative of all the metals. The cost of a ton is only about a tenth of what it was 200 years ago. There is evidence that oil—the most worrisome of resources because it is a depletable resource and therefore cannot be recycled—has actually been getting cheaper to produce. On the one hand, the falling price of oil throughout the 20th century was proof that the overall cost of obtaining oil had to be falling. On the other hand, wells were being drilled deeper and deeper, which called into question whether the physical production costs were rising in some important parts of the industry. But industry data reported in *Business Week* show that the worldwide production cost per barrel has been falling since 1980. So not only is more oil being found, it is getting cheaper and not more expensive to find.

The Status of Women and Minorities: In December 1900 Booker T. Washington wrote in the *Atlanta Journal*: "I pray that the white people in every part of this country will bear in mind that they cannot oppress the Negro without the white race becoming degraded." One of the most heartening findings in this book is that the gains we found for all Americans have tended to be most pronounced for women and blacks. Gaps on the basis of sex and race are narrowing, not widening. The average wage for black men was about 30 to 40 percent of the white man's wage (versus about 70 percent today.) In the 19th century women who were permitted to work outside the home (the average homemaker worked 70 hours a week doing household chores) earned about half of a man's salary, versus at least 80 to 90 percent today. To attend high school was rare for women and blacks; college was almost exclusively the birthright of rich, privileged white males.

How Freedom Promotes Progress

We focus in this book primarily on the experience of the United States, because in our view it has been clearly on these shores that the eruption of progress and invention has been singularly most impressive. (It is also more feasible to obtain reliable time series data for the United States.) "In the 20th century, America led in virtually everything," *The Economist* magazine recently noted, "growth, productivity and incomes, new products and new processes, applying new indeas first or most effectively even if it did not invent them." We sometimes forget that at the start of the century, per capita incomes were higher in the United Kingdom and even Australia than in the United States. By the end of the century, U.S. incomes were substantially higher than in those two nations. In addition, U.S. industry had grown so internationally dominant that the United States is now recognized as the sole global economic and military superpower.

The obvious query is, Why? Why did so much of the progress of the past 100 years originate in the United States? Our shorthand answer is, Freedom works. The unique American formula of individual liberty and free enterprise has cultivated risk taking, experimentation, innovation, and scientific exploration on a grand scale that has never occurred anywhere before.

Economic freedom and freedom from government repression, in particular, are necessary ingredients for human progress. In the United States, for the most part and at least more than nearly anywhere else of consequence on the globe, the government has set down a reasonable rule of law, providing a well-balanced equilibrium between liberty and order, and then gotten out of the way. In the post–World War II period when Europe, America's closest economic rival, experimented with socialism in the west and totalitarianism in the east, the United States wisely continued to pursue free-market capitalism, thus widening the U.S. lead in economic prosperity.

We would add to this that the United States enjoys a unique advantage over other nations because it is a nation that remakes itself through the new blood of immigrants. The tens of millions of new Americans who came through Ellis Island or across the Rio Grande have represented the cream of the rest of the world. Americans are self-selected problem solvers and progress seekers.

Historians used to speculate that one main reason the United States became so wealthy so quickly was that the North American continent is so richly endowed in natural resources. Indeed, it is. Alexis de Tocqueville once described America as "the noblest habitation prepared by God for man." But at least for the latter half of the 20th century, natural resources have had little to do with America's bountiful economic growth. Almost all progress since 1950 has been a result of the human intellect, not resources dug from the earth. (Russia is a nation that is one of the richest in the world in natural resources. However, few places on earth experienced less improvement during the 20th century.)

America got rich at such a faster pace than other nations in the 20th century quite simply because no other place on earth cultivates the entrepreneurial, inventive spirit of human beings more than the United States does. Government has grown enormously over the past century in the United States, much more than we believe is optimal, but compared with other nations and with the heavy hand of government that restricted individual freedom in past eras (about one-half the world's population was slave or serf), Americans today enjoy an unprecedented degree of political and economic freedom. This provides Americans with the ability and the incentive to build, create, innovate, and prosper.

The tragedy of the past 100 years is that humankind has had to relearn the lesson of history again and again—most recently in the former Soviet Union where life expectancies have tragically fallen and in China where tens of millions have starved to death under collectivist agricultural policies—that repression by government short-circuits the human spirit and produces sustained periods of stagnation and even anti-progress. The figure shows a strong positive relationship between economic freedom and economic prosperity. The free countries are the rich countries. Over the past 30 years the freest nations have had the fastest economic growth rate: about 2.5 percent per year per capita. The least free nations have actually had negative growth rates over that same period. This connection between economic freedom and growth may seem intuitively obvious. The figure also shows that health and freedom go hand in hand. Life expectancies are 21 years longer for those born in free nations than for those born in non-free nations.

Free Countries Are Wealthier and Healthier

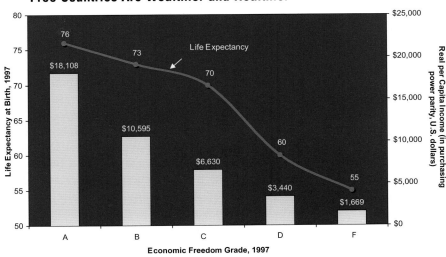

SOURCES: DKT International; James Gwartney and Robert Lawson, *Economic Freedom of the World 2000;* and World Bank, *1999 World Development Indicators.*

Annual Average Growth Rate of GDP during the 1990s

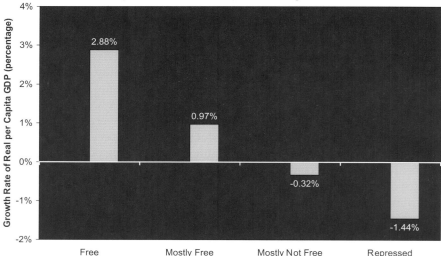

SOURCE: Gwartney and Lawson.

Skeptics have challenged this conclusion. These skeptics argue that the United States has experienced gains because it has more government now than 100 years ago. David Corn of the *Nation* writes that Simon and Moore:

> . . .credit free enterprise for our 20th century success, and cite an increase in the size of government as one of the few negative trends of the past 10 decades. But if one thinks about their list of positive trends for a moment, Cato's view—government bad/commerce good—is undermined. The air, [Simon and Moore] say, is 97 percent cleaner. But it was government agencies, such as the Environmental Protection Agency, that forced polluting companies to clean up. Wages are up since 1900. No credit is given to the minimum wage laws that fuel wage growth. . . . Deaths from infectious diseases are down. Let's give credit to public health measures. . . . Accidental deaths are down, yet they have never cheered the Occupational Safety and Health Administration and workplace safety standards. The income of African-Americans has increased ten-fold. But would they be that high if it had not been for affirmative action? . . .

There are kernels of truth here. And we are not arguing that all government regulation is unwise. For example, we are not opposed to wise environmental laws and applaud the achievement of a more colorblind society. But to maintain that government rules and agencies yielded the tremendous gains of the past century is to fundamentally misunderstand history and the engine of progress. Albert Einstein and Thomas Edison were not creatures of the government. Government did not build the Model T or invent the microchip.

Income gains were most impressive long before there was such a thing as a minimum wage and, if anything, wages have grown more slowly since the advent of the minimum wage. Occupational safety was improving for decades long before there was an Occupational Safety and Health Administration (see Section XIII on occupational accidents). Most of the great advances in medicine over the past century have been privately financed and developed. Government regulation of the drug industry creates lengthy delays in life-saving medical treatments. Milton Friedman believes that the Food and Drug Administration's regulations have led to a net loss of human life. African-American incomes rose steadily long before affirmative action and even the civil rights movement. What we are saying is that nations with a heavier burden of regulation, more obese welfare states, and higher tax rates have developed far more slowly than we have. Nations that have tried to use central planning as a formula for creating prosperity have been miserable failures.

It is true that we now have lots of prosperity and lots of government, but the government has been a consequence, not the cause of our economic growth. We devote unprecedented amounts of resources today to health, environmental protection, and safety, precisely because we are an affluent and productive society. But when government gets too big and intrusive, it can kill the goose of private enterprise that lays the golden eggs. Nobel prize–winning economist Amartya Sen reminds us in his latest book, *Development as Freedom*, that "the expansion of freedom is both the primary end and . . . principal means of development." We agree.

Most important of all, almost every great tragedy of the 20th century has been a result of too much government, not too little. As the table shows, Nazism, socialism, communism, Marxism, and apartheid were all simply fancy names for statism—for unreasonable government control over the lives and liberties of the citizenry. F. A. Hayek, winner of the Nobel prize in economics, recognized that socialism and Nazism were simply mirror-image forms of tyranny. The result of these experiments, almost always applauded by the intelligentsia, has been untold human suffering. This has been a great century, yes. But Hitler killed 6 million Jews and other Eastern Europeans in the Holocaust; Mao murdered an estimated 30 to 40 million people; Stalin's purges account for the extermination of between 20 and 60 million people; the killing fields of Cambodia held roughly 2 million bodies. The enduring lesson of the 20th century is that the only real restraint on progress is a government that smothers the human spirit.

The Death Toll from Statism
(civilians killed by governments, excluding war)

China (communist)	35 million
Germany (total, 20th century)	21 million
The Holocaust (1938–1945)	6 million
Soviet Union (total, 20th century)	62 million
Stalinist Purges (1930–1938)	20–60 million (est.)
Cambodia (1975–1979)	1–2 million

SOURCES: David Wallechinsky, *The People's Almanac Presents the Twentieth Century* (New York: Little, Brown, and Company, 1995); and "Statistics of Democide," by Rudy J. Rummel, as cited in *The Economist* magazine.

Are There Limits to Growth?

The record of humanity shows that, on average, each generation creates a bit more than they consume. Not only must this be true to account for the increase in our wealth and numbers, but if it were not—if we consumed a bit more than we created, and our assets deteriorated like an often patched tire deteriorates until it is no longer useful—we simply would have become extinct as a species. The essential condition of fitness for survival of our species is that each generation creates a net surplus on average, or at least breaks even. Since we have survived and increased, this condition must have been present.

The question then immediately arises: Must not we, like other species, cease our growth when we have filled up our niche—that is, reached the limit of the available resources? One cannot answer this question with assurance, of course, because with each increase of wealth and numbers, we proceed into a situation with which we have no prior experience.

But as can be seen in the evidence of the increasing availability of natural resources throughout history as measured by their declining prices—especially food, metals, and energy—there

16

apparently is no fixed limit on our resources in the future. There are limits at any moment, but the limits continually expand, and constrain us less with each passing generation. In this, we are quite unlike all other animals. The great 19th century economist Henry George once wrote the following parable about the uniqueness of the human species as a net resource creator: "Both the jayhawk and the man eat chickens, but the more jayhawks the fewer chickens, while the more men, the more chickens."

The pessimists wonder whether our present glorious age is just another blip in history, like the Egyptian, Persian, and Roman empires and the Golden Age of Greece. The doubters ask why we should believe that the progress we have experienced since 1750 is an irreversible breakthrough. They suggest that we simply may be living through an episode of glory that will soon be eclipsed, as were previous Roman, Greek, and Chinese civilizations.

We doubt it. The advanced civilization that we are now living through is different from those of earlier times. Ours is the first age in which affluence has been enjoyed by more than just a tiny fraction, typically just 5 or 10 percent, of the population. In other great empires, at least 90 percent of the populace remained at a Malthusian level of subsistence existence. Never before have quality of life improvements been spread to virtually every segment of the population as has happened in the United States in this century.

A second reason we are optimistic is that unlike previous eras of progress, the gains that have been made in the 20th century are truly irreversible because they are primarily the result of the wondrous advances in the storehouse of human knowledge that have accumulated in this century. That knowledge can never be erased even if barbarians or Luddites were to burn every library to the ground. Encyclopedias of knowledge can now be stored on a $10 computer disk. If, God forbid, a bomb were to destroy all the physical capital and infrastructure of the United States, they could be rebuilt in a generation provided people were still around to do the rebuilding. (Consider how quickly Germany was resurrected after World War II.) Moreover, the information age makes it more futile than ever for a repressive government, like the former Soviet Union, to try to restrain freedom through military might, as many did in previous eras.

Finally, we are convinced that 20th century progress has not been a mere historical blip but rather the start of a long-term trend of improved life on earth, because even poor nations are making spectacular strides in health, education, incomes, and equality. India's and China's per capita incomes, for example, have more than doubled in just the past 30 years. That is to say, income gains have been more dramatic in China and India in the past 30 years than in the previous 3,000 years. Our prediction is that within the next 50 years most people in the world will attain an income level similar to that of the middle class in the United States today. In other words, on the basis of current trends, within the next half century, most people in the world will be lifted out of poverty, and material deprivation will be a thing of the past.

We now stand on the shoulders of our ancestors and are able to draw upon the accumulated knowledge and know-how of the past two centuries. This knowledge is our communal wealth. Much more than the power to enjoy gadgets, our wealth represents the power to mobilize nature to our advantage, rather than to just accept the random fates of nature. There is no turning back the clock, only boundless opportunity for future advancement.

The Troubling Trends

The trends discussed in this book deal with our measurable and material well-being. The trends do not mean that people will be more or less "happy" about their own lives; about that we have no prediction. Similarly, whether people are spiritually better off today than in the past is impossible to gauge objectively. Nor are we ignoring contemporary social ills: mass graves in Bosnia, AIDS and other diseases, sexual exploitation of children, and the like.

Although we are hard-pressed to find more than a small handful of areas of life in the United States that have gotten worse, these troubling trends indicate that improvements in life have not been universal. Here are a few areas in which there is evidence of regression:

- Taxes are higher and government is much bigger than it was 100 years ago (as discussed earlier). In the early years of the 20th century, government spending ranged from less than 10 percent of GDP in the United States to about 15 percent in Germany and France. By the end of the century, federal spending ranged from 34 percent of GDP in the United States to a range of 40 to 65 percent in Europe. But even that trend is showing signs of reversing. For example, in the United States federal spending as a percent of GDP has now dipped to its lowest level in 25 years—suggesting perhaps that Bill Clinton

18

was right to concede that "the era of big government is over."

- Various social trends indicate deterioration not improvement over the past 30 to 40 years, as scholars like William Bennett and Robert Bork have emphasized. The family seems to be in a state of crisis in the United States today. Divorce rates have skyrocketed since the 1950s. In 1950, 13 percent of births to teen-aged girls were out-of-wedlock; in 1970, 30 percent were, and by 1995, 75 percent were. But even here there are glimmers of good news. In recent years, even most of these troubling trends of social decay have moved in the direction of progress.
- Educational quantity has soared in this century. But in recent decades educational quality has deteriorated. Average Scholastic Aptitude Test scores have fallen significantly since the 1960s.
- Violent crime rates have drifted upward—in the 1920s, 1960s, and 1970s, for example—and downwards—in the 1930s and 1990s, for example—with no hopeful trend of long-term improvement.
- Suicide is the ultimate expression of human despair. It is troubling therefore to report that despite all of the material progress of the past 50 to 100 years, a larger percentage of Americans take their lives today than was true in 1900. Teen suicide has risen at an especially disheartening rate.

Our hope is that Americans will strive in the years ahead to permanently reverse each of these unhappy trends. The good news is that in very recent years signs indicate that we have already started to turn the corner in each of these areas of decline, but we hesitate to read too much into any short-term trend—positive or negative.

Why Do We Believe the Doomsayers?

Over the last 200 years, there has been one constant: pessimistic forecasts about human prospects based on anecdotes about social ills have been repudiated by the reality of material progress. The most mistaken forecast of all time was made by English economist Thomas Malthus in 1798 when he predicted in "An Essay on the Principle of Population" that population growth was an inexorable juggernaut that would keep the mass of mankind in misery forever. In fact, at the very time that Malthus wrote, the advanced countries of the world were lifting off into an astonishing period of progress that continues to this day. To Malthus's credit, after his dismally wrong first edition based on nothing but arithmetic and speculation, he educated himself and reversed his original conclusions. Unfortunately, almost no one pays attention to Malthus's correction of his own theory. Instead "Malthusian" has come into the language to describe what Malthus wrote while still in a state of scientific ignorance.

One paradox of this century is that the better things get, the more attention we pay to those who preach that doomsday is right around the corner. Here is a depressing reminder of how an official 1980 U.S. government report, *Global 2000*, depicted life on earth today, as reported by *Newsweek* magazine:

> The year: 2000. The place: Earth, a desolate planet slowly dying of its own accumulating follies. Half the forests are gone; sand dunes spread where fertile lands once lay. Nearly 2 million species of plants, birds, insects, and animals have vanished. Yet man is propagating so fast that his cities have grown as large as his nations of a century before.

That multi-million-dollar report was translated into eight languages (unfortunately, English was one of them) and sold 1.5 million copies. Its "Chicken Little" warnings commanded newspaper headlines across the world, and the TV networks broadcast its dreary forecasts into every American living room. The report came on the heels of an even more infamous report by the Club of Rome entitled "The Limits to Growth." That report explained to a world audience that lifeboat earth had become so weighted down with humans that food, minerals, forests, water, energy, and, well, just about everything that we depend on for survival was running out. It is no wonder that one of the hot-selling bumper stickers in the 1970s read: "Stop the Planet! I Want to Get Off."

One of us (Simon) had a famous $1,000 bet in 1980 with one of the leading pessimists of our time, Stanford biologist Paul Ehrlich. The bet was on whether 5 natural resources of Ehrlich's choosing would fall or rise in price in 10 years' time. By 1990 not only had the optimist (Simon) won the bet, but every one of the resources had fallen in price, which, of course, is another way of saying that the resources had become less scarce, not more. A few years before that Ehrlich wrote: "I would take even money that England will not exist in the year 2000." He wrote in 1969, the eve of the green revolution, that "the battle to feed humanity is over. In the 1970s the world will undergo famines. Hundreds of millions of people will starve to death." Although Professor Ehrlich continues to make dimwitted statements like this, he is still taken quite seriously by the American intelligentsia. He even won a MacArthur Foundation "genius" award after he made these screwball predictions.

One of the most confounding mysteries of modern life is why Americans reflexively believe that things used to be better yesterday than they are today. Perhaps it was the great comedian Jackie Gleason who best put his finger on the great divide between reality and nostalgia when he said, "the past remembers better than it lived." The nostalgia that many Americans express nowadays for the 1950s is a notable example. Let us call this "the Pat Buchanan myth." The objective reality is that for the vast majority of Americans, life on earth was not better in the 1950s than it is today. We are healthier; we live longer; we are richer; we can afford to purchase far more things; we have better jobs at better pay; we have more time and money for recreation, sports, the arts; we have bigger and better homes; we are at much less risk of catastrophic accidents; we breath cleaner air and drink safer water; the list could go on and on. "Back in those golden fifties," notes *Fortune* magazine, "most Americans did not notice or care that one-third of the elderly and one-half of black people were destitute."

Ironically, many of the very measurable trends that have shown the greatest improvement over the past 50 to 100 years are in areas that Americans fret about having gotten worse. Here are some examples:

- Many Americans believe that the environment is in worse condition today than it was in the past, when in fact the past 30 years have seen stunning improvements in the quality of air and water.
- Many Americans think that food and other consumer items are more expensive, when in fact they tend to be much more affordable.
- Many Americans think income inequality is worse than it was 100 years ago, when in fact the divide between rich and poor was wider.
- Opinion polls indicate that Americans believe that the risks of dying from accidents or natural disasters are greater than they were in previous eras, when in fact the risks have fallen by about two-thirds.
- Many Americans believe that technological change is a negative development, when in fact technology is making life better in almost every way.

In 1984 Ben Wattenberg of the American Enterprise Institute aptly entitled one of his books *The Good News Is the Bad News Is Wrong*. In noting the paradox that as the quality of our health has improved by light years, the American public is as worried as ever about getting sick, Dr. Lewis Thomas wrote several years ago in the *New England Journal of Medicine* that we Americans are in danger "of becoming a nation of healthy hypochondriacs, worrying ourselves to death." Or to put it another way, all we have to fear is fear itself.

False scares are often propagated as a means of inspiring public outrage and thus government action, but exaggerated fears can be immensely costly in terms of resources wrongly deployed and even lives lost. One of the best examples of this was the DDT scare prompted by Rachel Carson's environmental creed as expressed in *Silent Spring*. On the basis of faulty and unproven science, Carson contended that the pesticide was killing enormous numbers of birds. DDT was banned even though this chemical was one of the great life savers of the 20th century, reducing malaria deaths estimated in the millions. Economist Roger Meiners of the University of Texas relates the following story of the deadly impact of the false furor over DDT: "Before large-scale DDT programs were introduced in 1962 in Ceylon (now Sri Lanka), there were some 2 million cases of malaria reported for the country. During the DDT program, the number of new cases fell to 17 in 1963. In 1964, pressure from western nations brought an end to the use of DDT. By 1969, 2.5 million people in Sri Lanka were suffering from the disease, partly because it was not politic to admit that wise leaders do not know their environmental science and are willing to inflict massive suffering on tens of millions of people in lesser developed countries."

The media play a central role in shaping our perceptions and reinforcing our natural nostalgia for the better times of the past. (One of the possible reasons why we all pine for the past is that we were younger back then.) Here is one recent example of how the media accentuates the negative and ignores the positive. In 1998 there was not a single commercial airline crash out of the hundreds of thousands of commercial flights and billions of air passenger-miles traveled. But there was almost no major news coverage of this truly miraculous safety record. By contrast, in 1999 the crash of an Egyptian airliner that killed 250 people was headline news for days and remained one of the major news stories for weeks afterward. Is there any wonder that Americans fear flying? For the media, good news is a contradiction in terms.

Michael Prowse of the *Financial Times* of London recently provided another intriguing explanation for why Americans are unduly pessimistic about the state of affairs. Unlike virtually all other nations, we Americans flaunt our vices for all the world to see. After living in and writing about the United States for more than a decade, Prowse wrote as follows:

> The United States has a much worse reputation than it deserves. Commercial television and cinema present a grotesquely distorted image of modern American life. The tendency of foreigners to bash the U.S is encouraged by the very openness of the society, which ensures that every possible vice—from political corruption to low school test scores—is paraded before the world. Other countries try to hide their sins in the interest of progress. Americans take a delight in exposing theirs.

The Dawn of Progress

Winston Churchill once said that "the further back you look, the further ahead in the future you can see." As we look into the future, we see continued sustainable progress. Here are a few predictions that we make with reasonable confidence for the next 100 years:

1. The wealth and health that have been attained in the United States today will be spread to the rest of the world in the next 50 years. We are in the first stages of a worldwide boom in wealth.
2. The price of natural resources will continue to fall, representing less constraint on growth than ever before.
3. Continued improvements in agriculture—particularly in the area of bioengineering—will mean bountiful food production that far outpaces population growth.
4. Many, if not most, of the remaining diseases that threaten us today—cancer, Alzheimer's, multiple sclerosis, arthritis, AIDS, diabetes, and ALS—will be treatable, survivable, and perhaps even eradicated.
5. The information age will cause a continued surge in productivity and output, enabling most middle-class Americans to become millionaires. (The number of American millionaires tripled in just the past 10 years.)
6. In the coming era of global free-market capitalism, we will witness what former Citibank chairman Walter Wriston

described as "the twilight of sovereignty": taxes will be lower, regulations will be more reasonable, central governments will be less intrusive, minority groups will demand and receive greater civil rights, and people will have more political freedom than they do today.

7. The modern doomsayers who now warn of impending global catastrophe will be proven as wrong as the Club of Rome, the Paul Ehrlichs, and the Thomas Malthuses have in earlier times.

Our hope is that the 100 great trends of human achievement recorded in these pages will persuade all but the unpersuadable that this is the best time on earth to have ever lived—except for tomorrow. The data and analysis should also convince all but the deepest skeptics that the past 100 years have truly been the American century. Will the next 100 years be too? We suggest they will be. Here is how the great American comedian/philosopher Will Rogers summarized his views (which we share) about America's future:

> Trying to stop this country now would be like spitting on a railroad track. No politician, no party, not Congress or the Senate, can really hurt this country now. And we're not where we are on account of any one man. We're here on account of the common sense of the big normal majority. This country is bigger than any man or any party. They couldn't ruin it even if they tried.

SECTION I. HEALTH

"Health is the first wealth," Emerson once wrote. The health of Americans improved in ways during the 20th century that can only be described as miraculous. Death and infant mortality rates plunged; life expectancy rose by 64 percent; and almost all of the killer diseases throughout human existence were conquered over the course of the century. This was a century that can and should be celebrated as "an epidemic of life." Yes, health is the first wealth, and in few other areas of life has the human condition improved so universally.

In the 1980s and 1990s the AIDS virus has understandably frightened the public because of its fatal consequences. AIDS has served as a humbling reminder of the vulnerability of human beings to deadly contagious diseases. Throughout most of history plagues and epidemics were killers of much greater magnitude than they are today. In some cases plagues and diseases could wipe out a fourth to a half of a country's population in the span of a decade. Even as recently as the beginning of the 20th century, the death toll from infectious diseases was about 700 per 100,000 population per year. Today, despite new diseases such as AIDS, infectious diseases kill about 50 per 100,000—a stunning 14-fold reduction in death from infectious disease in this century.

Here is another example of modern health improvement. For about the past 30 years, sudden infant death syndrome (SIDS) has been an indiscriminate, traumatizing, and mysterious killer of newborns. However, better education and prevention have resulted in a threefold decline in the SIDS death rate of children under age 5 over the past 15 years and have provided huge relief and comfort to their to parents.

Humankind has made gigantic progress in enabling us to live longer and healthier lives as a result of advancements in modern medicine.

1. Lengthening Human Life

Throughout most of human history, death came at an early age—25 to 30 years was a typical lifespan. The essential element of the human condition was a day-to-day struggle to fend off death. Hence, the most amazing demographic fact—and the greatest human achievement in history in our view—is that human beings have almost won the battle against early death. We are not alone in this assessment. Several years ago the *New York Times Magazine* called the doubling of life expectancy since the start of the industrial revolution "the greatest miracle in the history of our species."

Longer life expectancy reflects a multitude of improvements in health care, nutrition, sanitation, safety, and wealth. Increasing life expectancy at birth from the lower 20s to the high 20s around 1750 took thousands of years. Over the next two centuries, life expectancy in the richest countries suddenly accelerated and tripled. From the mid-18th century to today, life spans in the advanced countries jumped from less than 30 years to about 75 years.

In 1900 the average life expectancy in the United States was just under 50 years. Today it is 77 years. This means that we have expanded the time horizon for a typical human life by 50 percent in the past 100 years. And life expectancy for blacks has moved up from only 30 years in 1900 to a bit less than that of whites.

Women have made greater gains in life expectancy than men in this century. In 1900 women on average lived two years longer than men. In 1950 they lived 5 years longer and today women on average live 6 years longer than men.

Life expectancy has also increased at every age. For example, a 45-year-old American could have expected to live 25 more years in 1900. Now a 45-year-old can expect to live 34 more years, as shown in the table.

The gains in life spans in industrialized countries are now also showing up in the poorest nations as well. As recently as 1950, the life expectancy of a citizen of a less developed country like China or India was about 40 years. Today it is 63 years. This is a stunning 50 percent gain in life expectancy in just 50 years.

Life Expectancy in the 20th Century

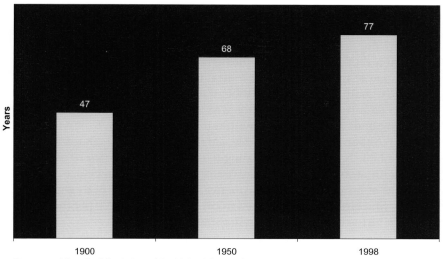

SOURCES: *Historical Statistics of the United States*, Series B 107-115; and *Health, United States, 2000*, Table 28.

Life Expectancy Has Increased at Every Age

Age	1901	1954	1968	1977	1990	1996
0	49	70	70	73	76	76
15	62	72	72	75	77	77
45	70	74	75	77	79	79
65	77	79	80	81	82	83
75	82	84	84	85	86	86

SOURCES: Data for 1901, *U.S. Life Tables, 1890, 1901, and 1901–1910*, Department of Commerce (Washington: U.S. Government Printing Office, 1921), pp. 52–53. Data for 1940–1996, Vital Statistics of the United States (Hyattsville, Md.: National Center for Health Statistics, DHEW, selected years).

2. Reducing Infant Death

Dear to the hearts of all parents is the safety of their children. Parents who have experienced the joy of bringing a healthy baby into the world can imagine the agony that other parents suffer when they lose a baby at birth. The figure shows the heartening course of the rate of infant mortality in the United States. In 1900, early death was the fate of more than 1 birth in 10. In some areas of the country infant mortality was as high as 1 in 4. Today, only 1 in about 150 babies dies within the first year.

Although solidly reliable data for the United States are not available before 1915, according to Kenneth Hill, professor of public health at Johns Hopkins University, "In the now-developed countries of Europe and North America, the probability of dying before the first birthday has declined from, in many cases, 200 per thousand live births to less than 10 in the span of 100 years."

The infant mortality for black Americans (18 per 1,000 live births) is about double the rate for white Americans (9 per 1,000). That is the bad news.

The good news is that the rate of improvement in infant mortality for black Americans has been tremendous over the past century—even outpacing the improvement for whites. The black infant mortality rate is one-tenth what it was 100 years ago. This means that the gap between black and white infant mortality has closed steadily over the past century.

The decline in infant mortality and death rates during childhood is a result of vast improvements in education, nutrition, incomes, environmental conditions, and most of all modern health care.

Throughout most of history a child had about a 40–50 percent chance of dying before the age of 5. (The probabilities were 5 to 10 percentage points higher for girls and lower for boys.) The next figure shows the long-term plunge in infant death rates in the poorer countries of the world. In countries like India, Indonesia, and Mexico, a huge amount of progress has been recorded in just the past 20 years. According to *The Economist*, "Between 1980 and 1996 India almost halved its rate of child mortality. In 1980, 173 of every 1,000 Indian children died before the age of 5; in 1996 the figure was 85."

Infant Mortality Rates

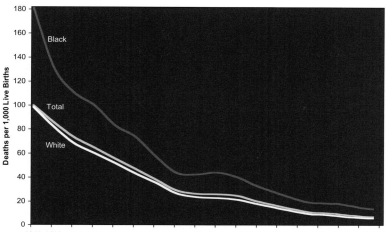

SOURCES: *Historical Statistics of the United States*, Table B 142-144; and *Health, United States, 2000*, Table 23.

Mortality Rates of Children under Age Five

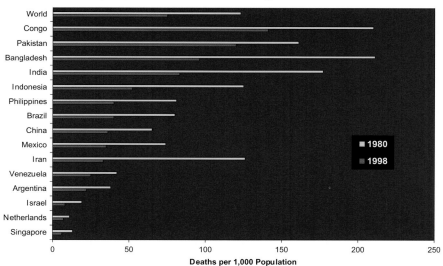

SOURCE: World Bank, *World Development Indicators 2000*, pp.106–8.

3. Fewer Mothers Die Giving Birth

These days Americans complain about drive-in child deliveries in which women are pushed in and out of the hospital within 24 hours. But childbirth is much safer for women today than in earlier times. Throughout the ages, it was not just the babies that failed to survive at birth. Historically, childbearing has been extraordinarily dangerous for women. In the 19th century as many as 1 in 100 women died during pregnancy. One hundred years ago, the maternal death rate was 100 times higher than it is today. In 1950 the maternal death rate was 10 times greater than it is today. By the 1980s only 1 in 10,000 women died giving birth.

Prior to the second half of the 20th century, safe procedures such as epidurals, Caesarean sections, and other medical technologies enhancing childbirth safety for the child and mother were not available. According to Elizabeth Whelan, executive director of the American Council on Science and Health, the plunge in maternal death rates is primarily a result of "increased prenatal care, new drugs to combat infection, and improved obstetric and prenatal practices."

The Centers for Disease Control reports that prenatal care is much more universally available today than ever before. The percentage of women who do not receive prenatal care before the third trimester of pregnancy has fallen by half—from 8 to 4 percent—in just the past 30 years.

Age-Adjusted Maternal Mortality Rates

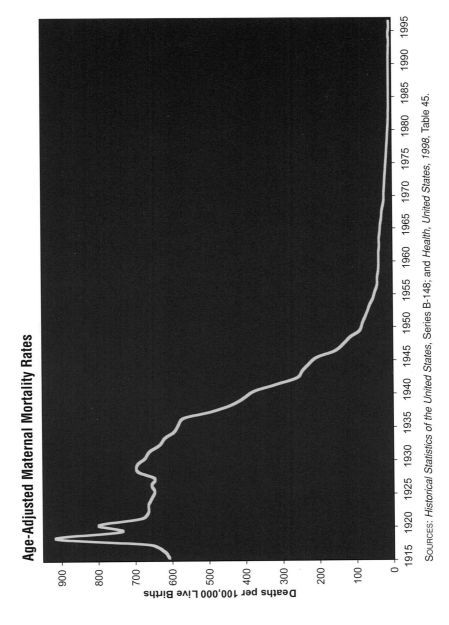

SOURCES: *Historical Statistics of the United States, Series B-148; and Health, United States, 1998, Table 45.*

4. Combating Death at Every Age

For our ancestors, human life was a constant struggle against death—particularly death at an early age. So it is good news indeed that the death rate (number of deaths per 1,000 population) has been falling steadily for at least the past 100 years. In 1900, the overall "crude death rate" was about 17 per 1,000 Americans; most recently, it is closer to 9 per 1,000 as the figure shows.

Impressive as this trend is, the crude death rate data understate the dramatic progress in conquering death in this century. The "age-adjusted death rate," for Americans fell by an astounding 53 percent from 1900 to 1950. Then it fell another 27 percent from 1950 to 1977 according to data compiled by the Centers for Disease Control.

Children between the ages of 1 and 14 are at least 10 times less likely to die than was true at the turn of the century and about one-third less likely to die today than was true in 1950.

For those in their preadult years, between the ages of 15 and 24, the death rate has plummeted sixfold since the turn of the century. Since 1950 death rates for this age group have declined by about one-third. For those in their working years, 25 to 64, death rates are half what they were at the turn of the century.

Amazingly, even for senior citizens, death rates have tumbled by nearly half despite increased worries of cancer, Alzheimer's, and other diseases associated with old age. According to Dr. Alan Fisher of the American Council on Science and Health, "Although methods of combating infectious diseases have made the most dramatic change in death rates, the contributions of 20th century medical knowledge to saving lives go further than that. If you've ever had ulcers, almost any kind of elective surgery such as an appendectomy, hypertension, diabetes, acute allergies, or problems during childbirth, modern medicine may well be responsible for your being alive today. In addition to life and death issues, current medical knowledge contributes to improving the quality of life. It does this through things as diverse as drugs for pain and physical therapy for rehabilitation."

Death Rates

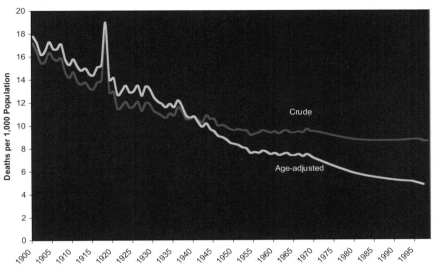

SOURCES: *Historical Statistics of the United States*, Series B 181-92; and *Statistical Abstract of the United States*, No. 131.

Death Rates at Selected Ages

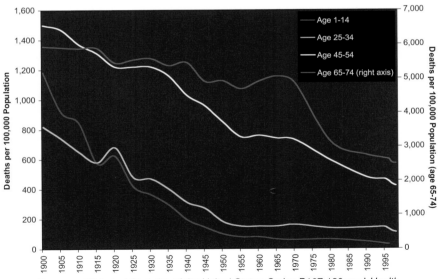

SOURCES: *Historical Statistics of the United States*, Series B167-180; and *Health, United States, 1999*, Table 36.

5. Eradicating the Killer Diseases throughout the Ages

The United States and other rich countries have now experienced the almost complete disappearance of the major diseases that have killed billions throughout human history. The figure shows the decline in infectious diseases which started late in the 1800s. Success was so complete that young people today are not even aware of the scourges of typhoid fever, cholera, typhus, plague, smallpox, and the other terrifying killers of humankind resulting from the filth and unsanitary conditions that were commonplace in the past.

Before 1900 major killers included such infectious diseases as tuberculosis, smallpox, diphtheria, polio, influenza, and bronchitis. Just three infectious diseases—tuberculosis, pneumonia, and diarrhea—accounted for almost half of all deaths in 1900. Now few Americans die from these diseases, and many diseases have been completely eradicated due to a medley of modern medicines. The figure compares what we died of at the beginning of the century with what we die of today.

Since 1900 the childhood death rate from pneumonia and influenza has fallen by an astonishing 93 percent.

AIDS was a disease that exploded onto the public health scene in the mid-1980s. Although AIDS is a horrid epidemic in Africa, the incidence of AIDS in the United States hit its peak in 1992 when 85,000 Americans were diagnosed with the virus. By 1997 that number had dropped to about 30,000 cases. The decline in AIDS in the United States is a result of better education, behavioral changes, and a range of public health measures. Amazingly, the death rate from AIDS has fallen by half in just the past 3 years.

In the past decade, syphilis cases have dropped by more than 80 percent. Dr. Judith Wasserheit of the Center for Disease Control predicts that "if we can build on the success that we have had so far, we should be able to eliminate syphilis in the United States by 2005."

Incidence of Selected Diseases in the United States

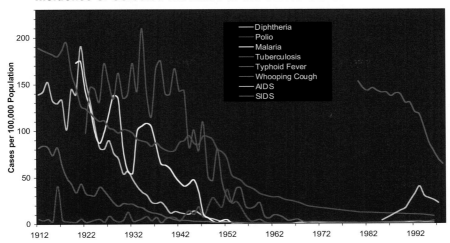

SOURCES: *Historical Statistics of the United States*, Series B 149, B 291, B 295, B 299-300, B 303; *Health, United States, 1999*, Table 53; and American SIDS Institute, www.sids.org/rsearch/webrate/sld001.htm.

NOTE: SIDS rate is per 100,000 live births. AIDS definition was substantially expanded in 1985, 1987, and 1993. TB rate prior to 1930 is estimated as 1.3 times the mortality rate.

Disappearing Diseases

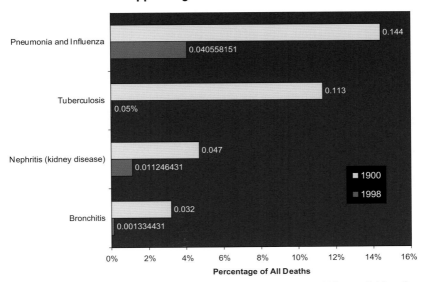

SOURCES: Centers for Disease Control, *Morbidity and Mortality Weekly Report*, v8, v29; and National Center for Health Statistics, *National Vital Statistics Report*, v47, n25.

35

6. Vaccines and Drugs: The Miracle Cures

In 1918 an outbreak of a tragic influenza virus killed an estimated 3 million Americans and between 20 million and 100 million people worldwide. It targeted its lethal fury at young, healthy males mostly between the ages of 20 and 40. More Americans were killed by the 1918 influenza pandemic than were killed in combat during World War I. Could such a killer flu virus strike again? Perhaps. But as *New York Times* writer Gina Kolata, author of a recent book on the 1918 killer influenza, comfortingly assures us, "We now have antibiotics that can block the pneumonia-causing bacteria that overwhelmed us in 1918, new drugs to lessen the effect of influenza infections . . . and vigilant surveillance to protect us from the most quotidian of infections."

The awful episode of the 1918 virus reminds us of how precarious life can be. It also helps us appreciate how many lives have been saved in this century by drugs. The greatest life-saving invention of the 20th century has been the vaccine. In fact, vaccines have been one of the greatest life savers in world history. Scientists generally attribute up to half the increase in life expectancy in this century to improved drugs, vaccines, and other medical treatment breakthroughs.

The figure shows the impact of vaccines on reducing four major diseases of the first half of the 20th century. Thanks to widespread vaccination, most of those diseases have nearly disappeared as health threats.

Diphtheria accounted for about 15 percent of all deaths in 1900. The figure below shows that the number of diphtheria cases fell sharply after the first vaccine was widely introduced in 1933 and then dropped almost out of existence after the DTP vaccine around 1950.

Whooping cough was also a major health problem in the first half of the century. But the number of cases fell almost tenfold from 1950 to 1960.

The number of polio cases fell from its peak in 1950–52 with more than 50,000 deaths per year down to about 5,000 in 1956 after the Salk vaccine was invented, down to 33 cases in 1970, and finally to zero cases in 1998.

Incidence of Selected Vaccine-Preventable Diseases

SOURCES: *Historical Statistics of the United States*, Series B 299, B 300, B 301, B 304; and *Health, United States, 1998*, Table 54.

7. Winning the Race for the Cancer Cure

Alas, we all have to die of something eventually. In this century, eradicating many of the most horrible and deadly infectious diseases—diseases that often afflicted children—has meant that the death rate from chronic and degenerative diseases associated with growing old—for example, heart disease and cancer—has risen accordingly. For example, 100 years ago cancer and heart disease were the cause of about one-quarter of all deaths. Today, they account for well over half of all deaths.

These days nearly everyone has a friend or family member who is battling cancer. This dreaded affliction seems to strike indiscriminately—against the young and the old, the strong and the weak. One American every minute of every day is a cancer casualty. But the good news is that we are making huge strides in preventing and treating cancer and heart disease as well.

The age-adjusted death rate from cancer is falling in the United States and much of the rest of the world. That is to say, for any particular age group—particularly the young—cancer is less threatening than ever before. This is true of almost every type of cancer, including leukemia—which is a killer of children. The most impressive strides have been made in reducing cancer deaths for women. The age-standardized death rate for women has fallen by more than 30 percent over the past 50 years.

One of the prevalent myths about cancer is that environmental factors—such as air pollution—have caused a cancer epidemic. The truth is that improvements in air and water quality over the past 30 years have contributed to the decline in cancer death rates.

At one time, to contract cancer was to receive a death warrant. Not so any more. We may not have a cure or any fail-safe prevention measure, but modern medical treatment has reduced death rates considerably in just the past generation. The figure summarizes the impressive gains in the span of just 30 years. For whites, the survival rate for cancer is up from 39 percent in 1960–63 to 62 percent by 1994. For blacks the probability of survival has roughly risen from one in four in the early 1960s to one in two today. Although good data do not exist before the early 1960s, it is a virtual certainty that cancer survival rates were much lower in the first half of the century.

Five-Year Relative Cancer Survival Rates

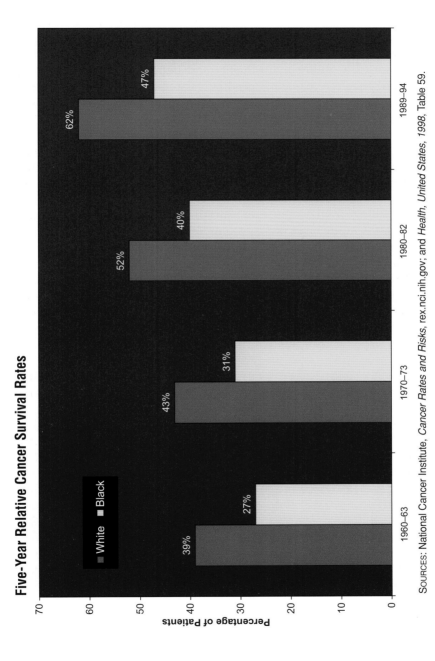

SOURCES: National Cancer Institute, *Cancer Rates and Risks*, rex.nci.nih.gov; and *Health, United States, 1998*, Table 59.

39

8. Surviving Heart Disease

There is exceptionally good news regarding the fight against heart disease. The latest health research indicates that "Americans' heart attacks are becoming smaller and less lethal, probably as a result of healthier living habits and better medicines. Although heart attacks remain an exceedingly common and serious problem, the data suggest that people's chances of surviving them have increased dramatically."

Modern medical procedures and drugs have wondrously reduced the long-term fatality rate for heart disease. The death rate from heart attacks and heart failure has declined from 307 per 100,000 Americans in 1950 to 126 today.

These heart disease gains are even more impressive when age adjusting. Total deaths from heart disease and strokes have risen to 500,000, an increase of 37 percent since 1950, but this is a result of the increased number of elderly in the population.

The most impressive gains in reduced cardiovascular disease have been for stroke and hypertension. Age-adjusted death rates for both of these diseases has fallen by more than half over the past 50 years.

Age-Adjusted Heart Disease Death Rates

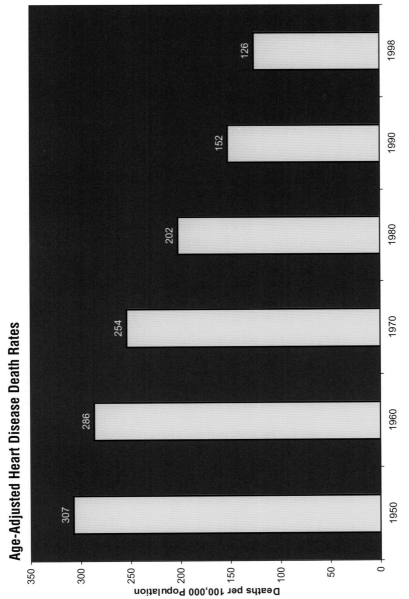

SOURCES: *Health, United States, 1998*, Table 30; and National Center for Health Statistics, *National Vital Statistics Reports, v47, n25.*

41

9. Better Dental Care, More Teeth

The father of our country, George Washington, had wooden teeth. Most of our grandparents wore dentures (if they could afford them) because their teeth had rotted away. But due to modern dental care, better oral hygiene, and fluoridated water, far fewer Americans than ever before lose their teeth. The number of Americans without their real teeth fell from 9.9 percent in 1970 to 3.8 percent by 1985—a decline of 3.6 million toothless Americans in just 15 years.

Average Americans have 3 more teeth today than they did in 1970 (21 then, versus 24 now). Americans in general keep their teeth about 10 years longer than they did in the 1960s. The number of children who have never had a cavity nearly doubled from 1971 to 1988, from 26 percent to 55 percent.

The gains in improved dental care have been most impressive among older Americans. For those between 55 and 64 years of age, the toothless rate has fallen by half—from 30 to 15 percent since 1970. The average 55 to 64-year-old persons now have 4 more of their real teeth than they did 20 years ago.

One factor behind the improved dental hygiene in the United States has been fluoridated water systems. In 1900 there was no fluoride in water. By 1950 about 20 percent of the U.S. population was served; by 1995 that number had grown to more than 70 percent.

Another factor has been the increased access to quality dental care. Dental care is a luxury good: spending goes up faster than income. In 1929 Americans spent $482 million on dentists. That expense fell to $300 million by the middle of the Depression, but by 1950 dental-care spending was just shy of $1 billion. By 1996 Americans spent $48 billion on dental care.

Here is how the American Council on Science and Health has described the progress in our oral hygiene over the past century: "In 1900 scientists had little understanding of what caused tooth decay—acids produced by bacteria-fermenting nutrients on the tooth surface. Today, we have significantly reduced tooth decay. The widespread use of fluoride in community water supplies and toothpastes is largely responsible for these gains. As a result, tooth-lessness has almost been eliminated in middle-aged adults."

Dental Health

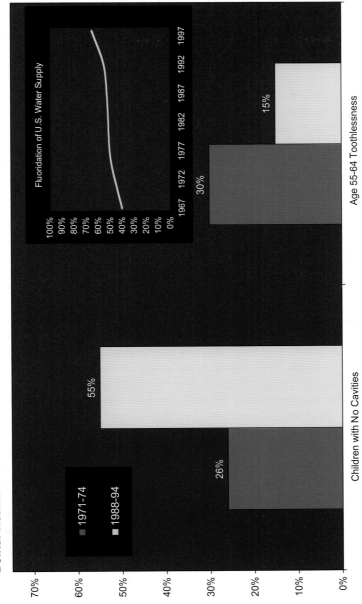

Fluoridation of U.S. Water Supply

100%
90%
80%
70%
60%
50%
40%
30%
20%
10%
0%

1967 1972 1977 1982 1987 1992 1997

■ 1971-74
■ 1988-94

70%
60%
50%
40%
30%
20%
10%
0%

55%

26%

30%

15%

Children with No Cavities

Age 55-64 Toothlessness

SOURCES: American Dental Association, "Number of Children without Cavities Doubles in Two Decades," Summary of *Journal of American Dental Association* article, March 1996; and Centers for Disease Control, "Achievements in Public Health, 1900–1999: Fluoridation of Drinking Water to Prevent Dental Caries," *Morbidity and Mortality Weekly Report*, October 22, 1999, pp. 933–40.

43

10. A Future Free of Ailments and Disease

Because of the giant leaps in medical know-how in just the past 20 years, we can now forecast a nearly disease-free future. Scientists are nearing major breakthroughs in solving the baffling biological puzzles behind AIDS, cancer, diabetes, Lou Gehrig's disease, arthritis, multiple sclerosis, and even Alzheimer's disease. The Wall Street Journal recently reported the exciting news that initial attempts to develop "custom vaccines" for cancer "though far from conclusive, are promising." One patient who successfully used the vaccine to treat his cancer noted, "Compared to chemotherapy, this was paradise." New arthritis treatments have emerged that literally enable disabled persons to walk away from their wheelchairs. Today, through massive funding of biomedical research, the gates have been opened to major breakthroughs in the next century.

There are now an estimated 1,300 companies, 100,000 people, and $13 billion a year devoted to biotechnology. This industry, which did not even exist 20 years ago, is dedicated to one end: finding the biological explanation for disease. By doing so, life can be prolonged and pain, suffering, and debilitating disease can be reduced.

The most promising and exciting project of all is the race to decode all human genes to discover the secrets of disease and aging. Celera Genomics Group, the private biotechnology firm, announced in 1999 that it leads the race in decoding and sequencing human genes. The human body contains an estimated 100,000 genes and some 3 billion to 5 billion base pairs of unique genetic code. Scientists are close to completely mapping the location and sequence of some of the 100,000 genes that would allow medical science to eventually unlock the DNA code of the human body. Scientists have already located the genes responsible for Lou Gehrig's disease and Huntington's disease. Soon they hope to isolate the genes responsible for Alzheimer's disease and breast cancer.

As of the end of 1999 scientists had mapped some 16,000 genes. In the early 1970s, geneticists had identified less than 100.

Scientists now predict that by 2005 most human genes will be identified. Although gene therapy introduces confounding new ethical issues—cloning, for example—the fact remains that tens of millions of Americans have already benefited from genetically engineered medicines and treatments for arthritis, stroke, heart disease, and cancer.

Health Research and Development Spending

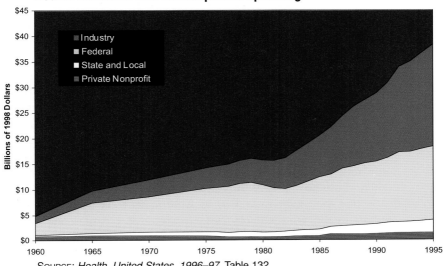

SOURCE: *Health, United States, 1996–97,* Table 132.

Mapping the Human Genome

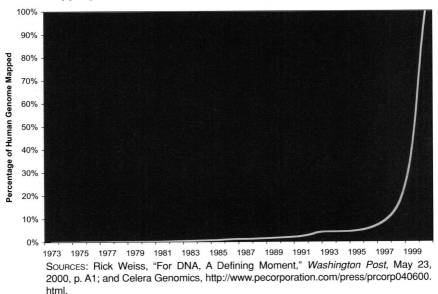

SOURCES: Rick Weiss, "For DNA, A Defining Moment," *Washington Post*, May 23, 2000, p. A1; and Celera Genomics, http://www.pecorporation.com/press/prcorp040600.html.

45

11. Better Hygiene

Cleanliness is next to godliness, or so the saying goes. Americans' hygiene has improved dramatically over the past half-century, partly because nowadays almost all Americans have the means to stay clean and odor-free. Moreover, poor hygiene was a contributing factor to diseases like polio that could be spread by germs on unwashed hands. Modern plumbing, bathtubs, showers, and washers and dryers have improved our hygiene, our appearance, and our health.

• A novelty at the start of the century, bathtubs, showers, and plumbing became standard features in American homes before 1950 and are now nearly universal in homes.

• In 1950 fewer than 3 in 10 Americans took a daily bath or shower in the winter every day. Today, 3 of 4 Americans take a shower in the winter every day. Seventeen percent of Americans bathed just once a week in 1950, compared with only 1 percent of Americans today who bathe this infrequently.

• Americans' spending on personal care has increased more than sixfold since 1900.

How Often Do You Take a Bath or Shower in the Winter?

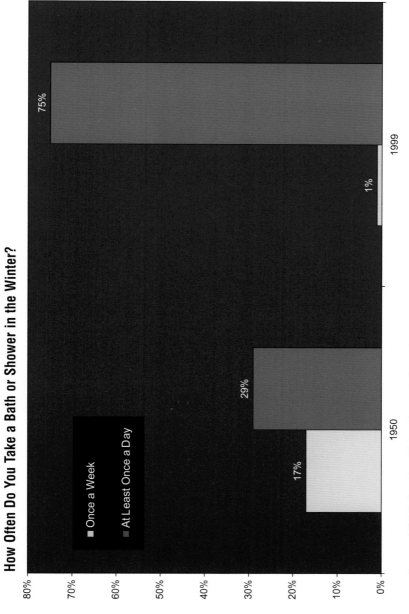

SOURCE: *USA Today,* "How We've Changed," December 31, 1999.

SECTION II. DIETS AND NUTRITION

Throughout history, people's preeminent quest has been to feed themselves. Famines have taken a horrid toll through the ages, in some cases wiping out as much as one-quarter of whole populations. The great potato famine in 19th century Ireland, for example, caused more than a million deaths. Even when people did not starve to death, hunger and malnutrition have been a routine part of human existence for most people throughout most of history. In this century, food supply and consumption has increased rapidly. Food safety has improved immeasurably in the past century. Today, Americans are obsessed with minor risks associated with pesticides, irradiation, and unsafe food-handling, and rare maladies such as "mad cow" disease. But before the 20th century, food poisoning was common, and milk was the carrier of tuberculosis and typhoid until pasteurization all but ended those risks. Consider journalist Michael Fumento's unappetizing description of the quality of food that was eaten before the modern industrial era began:

> At first the medieval food market seems like a beautiful fairy tale, as we so often fantasize the Middle Ages today. But then we see mounds of food—including meat—left out in a state in which it must certainly be putrefying. After it is bought and taken home this food will continue to spoil, right up until the moment before consumption. Such food, of course, was terribly dangerous. People eating this fare dropped like flies. They died of e. coli, shigellosis, and all sorts of horrible food-borne diseases hardly anyone today has even heard of. And when they weren't dying, they were vomiting or suffering horrible or sometimes deadly bouts of diarrhea. Most of these diseases concentrated their effects on children and the elderly, both of whom suffered the most and died in the greatest numbers.

12. Getting Enough to Eat

Americans do not eat substantially more than their ancestors did 100 years ago, but they do eat better—both in terms of nutritional value and taste. Between 1910 and 1990 caloric intake rose very little. Americans eat about half as much bland grain products, cereals, and potatoes, and slightly less dairy products (excluding ice cream) and red meat. They eat far more fresh fruit, poultry, and sugar, and they drink more coffee. They consume a lot more fat, and eat out a lot more. They also consume more vitamins.

The figure shows the long-term trend for meat consumption in six countries. The huge surge in animal protein indicates the long-run marked improvement in dietary consumption for humans over the past two centuries. One indication of improved American diets is the decline in nutritional deficiency diseases. In the 19th century many Americans suffered from pellagra, goiter, and rickets. Today's major nutritional problem is obesity.

Before the beginning of the 20th century, sugar was a luxury food item. Nowadays, sugar is one of the cheapest and most plentiful food items, and the problem in the United States is too much sugar in our diets, not too little. Sugar consumption has risen by about 50 percent since the turn of the century.

Eating is fun. Today, we can be choosy and buy what we like most. For example, many Americans now start their workday with gourmet coffees or a cappuccino. Or consider ice-cream consumption. At the start of the century, Americans ate very little ice cream—a total of about 2 pounds per person, per year. This was partly because ice cream was expensive, and partly because few Americans had freezers to keep it from melting. Now Americans eat about 30 pounds of ice cream per capita in a year. We have far more exotic flavors to choose from too, including Ben & Jerry's "Rainforest Crunch," Haagen-Daaz chocolate chip cookie dough, and Baskin-Robbins strawberry cheesecake.

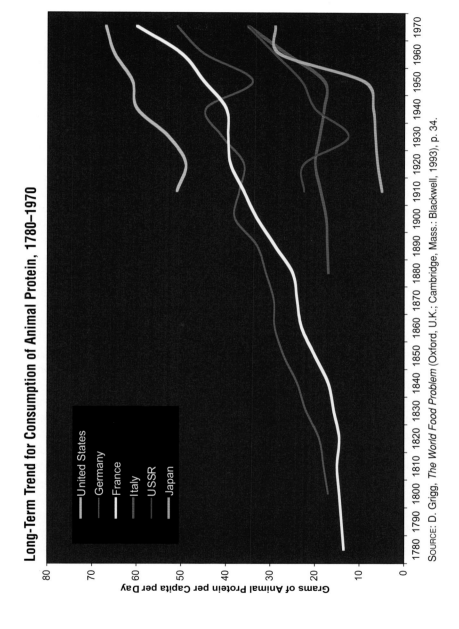

Long-Term Trend for Consumption of Animal Protein, 1780–1970

Grams of Animal Protein per Capita per Day

80 70 60 50 40 30 20 10 0

1780 1790 1800 1810 1820 1830 1840 1850 1860 1870 1880 1890 1900 1910 1920 1930 1940 1950 1960 1970

Legend:
- United States
- Germany
- France
- Italy
- USSR
- Japan

SOURCE: D. Grigg, *The World Food Problem* (Oxford, U.K.; Cambridge, Mass.: Blackwell, 1993), p. 34.

51

13. The Declining Cost of Food

Never before in history and in no other society has the common working man been able to afford such a bountiful basket of tasty foods to put on the kitchen table as Americans can today. Even though they eat better than ever before in terms of food quality, variety, and taste, Americans nonetheless devote less and less of their family budgets to food as time goes by. Americans devoted almost 50 percent of their incomes to putting food on the table in the early 1900s compared with 10 percent in the late 1900s.

According to an analysis of food costs by Wesleyan University economist Stanley Lebergott, "Because food in the United States costs less and less over time in real terms, during periodic economic recessions, Americans could and did leave their nutrition unchanged, but cut spending for less urgent items—autos, appliances, home purchases, recreation and clothing." In other words, due to lower food costs, middle-class and even poor Americans rarely go hungry during tough economic times.

The cost of purchasing food in terms of time worked has fallen about fivefold to tenfold over this century. For example, according to research by the Federal Reserve Bank of Dallas, in 1920 the average American had to work 2 hours to purchase a chicken at the store compared with an average of 15 to 20 minutes worked to buy a chicken today. A candy bar or a soft drink required 20 minutes of work, versus 2 minutes today. A dozen eggs required an hour and 20 minutes of work in 1919 versus 5 minutes today.

Americans work much less than residents of other nations to buy food. The Germans and Japanese devote more than 60 percent more of their income to food than Americans do.

According to a recent study examining U.S. Census Bureau data by welfare specialist Robert Rector of the Heritage Foundation, "The average consumption of protein, minerals and vitamins is virtually the same for poor and middle income children, and in most cases is well above recommended norms for all children. Most poor children today are in fact overnourished."

Eating Out and Spending Less

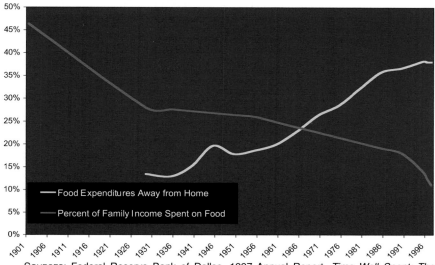

SOURCES: Federal Reserve Bank of Dallas, 1997 Annual Report, *Time Well Spent: The Declining Real Costs of Living in America*, p. 15; *Historical Statistics of the United States*, Series G 460; and *Statistical Abstract of the United States: 1998,* No. 723.

Consumer Expenditures

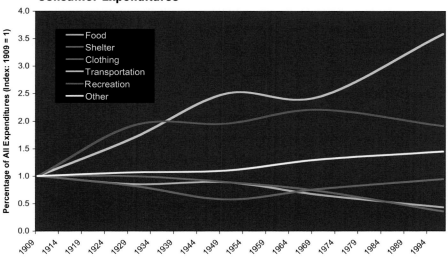

SOURCES: *Historical Statistics of the United States*, Series G 416, 419, 424, 429, 446, 452; and *Statistical Abstract of the United States: 1999*, No. 740.

53

14. Bigger, Taller, Stronger Americans

One of the best indicators of whether a society is malnourished or chronically hungry is the change in a population's average height. According to Nobel laureate Robert Fogel, "Changes in height during the growing years measure current levels of nutrition, while mean final height reflects the accumulated past nutritional experience of individuals over all of their growing years, including the fetal period." Professor Fogel also notes that "Extensive clinical and epidemiological studies show that height at given ages, and weight for height, are effective predictors of morbidity and mortality." If a society is growing taller, then nutrition and health are improving. One distressing recent example of the impact of hunger on height is in North Korea where severely underfed teen-agers are now well below 4 feet in height and resemble children in their appearance.

The average height of Americans has risen by several inches since the 19th century. Americans on average are now roughly 2 inches taller than their grandparents.

The average height of poor Americans has risen too. According to a recent Heritage Foundation study, "Poor boys grow up to be about 1 inch taller and 10 pounds heavier than the GIs who stormed the beaches at Normandy in World War II." The average height of people living in Europe also rose by an average of about 2.5 inches between 1850 and 1950.

Only about 4 percent of Americans are underweight today. The major nutritional problem in the United States and many other developed nations today is obesity, the opposite problem of people throughout the ages. The traditionally underfed Chinese also now have obesity problems.

Average Heights of White, Native-Born Men by Birth Cohort, 1900–70

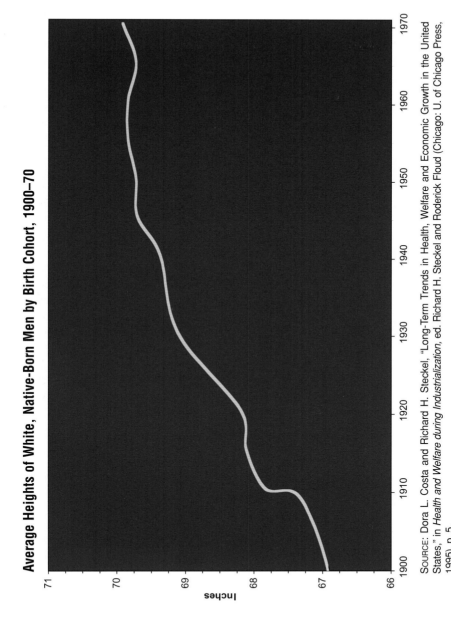

Source: Dora L. Costa and Richard H. Steckel, "Long-Term Trends in Health, Welfare and Economic Growth in the United States," in *Health and Welfare during Industrialization*, ed. Richard H. Steckel and Roderick Floud (Chicago: U. of Chicago Press, 1995), p. 5.

SECTION III. WEALTH

The late Harvard economic historian Simon Kuznets once proclaimed in wonderment: "We Americans are so used to sustained economic growth in per capita product that we tend to take it for granted—not realizing how exceptional growth of this magnitude is on the scale of human history."

Kuznets marveled at the way the United States transformed itself into a wealth-creation machine in the 20th century—setting a frantic economic pace never before equaled in history. The U.S. standard of living, for example, has rocketed upward at least sixfold over the past century. The gains have been broadly shared. Between 1900 and 1920 the United States surpassed Britain and Australia in per capita output, and since then the disparity has steadily widened. Even the poorest Americans live substantially better than most of the rest of the residents of the world and far better than the poor in times past. There is much truth to the adage that if one has to be poor, America is a good place to be.

The result of rapid economic growth in this century is that the birthright of every working-class American is to attain a standard of living greater than most members of royalty could enjoy in other nations before the century began.

15. Expanding Economic Output

The broadest measure of a nation's overall economic performance is the rise in its national output, or what is now commonly called its gross domestic product (GDP). The U.S. real GDP has grown from $0.5 trillion in 1900 to about $8.5 trillion in 1998 (in constant dollars).

At the start of the century, the growth was spurred by harnessing the awesome productivity gains from the middle phase of the industrial revolution and the widespread implementation of innovations such as Henry Ford's factory assembly lines. By the end of the century, rapid economic growth was propelled by the computer and the information age. The contribution of the industrial and computer revolutions has been to create huge amounts of value added output with ever declining levels of workforce and other resource inputs required.

Over the past century, real U.S. GDP growth outpaced population growth and inflation by about sevenfold. In 1900 per capita GDP was about $4,800 compared with $32,000 in real dollars at the end of the century (2000). Going back to 1820, per capita GDP was about $1,500 or about 1/16 of its current level.

America's annual real per capita GDP grew over the past century at an impressive 2 percent per year. The rapid economic growth of the 20th century contrasts with the economic performance of the world over the previous 2,000 years when, according to economic historian Angus Maddison, the per capita economic growth rate worldwide was "virtually nonexistent." Growth rates from 1500 to 1700, the eve of the industrial revolution, averaged just 0.1 percent per year—a growth rate that was about 1/10 as rapid as today's growth rate worldwide.

Economist Edward Denison has estimated that about two-thirds of the economic output in the post–World War II era in the United States is attributable to the increased size of the workforce and that workforce's greater pool of knowledge. In other words, human capital accounts for a huge share of the increased efficiency of the American economy.

Gross Domestic Product

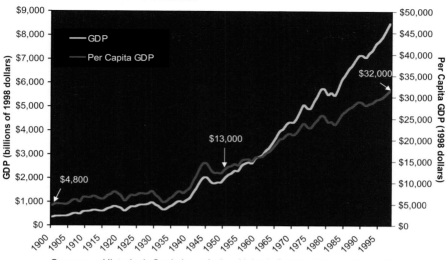

SOURCES: *Historical Statistics of the United States*, Series F1; and
U.S. Department of Commerce, Bureau of Economic Analysis,
www.bea.doc.gov/bea/dn/gdplev.htm.

Average Income Levels

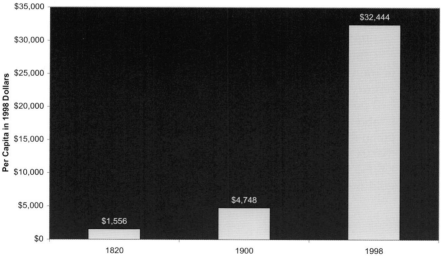

SOURCE: Joint Economic Committee, *The U.S. Economy at the Beginning and End of
the 20th Century, Chartbook*, p. 13.

59

16. The United States Emerges as an Economic Superpower

As the data in the previous section illustrate, the 20th century from an economic standpoint was truly. . . American century. One way to appreciate the economic gains is to compare U.S. economic performance over the past century with that of other advanced nations. At the start of the century, Australia and Great Britain had slightly higher per capita incomes than the United States. By around 1903, the United States had become the richest country in the world. Since then, despite wide fluctuations in United States economic performance, the United States has remained the richest nation on earth. In the 1990s the United States far outperformed other industrialized countries and solidified its status as the world's number one economic superpower.

From 1850 to1950 the United States had the highest economic growth rate in the world. U.S. per capita GDP grew by 1.9 percent per year, compared with about 1.0 percent for Germany and the United Kingdom and 1.3 percent for France and Denmark, and about 1.8 percent for Japan.

The U.S. GDP share of the world economy expanded from 17 to 21 percent of total output in the 20th century. With just 5 percent of the world's population, the United States produced more than one-fifth of total world output.

The figure shows the change in the relative living standards in the United States and other advanced economies over the past century. In the period from 1900 to 1998 the United States moved to first position from third. While Canada has a per capita income that is about 90 percent of that of the United States, Germany and Japan—two of our greatest economic rivals—have per capita output that is still less than 80 percent of that of the United States. The United States does not look as though it will be surrendering its gold-medal economic status anytime soon.

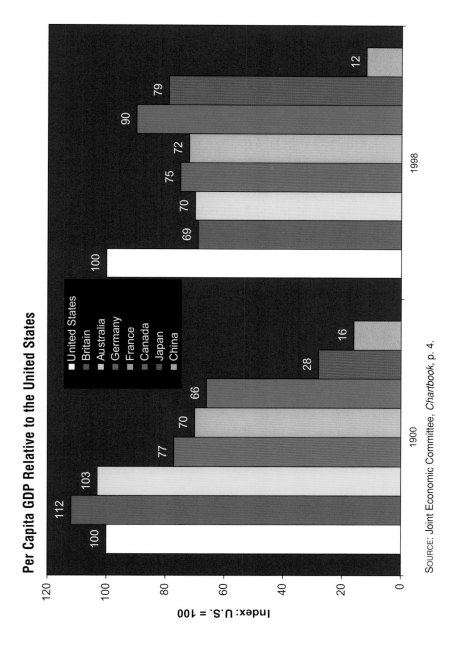

Per Capita GDP Relative to the United States

Index: U.S. = 100

Legend: United States, Britain, Australia, Germany, France, Canada, Japan, China

1900: 100, 112, 103, 77, 70, 66, 28, 16

1998: 100, 69, 70, 75, 72, 90, 79, 12

SOURCE: Joint Economic Committee, *Chartbook*, p. 4.

61

17. The Rising Affluence of the Middle Class

Barbara Ehrenreich recently asked in the *New York Times*, "Is the Middle Class Doomed?" She then notes that "some economists have predicted that the middle class . . . will disappear altogether, leaving the country torn, like many third-world countries, between an affluent minority and throngs of the desperately poor." Fortunately, the middle class is anything but doomed in America. Not all of the wealth created in the 20th century was hoarded by the Carnegies, the Mellons, the Rockefellers, and the Gateses. Just the opposite. The United States and Britain are populated perhaps by the first genuinely prosperous and upwardly mobile middle-class societies in world history. The U.S. Census Bureau provides reliable data on median family income back to 1950. The Census Bureau reports that after adjusting for inflation, median family income in the United States has more than doubled since 1950.

If proper adjustments were made for inflation, the 122 percent gain in family income would be closer to a 150 percent gain.

The common claim that income growth for the middle class has stalled in the United States since the 1970s is erroneous. This is the so-called treadmill hypothesis—that working-class Americans are working longer and harder to stay in place. The truth is that when adjusting for the decline in family size over the past 25 years, incomes have continued their general pattern of ascent over the past 100 years. The Census Bureau says, "Since 1967 average family size has declined by more than 12 percent, during which time median family income grew 27 percent."

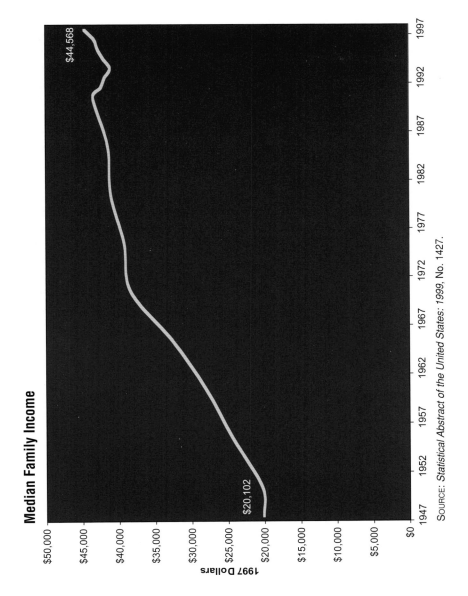

Median Family Income

$44,568

$20,102

1997 Dollars

SOURCE: *Statistical Abstract of the United States: 1999, No. 1427.*

63

18. The Millionaire Next Door

A recent bestseller titled *The Millionaire Next Door* describes how middle-income workers are rising into the ranks of asset millionaires. Through a combination of thrift, hard work, and wise investment, a level of wealth that was once only attainable by a handful of the super-rich (less than 5,000 Americans, or less than 0.1 percent of households, were millionaires in 1900) is now becoming commonplace. Today, there are almost 8 million millionaire households in the United States, a twentyfold increase in just the past 25 years.

Even after adjusting for inflation, the number of millionaire households has doubled in just the past decade.

Only about one in four millionaires today inherited their fortunes. The vast majority of today's rich are self-made men and women.

One notable example of the "millionaire next door" is Theodore R. Johnson who, according to a 1991 Associated Press article, never made more than $14,000 a year working at United Parcel Service. But he plowed every penny of savings he had back into UPS stock (he really should have diversified), and when he reached the age of 90 in 1992 he shocked his relatives and friends by announcing that his net worth was close to $70 million.

Millionaire Households in the United States (current dollars)

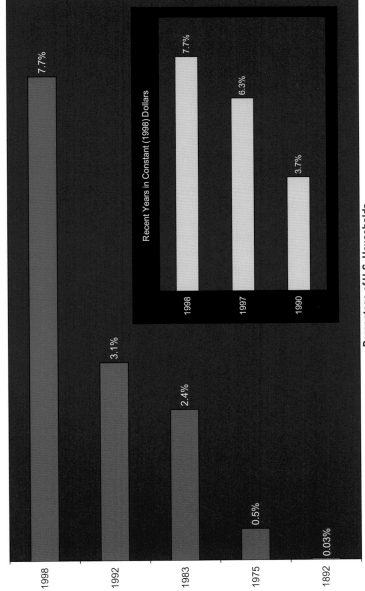

Recent Years in Constant (1998) Dollars

Percentage of U.S. Households

SOURCES: *1998 Affluent Market Research Program* (Hartford, Conn.: Spectrem Group, 1998); Affluent Market Institute; and Thomas Stanley and William Danko, *The Millionaire Next Door* (New York: Simon and Schuster, 1998). Inset source: Spectrem Group.

65

19. The Great Bull Market of the 20th Century

The stock market is an ideal barometer of U.S. industrial health and the competitiveness of the U.S. economy. Despite wide fluctuations in stock values in the 20th century—and two dreadful bear markets, 1929 to 1939 and 1966 to 1982—the stock market has risen 150-fold since 1920. In 1920 the Dow was at 72. In 1999 the Dow closed at over 10,000. The Standard & Poor's composite index rose from 6 in 1900 to over 1400 at the end of 1999.

Jeremy Siegel's new "bible" on the financial markets, *Stocks for the Long Run*, reports that for roughly the past 150 years the average annual rate of return in the stock market has been more than 10 percent. There has never been a 40-year period in U.S. history when the markets have deviated significantly from that long-term trend.

Albert Einstein once declared that "the most powerful force in the universe is compound interest." He might have been talking about the U.S. stock market. Because of the compounding effects of New York Stock Exchange gains, $100 invested in the stock market in 1926 would be worth $266,139 today. But if $100 had been invested each and every year in the stock market since 1926, that account would be worth $2.36 million today.

Rising Stock

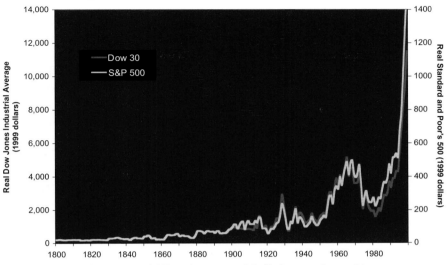

SOURCE: Global Financial Data, http://www.globalfindata.com/freesm.htm.

$100 Annual Investment through 1999

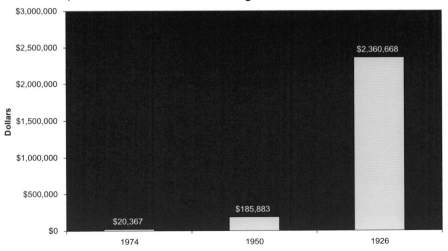

SOURCE: Savers and Investors League, www.savers.org.

67

20. The Wealthiest Society

The rise in the stock market has meant an enormous increase in the financial wealth of Americans. It is amazing but true that more financial wealth has been generated in the United States over the past 50 years than was created in all the rest of the world in all the centuries before 1950. Fifty years ago real financial wealth was about $5 trillion in 1998 dollars. By 1970 that financial wealth had doubled to $10 trillion. Since then the value of Americans' financial wealth has tripled to $30 trillion.

When we combine the burst in financial wealth with the sevenfold increase in housing equity owned by Americans, we discover that the nation's assets have risen from about $6 trillion to more than $40 trillion in real terms in the past half century.

Of course, one American alone, Bill Gates, holds about $100 billion of this wealth—which is a greater net worth than most entire nations own. Unquestionably, there are far more wealthy Americans today than there were just 15 years ago. The wealth needed to be on the prestigious Forbes 400 list rose fivefold between 1982 and 1997.

But wealth in America is widely disbursed. Median household wealth more than doubled from $29,000 to $59,000 between 1965 and 1995. In 1998 the Federal Reserve Board estimated that median household wealth rose to $71,600. Although we hear complaints about American indebtedness, asset values have risen at a much faster rate than has debt.

Wealth of U.S. Households

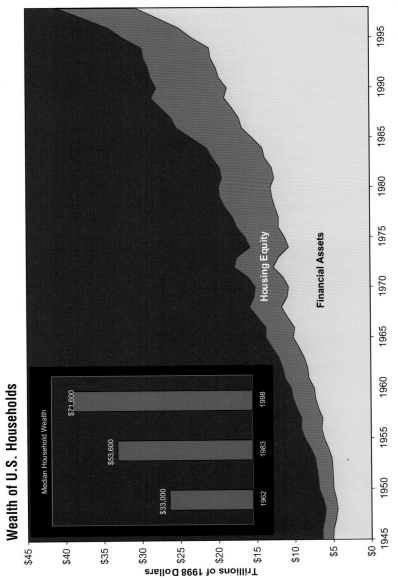

SOURCE: Federal Reserve Board, *Flow of Funds Accounts of the United States,* www.federalreserve.gov/releases/z1/Current/data.htm. Inset sources: For 1983, Federal Reserve Board, 1998 Survey of Consumer Finances. For 1962, Dorothy S. Projector and Gertrude S. Weiss, *Survey of Financial Characteristics of Consumers* (U.S. Board of Governors of the Federal Reserve System, 1966), p. 3.

21. A Nation of Owners

For capitalism to work, a nation must have capital and capitalists. Over the past quarter century the United States has transformed itself into a nation of worker-owners. The United States today, more so than any other country in history, is a nation of capitalists with broad-based ownership. At one time the stock market was the exclusive domain of the very richest Americans. As recently as 1965 only about one of seven Americans owned stock. Now more than half do, according to data accumulated by Peter Hart Associates. And about 55 percent of American shareholders have incomes below $50,000. We have been converted into a nation of owners, and the stock market is now one of the most democratic institutions in the world.

It is not true that financial equities are only owned by older Americans. According to Peter Hart Associates, the percentage of stockholders under the age of 35 has almost quintupled from 11 to 52 percent. In addition, there are now three times as many U.S. stockholders (52% of workers) as trade union members (14%).

Americans own stocks through direct ownership, defined contribution pension plans, IRAs, 401(k)s, and mutual funds. The first mutual fund debuted in 1924 sponsored by the Massachusetts Investor Trust. A $10,000 investment in that inaugural mutual fund would be worth $13 million now. Today there are 7,000 mutual funds with assets of $5 trillion and at least 75 million American investors.

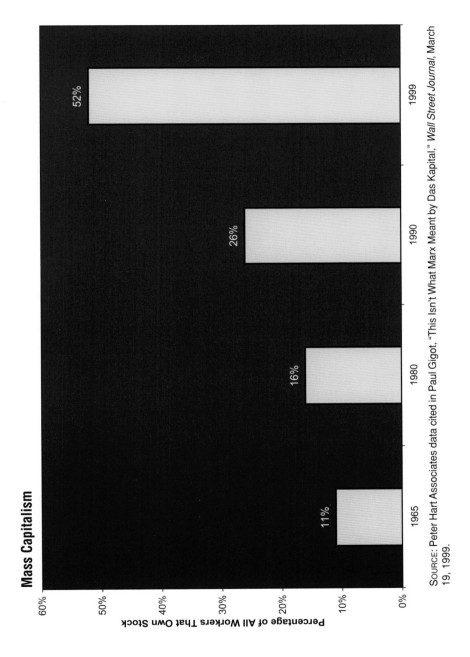

Mass Capitalism

Percentage of All Workers That Own Stock

1965: 11%
1980: 16%
1990: 26%
1999: 52%

SOURCE: Peter Hart Associates data cited in Paul Gigot, "This Isn't What Marx Meant by Das Kapital," *Wall Street Journal*, March 19, 1999.

71

SECTION IV. THE STATE OF POOR AMERICANS

The Bible tells us that the poor will always be among us. Fortunately, the percentage of Americans that are truly poor in terms of material deprivation relative to earlier times in our history is low. Why? Because of economic growth and rising overall incomes. The Great Society's war on poverty and other government programs designed to eradicate poverty in America clearly have had, at best, a minor impact in reducing the number of families that are poor and in reducing dependency. The welfare state has failed despite the federal government's spending about $5 trillion to fight poverty. The lesson learned is that the best antidote to poverty is a job and a rising tide of prosperity that lifts all boats. Some 30 million Americans are still officially classified as poor in the United States—but the poverty "rate" has fallen by more than half since 1950.

The good news is that even most of those who are classified as poor do not suffer material deprivation, and, in fact, the poor today own things that were considered luxuries in the first half of the century. Poverty expert Rebecca Blank of Northwestern University concludes, "The trends in income poverty in the United States over the past two decades give a more pessimistic picture of economic need than do alternative measures. Housing conditions, food consumption, access to health services, and general health status have improved among poor individuals in the United States over the past three decades by virtually all measures. Poverty indexes based on consumption rather than on income generally show a greater decline in need."

22. Abating Poverty

Before 1900, being poor for most poor Americans meant, in truth, surviving on a subsistence income—in some cases living on bread and water. In the 1920s poverty rates fell to about 20 percent and, on the eve of the Great Depression, Herbert Hoover notoriously declared that "we shall soon be in sight of the day when poverty will be banished in the nation." In the 1930s poverty rates surged to above 40 percent. Since the late 1950s poverty rates have declined by about 10 percentage points. For the past 20 years the "official" poverty rate, depending on the state of the economy, has fluctuated between 10 and 15 percent.

Official poverty estimates for the United States at the turn of the 20th century are not available, but unofficial measures suggest that poverty was substantially higher than today. In the late 1800s, 30 to 50 percent of families were in poverty. In 1950 the poverty rate was about 30 percent—or twice the current level. The century-long trend in poverty shows clear improvement.

The most impressive decline in poverty over the past half century has been among senior citizens. About one-half of seniors were in poverty in the early 1950s, compared with about 10 to 15 percent today.

Among the races, the greatest decline in poverty in recent decades has been for black Americans. In 1950 almost three of four black Americans lived in poverty. That rate declined to 40 percent in the 1960s and is today officially between 25 and 30 percent.

Political scientist James Q. Wilson points out that "You need only do three things to avoid poverty in this country: finish high school, marry before having a child, and produce the child after the age of 20. Only 8 percent of families who do this are poor; 79 percent of the those who fail to do this are poor. "

Economist Daniel T. Slesnick of the University of Texas has measured poverty on the basis of actual consumption levels of poor households. Slesnick finds that if we measured poverty on the basis of expenditures rather than reported income, which does not include noncash government benefits or payments that poor households receive but do not disclose to the government, then poverty rates would be about two-thirds below the "official rate."

Measuring Poverty

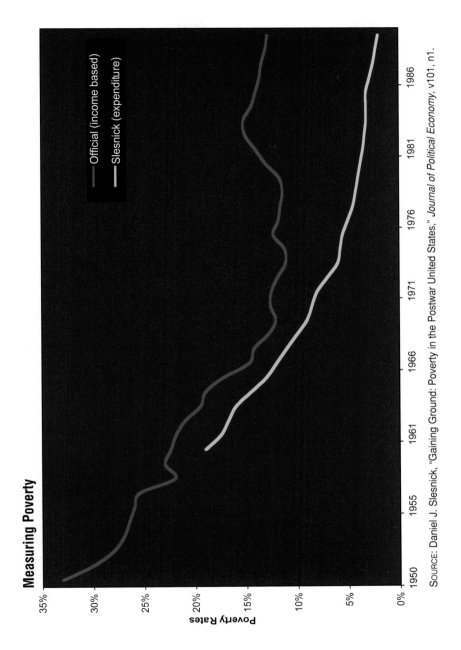

Poverty Rates

Legend: Official (income based) / Slesnick (expenditure)

Source: Daniel J. Slesnick, "Gaining Ground: Poverty in the Postwar United States," *Journal of Political Economy*, v101, n1.

23. Rising Living Standards for the Poor

Adam Smith once defined poverty as the lack of those necessities that "the customs of the nation render it indecent for creditable people, even of the lowest order, to be without." Today, we define poverty officially as the cash income to meet basic economic needs. But as the American society has seen an abundance of affluence in this century, we have begun to define "basic needs" much more broadly. Yes, there are still far too many Americans who live in material poverty. But most of the poor today have a living standard—based on what they can afford to own—that is higher than that of the middle class 50 years ago and higher than that of all but the richest Americans at the start of the century. The U.S. poverty threshold would be considered wealthy in most countries of the world today. The poverty level is more than three times the average income in the world today.

In 1995 the poverty level in the United States for a single person was about $7,800. In that year 155 countries had an average per capita income below the U.S. poverty level. In fact, 120 nations have per capita incomes that are *half* the poverty level of the United States. And there are some 50 nations with per capita income *one-tenth* the U.S. poverty level.

Poor Americans fare much better today than their counterparts 50 or 100 years ago. Almost 4 in 10 poor households today own their own homes. Almost 70 percent own a car or truck; 98 percent own a refrigerator; more than 95 percent of poor households own a television set, and almost one-third own two or more color television sets.

The rise in material affluence has been so great in this century that most poor households now own consumer and household appliances in higher percentages than the middle class did in the 1950s and that even most of the rich could not afford at the turn of the century. In 1930, for example, less than 10 percent of all American homes had refrigerators, compared with 98 percent of poor households today. In 1950 only about 2 percent of households had dishwashers, today over 20 percent of poor households own one.

The average poor household in the United States is more likely to own a color television set than the average income household in developed countries such as Ireland, France, Germany, and Italy.

Per Capita GDP (selected countries, 1998) vs. U.S. Poverty Level

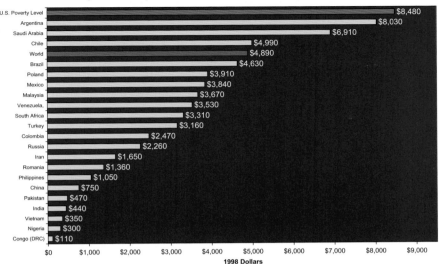

U.S. Poverty Level	$8,480
Argentina	$8,030
Saudi Arabia	$6,910
Chile	$4,990
World	$4,890
Brazil	$4,630
Poland	$3,910
Mexico	$3,840
Malaysia	$3,670
Venezuela,	$3,530
South Africa	$3,310
Turkey	$3,160
Colombia	$2,470
Russia	$2,260
Iran	$1,650
Romania	$1,360
Philippines	$1,050
China	$750
Pakistan	$470
India	$440
Vietnam	$350
Nigeria	$300
Congo (DRC)	$110

1998 Dollars

SOURCE: World Bank, World Development Indicators database, http://www.worldbank.org/data/databytopic/GNPPC.pdf.

Ownership of Poor Households vs. Ownership of All U.S. Households (1950)

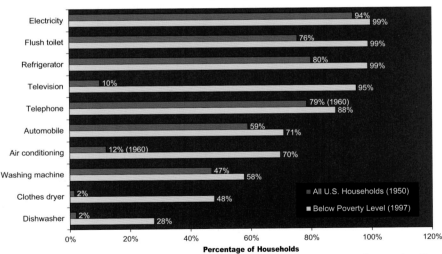

	All U.S. Households (1950)	Below Poverty Level (1997)
Electricity	94%	99%
Flush toilet	76%	99%
Refrigerator	80%	99%
Television	10%	95%
Telephone	79% (1960)	88%
Automobile	59%	71%
Air conditioning	12% (1960)	70%
Washing machine	47%	58%
Clothes dryer	2%	48%
Dishwasher	2%	28%

Percentage of Households

SOURCES: U.S. Bureau of the Census, *American Housing Survey for the United States in 1997*; U.S. Bureau of the Census, "Housing Then and Now," www.census.gov/hhes/www/housing/census/histcensushsg.html; and *Historical Statistics of the United States*, Series Q 175.

24. The World's First Universal Opportunity Society

In 1859 Abraham Lincoln described the uniquely American economic system of opportunity as follows: "The prudent, penniless beginner labors for wages awhile, saves a surplus with which to buy tools or land for himself; then labors on his own account for another while, and at length hires another new beginner to help him. This . . . is the just and generous and prosperous system, which opens the way for all—gives hope to all, and energy and progress, and improvement of conditions for all." The evidence from recent years in the United States indicates that this ability of Americans of all income classes to rise up by their bootstraps and gain wealth has never been more apparent.

According to a 1997 study by the Alexis de Tocqeuville Institute based on Census Bureau data covering the period 1975 to 1991, there is remarkable income mobility in the United States today. The study finds, "About 30 percent of the bottom fifth of income in 1975 were in the second fifth in 1991; 29 percent were in the top fifth, with an average income of about $50,000. The families in the lowest income tier in 1975 were five times as likely to have moved all the way up to the top fifth of income as they were to stay in the bottom fifth." Meanwhile, of those who were in the top 20 percent of income in 1975, 37.5 percent had fallen out of the richest fifth by 1991.

The evidence suggests that the United States more than at any time in the recent past is becoming ever more a dynamic opportunity society rather than a stagnant, permanent class-oriented economy. Between 1975 and 1991 the largest income gains in dollars were achieved by those who started in the lowest income group. For example, a household that was in the lowest income group in 1975 saw its income rise on average by $25,000 a year by 1991. On the other hand, a family that started the period in the highest income group saw its income grow by just $4,000 on average over the same period.

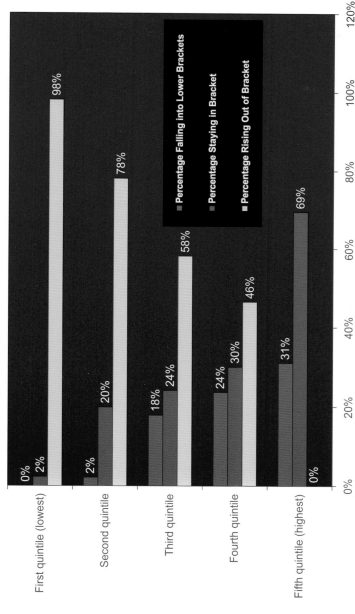

Income Mobility, 1975–91

First quintile (lowest)	0% / 2%	98%
Second quintile	2% / 20%	78%
Third quintile	18% / 24%	58%
Fourth quintile	24% / 30%	46%
Fifth quintile (highest)	31% / 69%	0%

Legend:
- Percentage Falling into Lower Brackets
- Percentage Staying in Bracket
- Percentage Rising Out of Bracket

SOURCE: University of Michigan data cited in W. Michael Cox and Richard Alm, *By Our Own Bootstraps: Economic Opportunity and the Dynamics of Income Distribution*, 1995 Annual Report, Federal Reserve Bank of Dallas, p. 14.

SECTION V. THE STATE OF CHILDREN AND TEENS

Our children are our passports to the future. How well they are fed, nurtured, taught, and loved are key factors in determining whether our society will be prosperous and whether our system of self-government will endure in future years. There are certainly trouble signs with respect to the state of our children. Reported cases of child abuse and neglect are on the rise (though we question whether actual abuse of children by parents has risen nearly as much as the reporting has; about two of three child abuse reports are eventually dismissed as "unfounded").

More children than ever are growing up without fathers in the home. It seems as though children spend more time engaged in unproductive activity—like watching TV—or destructive activity, like drug use and crime. Teen suicide rates are still distressingly high.

But on balance the material well-being and the health status of our children has improved so spectacularly over the past 50 to 100 years that it is highly misleading when social critics say that the state of our children has declined. Perhaps the single best indication of this improvement is the decline in the death rate of children documented in Section I. To repeat that benevolent finding: children are about 10 times less likely to die before the age of 12 today than 100 years ago, and about 3 times less likely to die than 50 years ago. Other socioeconomic indicators also signal improvement in our youths and teens: declining poverty; declining teen drinking, smoking, and drug use; and declining rates of teen pregnancy. To quote the rock group The Who: "The kids are alright."

25. Reducing Child Poverty

The economic well-being of children has unquestionably improved over the course of the century. Although children have the highest poverty rate of any age group, the percentage of poor children has fallen by more than half over the past half-century. In the early 1950s roughly 40 percent of American children lived in poverty. The rate of poverty was no doubt higher before that. In 1960 the child poverty rate had declined to about 25 to 30 percent. Today about 20 percent of U.S. children are poor as seen in the figure. This is too high for an affluent society, but we are moving in the right direction.

Child poverty is mostly a result of family breakup, not a failing economy. The Urban Institute has found that children are at least four times more likely to live in poverty if they are in a one-parent household than in an intact family. Only about 1 in 10 children in two-parent households are poor.

Clearly, the economic status of children is far better than in earlier times in history. *Washington Post* economic reporter Robert J. Samuelson recently described the condition of the young during the 19th century: "Until this century, children worked in homes, fields, and factories almost as soon as they could. Historians tell us that 55 percent of the cotton mill workers in Rhode Island in 1820 were children. In 1826 a 19 year old became a mill superintendent because he had already worked there 11 years. In the late 19th century rural families almost universally depended on the labor of their children."

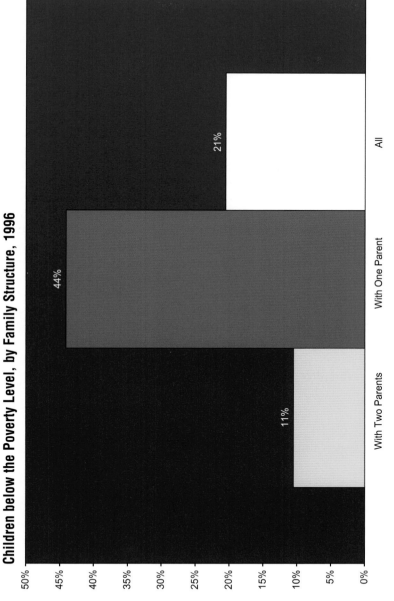

Children below the Poverty Level, by Family Structure, 1996

With Two Parents — 11%

With One Parent — 44%

All — 21%

SOURCE: Megan Gallagher and Sheila Zedlewski, "Income and Hardship: Poverty among Children," in *Snapshots of America's Families* (Washington: Urban Institute, 1999), http://newfederalism.urban.org/nsaf/tables/income_a2.htm.

26. The Toy Culture

Nintendo. Barbie dolls. Pokemon cards. Skateboards. And 12-speed mountain bicycles. The United States is awash in toys.

Toy production and sales surged over the course of the 20th century. In 1921 the nation spent around $2 billion on toys and sports equipment (in 1998 dollars). In 1950 the nation spent $8 billion. Today Americans spend $45 billion.

In 1999 the toy industry spent an estimated $6 billion promoting and producing just the toys and action figures related to the Star Wars prequel. That was more money than was spent in 1950 on all toys. American Demographics recently reported that advertisers must aim their marketing toward youths, because their increased buying power makes them a critical age group. In 1998 children spent $25 billion of their own money on purchases and directed another $187 billion of their parents' money. That's about $6,000 of spending for every child, which is about twice the per capita income of the world. In 1900 many parents could barely afford to purchase a doll for their daughters or a baseball and bat for their sons. Now we worry that kids have far too many toys, not too few.

Expenditures on Toys and Sports Equipment

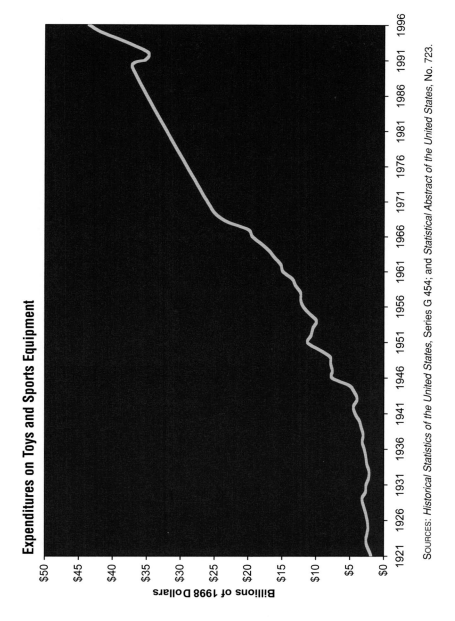

SOURCES: *Historical Statistics of the United States, Series G 454; and Statistical Abstract of the United States, No. 723.*

27. Teen Drinking, Smoking, and Drug Use on the Decline

Teenagers are naturally rebellious creatures. This rebellion and quest for independence is manifested in many ways that are sometimes socially and personally harmful. Thirty years ago one of the most alarming trends was the surge in illicit drug use and alcohol by U.S. youths. Good news: Teen drinking and drug use are way down from the height of the drug culture in the 1960s and 1970s. So is teen smoking.

Teen drinking has fallen substantially over the past 20 years. The percentage of 12 to 17 year olds who drink has declined steadily from half to less than one-quarter since 1979.

There has also been an encouraging decline in "binge drinking"—which the National Institute on Drug Abuse defines as "five or more drinks in a row in the last two weeks"—from 40 percent to 30 percent in the past 16 years.

Teen smoking has declined as well. In 1979 nearly 20 percent of high school seniors smoked at least half a pack a day, compared with 15 percent today.

The decline in cocaine use began in the early 1980s. Despite an increase in recent years due to the marketing of crack cocaine, cocaine use is still only half the levels of the 1970s.

Although marijuana use has been up in recent years, there is no reefer madness in the United States today. Fewer Americans are smoking pot today than at any time since the early 1960s. Marijuana use has fallen by almost 60 percent since the late 1970s. There has, however, been a slight increase in sales of marijuana to teenagers and arrests for marijuana use have risen.

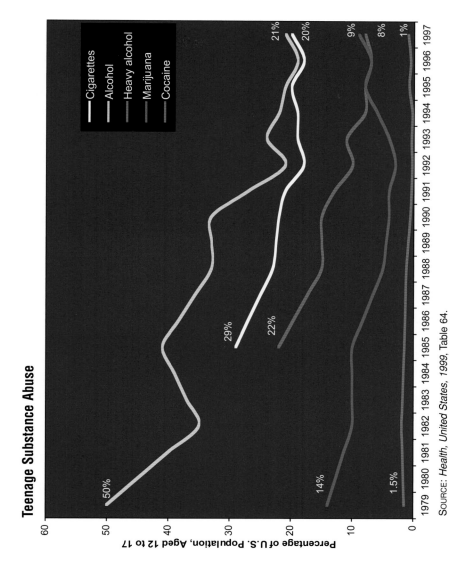

Teenage Substance Abuse

Percentage of U.S. Population, Aged 12 to 17

Legend:
- Cigarettes
- Alcohol
- Heavy alcohol
- Marijuana
- Cocaine

50%
29%
22%
14%
1.5%
21%
20%
9%
8%
1%

1979 1980 1981 1982 1983 1984 1985 1986 1987 1988 1989 1990 1991 1992 1993 1994 1995 1996 1997

SOURCE: *Health, United States, 1999*, Table 64.

87

28. Declining Rates of Teen Pregnancy

A general consensus in the United States today is that when teens end up having babies, it is a prescription for social decay and ruined lives for the teens and their babies. So it is good news that teen birth rates have been falling dramatically not only in the short term but also the long term. The use of contraceptives, of course, has contributed to a decline in teen births, as has abortion. In the past teenage girls were pressured to marry and have children at a young age, but that social norm has changed. The decline in the teen birth rate is especially encouraging because as health has improved markedly over the past 100 years, the age at which a teenager can conceive is much earlier as well.

In 1950 the teen birth rate was just over 80 live births per 1,000 teenage girls. Over the past 45 years that teen birth rate has declined to 54 live births, a 31 percent decline. Even for very young mothers, the 15- to 17-year-old girls, the birth rate has fallen since 1960.

Abortion is not primarily the explanation for lower teen birth rates, although teen abortions have risen. The teen pregnancy rate shows generally the same pattern as the teen birth rate. In 1955 there were about 250 pregnancies per 1,000 teen-age girls. By 1990 that rate had fallen to about 120 for 15 to 19-year-old girls.

The National Center for Health Statistics reports that children born to teenage mothers are likely to be less healthy than other children. The report finds that only about one-third of pregnant teens receive adequate prenatal care; that babies born to young mothers are more likely to be low birth-weight, and that they are "at risk of serious and long-term illness, developmental delays, and of dying in the first year of life."

Teenage pregnancy is not good for young mothers either. The National Center for Health Statistics reports that teenage girls who have children are much more likely to drop out of high school, are much less likely to ever go to college, and are much more prone to be poor in their twenties.

The teen birth rate has fallen in the 1990s as well. Between 1991 and 1997 the teen birth rates were down 6 percent for first births and down 21 percent for second births.

Teenage Birth Rate

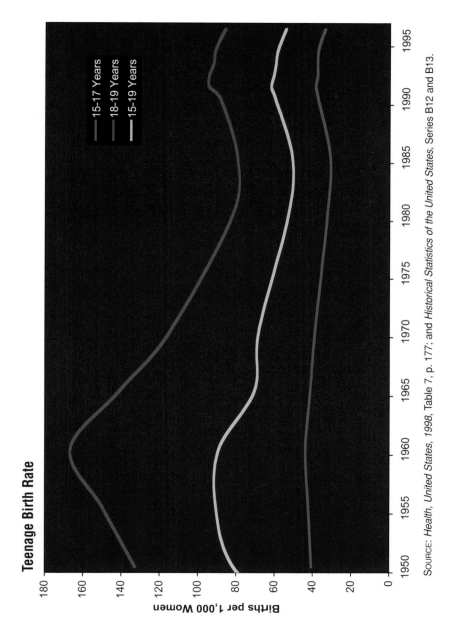

SOURCE: *Health, United States, 1998*, Table 7, p. 177; and *Historical Statistics of the United States*, Series B12 and B13.

SECTION VI. THE AMERICAN WORKER

Throughout the ages, man has been a beast of burden. Men and women toiled for long hours under gritty, dangerous, physically exhausting, and generally unpleasant working conditions. Before the start of the 20th century more than half of the world's residents were working in agriculture and typically produced a subsistence level of food. Now only 2 to 3 percent of Americans work on a farm. Work has changed much for the better in this century. Perhaps the best measure of that change is the shortened work-week. Other measures of improved life on the job include the elimination of child labor, more vacation time, and far fewer injuries and deaths on the job.

The primary explanation for the improved pay and working conditions for the American worker is what economists refer to as "the P word": productivity. Productivity improvements enable human beings to get more of what they want for less human effort. Productivity rises in a society because of technological innovation, capital investment, and increases in human capital—that is, an ever increasingly educated workforce. American workers are on average about 20 percent more productive than workers in other developed nations.

29. Workers Leave the Farm

One of the preconditions for increasing the standard of living of a nation is to reduce the percentage of the workforce devoted to feeding the population. Throughout most of human history, the vast majority of workers, about two-thirds in most societies, were employed in agriculture. The farmer's devotion to growing and gathering enough food left little time or energy for fulfilling other human needs.

In 1800 about 75 percent of Americans farmed. In 1900 that percentage had dropped to about 40 percent because of the industrial revolution. Today only about 2.5 out of 100 workers grow more than enough food for the entire nation and then enough to make the United States the world's breadbasket.

In 1900 there were roughly 12 million farmers in the United States. Today, there are slightly less than 4 million. Improvements in agricultural productivity now cause many to bemoan the disappearance of the family farmer. Despite the romantic vision of life on the farm, throughout most of history, farming involved long hours of backbreaking drudgery and toil in the fields.

Agricultural Labor Force

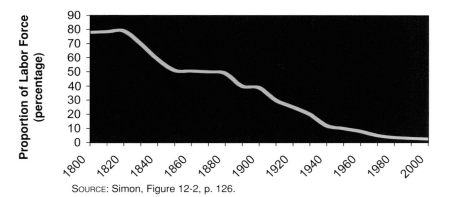

SOURCE: Simon, Figure 12-2, p. 126.

93

30. The Amazing Gains in Farm Productivity

Fewer farmers has not meant less food. The 20th century brought productivity-inducing technological changes on the farm that would have been unthinkable 100 years ago. Modern technologies—in farm equipment, pesticides, fertilizers, irrigation techniques, and bioengineering—have generated a fivefold to tenfold increase in farm output per work-hour worked in this century. Because of the surge in the American farmers' productivity, the United States is now called the breadbasket of the world. Today, the United States, with less than one-fifth of the world's population, produces almost 25 percent of the world's food.

The United States feeds three times as many people with one-third as many total farmers on one-third less farmland than in 1900.

One of the most important technological changes in agriculture was the transition to the modern tractor. It was not until the early 19th century that farmers discarded the hoe and the spade and could afford to purchase horses and mules for plowing. The transition from horses and mules to modern farm machinery for tilling the soil and harvesting the crop did not begin until the 1920s. In 1955, for the first time, more farm tractors than horses were used in agriculture.

One way to pay tribute to American farmers is to compare their productivity with that of farmers around the world. The American farmer is about 40 percent more productive than his closest rival, the European farmer. Over the past 20 years the U.S. productivity lead has widened.

A Colorado farmer named Bob Sakata recently told *National Geographic* about the gains in farm productivity. According to Mr. Sakata, "The only way you can stay in business as a farmer is to boost yield and reduce your costs. Fifty years ago, when we started here, an acre planted in onions would produce about 200 sacks. When we got that up to 350 sacks per acre we thought we were the hottest thing in farming. Today, if we don't produce 800 sacks per acre, we can't compete with the guy down the road."

U.S. Farm Labor Productivity

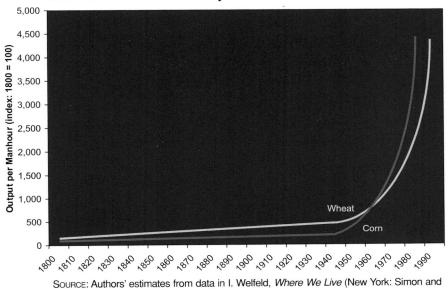

SOURCE: Authors' estimates from data in I. Welfeld, *Where We Live* (New York: Simon and Schuster, 1988).

Farm Motive Power

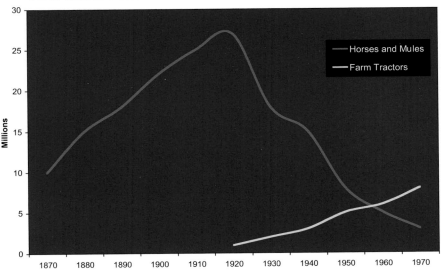

SOURCE: Marion Clawson, *America's Land and Its Uses* (Baltimore, Md.: Johns Hopkins University Press, 1972), p. 104.

31. The Most Productive Workers in the History of the World

American farmers are not the only ones who have become more efficient over the course of the 20th century. American workers today are astonishingly productive on the job—particularly when comparing them to workers in earlier periods of history. The surge in output produced per American worker is the driving force behind the dramatic rise in living standards in the United States. Ultimately, we can only be paid more and consume more if we produce more.

Around 1900 the typical American worker produced about $2 to $3 of output (in 1985 dollars) for every hour worked. By 1950 that had quadrupled to about $8 to $10 an hour. Today the average worker produces about $20 to $25 per hour of value-added product. That is roughly a ten-fold real increase in output in one century.

American workers are more productive for two reasons. First, they have greater know-how—workers are better educated and skilled. Second, technological improvement and modernized tools that Americans use on the job, including computers, machinery, scientific instruments, modernized communications, and so forth—enable them to produce more output with less time and less toil. Economists have estimated that more than 90 percent of the rise in worker productivity in this century is a result of workers' having more of this capital to work with on the job.

American workers are the most productive in the world. Most industrialized nations of Europe, for example, still only have productivity rates of about 80 percent of the U.S. level. The workers in Asian nations have less than 60 percent the productivity rate of American workers.

Total Labor and Factor Productivity, 1840–1997

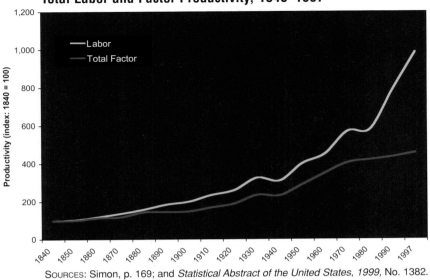

SOURCES: Simon, p. 169; and *Statistical Abstract of the United States, 1999,* No. 1382.

Labor Productivity (selected developed countries, 1996)

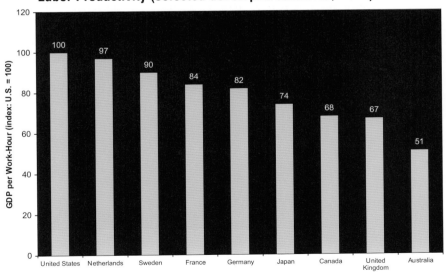

SOURCE: *Statistical Abstract of the United States, 1999,* No. 1381.

32. The Shrinking Workweek

The most important change in working conditions over time has been that Americans work substantially less and have much more leisure time. In 1850 the average workweek was 66 hours long—typically workers toiled for nearly 12 hours, 6 days a week. In 1900 the average workweek was still 60 hours—five 12-hour days. Since about 1950 the average workweek has been almost unchanged at 40 hours long. Moreover, because work required much more physical exertion in earlier eras than today, leisure time was often devoted to resting and convalescing.

The decline in the workweek does not mean Americans are suffering a loss of income by working less. A reduced workweek is a sign of growing affluence.

The workweek data understate the decline in lifetime hours worked because Americans are working fewer years. They start working later in life and end their careers earlier. Americans are increasing their years of schooling and also retiring at an earlier age even as life expectancy has increased dramatically. The average retirement age for workers has fallen from 66 to 60 over the past 50 years. This means that the average worker who reaches retirement can expect to spend 10 to 20 years in retirement.

Economist Michael Cox of the Federal Reserve Board of Dallas has assembled the following: Total lifetime hours worked on the job have declined about 25 percent in a little more than 100 years.

The average age for starting full-time work has increased from 13 in 1870 to 19 today.

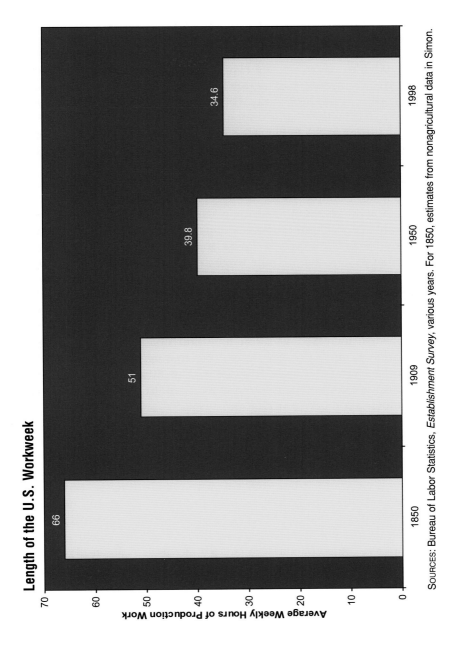

Length of the U.S. Workweek

SOURCES: Bureau of Labor Statistics, *Establishment Survey*, various years. For 1850, estimates from nonagricultural data in Simon.

33. Better Work for Better Pay

These days we often hear nostalgic talk about the good old days of the 1950s when it only took one parent's income to raise a family. Dad went to the office or factory. There was enough income for Mom to stay home and take care of the children. The '50s were an idyllic time long past, we are told, when good jobs were available at good wages. This portrayal of the '50s and '60s is partly true, and partly fairy tale. What is undoubtedly true is that the '50s and '60s saw a surge in the living standards of the typical American household. But it is a myth that wages and living standards were higher then than they are today. The average hourly compensation for a full-time worker is about 20 percent higher today than it was in the 1950s, for example. In some ways, *these* are the good old days.

The hourly manufacturing wage at the turn of the century was about $3.40 an hour in today's dollars. Today, the average wage is about $12.50 an hour—almost four times higher. Going back further in time, the average wage in 1800 was about $1.15 an hour or one-tenth of the current wage rates. The increase in real wages reflects monumental productivity improvements.

When we take into account the value of fringe benefits to workers—including employer-provided or mandated medical insurance, pensions, increased vacation time and holidays, unemployment insurance, and FICA taxes—we find that average hourly worker compensation has risen by more than 50 percent since 1950. Noncash income has grown from 5 percent to 19 percent of worker compensation between 1950 and 1995.

In recent years the official inflation rate has been overstated by about 1 percentage point per year. The inflation calculations have not properly accounted for improved quality of products and the dramatic decline in price for new products, such as cellular telephones and computer software. According to economist David Henderson of the Hoover Institute, "Assuming this minimum 1 percentage point bias for every year since 1973, real hourly wages since 1973 have actually increased by about 9.5 percent and real employee compensation since 1980 has increased by about 25 percent."

For most occupations the pay is better than ever. Teachers, service workers, steel workers, secretaries, and factory workers, just to name a few, fare substantially better financially than their counterparts did 40 years ago.

Rising Worker Pay

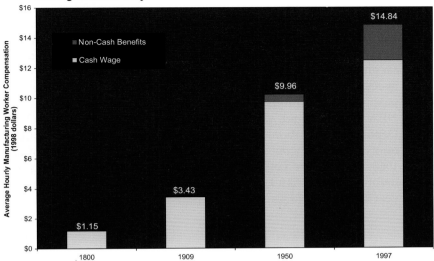

SOURCES: *Historical Statistics of the United States* , Series D 802; and *Statistical Abstract of the United States: 1998*, Table 867.

Median Income by Occupation (1997 dollars)

Year	Professor	Teacher	Lawyer	Doctor	Engineer	Manufacturing
1900		$6,404				$9,508
1930	$29,375	$13,650	$25,617	$36,123	$33,643	$14,303
1950	$29,001	$20,049	$38,113	$70,059	$32,305	$21,981
1995	$58,061	$39,374	$89,441	$92,342	$58,427	$29,411

SOURCES: *Historical Statistics of the United States*, Series D739-764; and Bureau of Labor Statistics, *National Compensation Survey*, various years.

34. The Reduction of Labor Unrest

In the first half of the 20th century, strikes against industrial giants were commonplace and oftentimes led to violence, sometimes injury, and always lost income for workers and lost output for employers. Such strikes are much less frequent now and would be less financially ruinous today than they would have been in the past, notwithstanding the famous strikes of the past decade by the NBA players and the major league baseball players. U.S. Department of Labor statistics indicate that, major work stoppages now occur at only one-quarter the frequency of the stoppage of the 1960s. During the peak year 1976 more than 400 strikes occurred involving more than 1,000 workers compared with less than 50 per year during the 1990s.

Work Stoppages

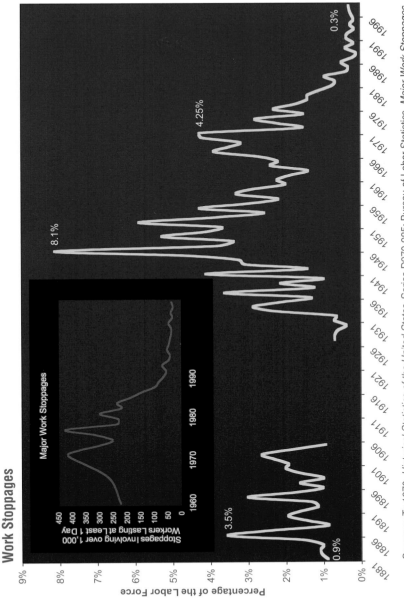

SOURCES: To 1970, *Historical Statistics of the United States*, Series D970-985; Bureau of Labor Statistics, *Major Work Stoppages*, various years; and data for 1971–98 based on *Statistical Abstract of the United States, 1999*, No. 717.

103

SECTION VII. LEISURE, RECREATION, AND ENTERTAINMENT

A prevailing opinion among Americans today is that we have less free time than ever. A recent best-selling book, *The Overworked American*, by Harvard economist Juliet B. Schor suggested that Americans are running endless circles around "the squirrel cage of capitalism." We are said to be stretched to the snapping point—juggling work, family responsibilities, housework, and other must-do activities—so that we have less free time than ever before. Parents are forever cramming their children into the van to drive them to their various activities. A new term has entered our lexicon to describe these harried individuals: soccer moms and dads. So it is understandable that many Americans think they have less leisure time than ever before. The actual evidence, however, shows that Americans spend less time at work and more time at discretionary activities than perhaps any other time in history. And certainly we spend more of our income on leisure activities than ever before.

Because we have more leisure and higher incomes, we spend more on recreation and entertainment than any other society in history. In fact, the United States in the second half of the 20th century became the world's first mass consumption society—so much so that now the complaint about Americans is that we consume too much. Today, the typical American consumes about four times more goods and services than our counterparts did 100 years ago. The reason is we produce about four times as much as our grandparents did.

One of the big growth areas for spending is entertainment. In the first half of the 20th century the major form of entertainment was radio and motion pictures. Since the 1950s TV has been king. It is common to denounce "the boob tube" as an invention that has eroded our sense and sensibility—perhaps diverting us from more productive activities like reading, exercising, working, and engaging in community events. But without a doubt, TV has transformed American life over the half century. One of the most memorable TV lines of the 20th century was, "Lucy, I'm home." For better or worse, Americans now watch more than six hours of television a day—tuning into soap operas, sitcoms, sporting events, game shows, and the nightly news.

35. Americans Have More Leisure Time

Sociologist John Robinson of the University of Maryland, the nation's leading authority on how Americans spend their time, has found that Americans gained on average about five extra hours of free time a week between 1965 and 1985.

In 1965 the average American had 34.5 hours of free time available during the week. By 1985 Americans had 40 hours a week for leisure. From 1965 to 1985 the greatest increase in free time was recorded for women who work in the labor force. Working women have on average one hour a day more free time than in the 1960s.

The long-term data are even more encouraging. The Dallas Federal Reserve Board study on work and leisure found that the average American has three times more leisure hours over his lifetime than his ancestors of the late 19th century did. Just over the past 20 years the average American gained 40,000 added lifetime hours of leisure.

The number of holidays and vacation days has more than doubled since 1960. Americans are also retiring about five years earlier than they did 30 years ago and they start work at least two years later.

Leisure Time

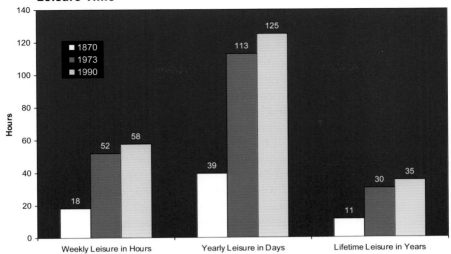

SOURCE: Authors' calculations based on Federal Reserve Bank of Dallas, *1993 Annual Report: These Are the Good Old Days*, pp. 7–8.

The Changing Content of Life and Time

	1870	1973	1990
Age starting work	13.0	18.5	19.1
Life expectancy	43.5	70.6	75.0
Retirement		6.6	11.4
Years on job	30.5	45.5	44.5
Annual hours on job	3,069	1,743	1,562
Annual hours work at home	1,825	1,391	1,278

SOURCE: Federal Reserve Bank of Dallas, *1993 Annual Report: These Are the Good Old Days*, pp. 4, 7–8.

36. Consumers Can Afford More of Everything

Today, even a low-income worker in the United States can afford a range of consumer and recreational items that goes beyond the imaginations of even the richest kings just a century ago. Most modern-day conveniences that we now take for granted either had not yet been invented before 1900 or were prohibitively expensive to produce for the common worker.

Ed Rubenstein of the Hudson Institute has measured the availability and cost of major consumer items over the course of the past century. The affordability of almost every standard consumer item has risen markedly over the past century. For example, in 1900 the average-income American had to work about 10 hours (or a full day's work) to afford a pair of Levi jeans. Now the average American has to work about 1 hour to purchase that same pair of pants.

Federal Reserve Board economist Michael Cox in his trenchent book on this subject, *The Myth of Rich and Poor*, has documented other examples: "The price of a 6.5 ounce bottle of Coca Cola, in terms of work required, has declined from 5.5 minutes in 1920 to 3.5 minutes in 1970 to 1.5 minutes of work today. In 1940 Californians paid 30 cents—nearly half an hour's wage—for the first McDonald's hamburger, one-eighth pound of ground beef. Today's one-fifth pound Big Mac costs $1.89, the equivalent of just 8.6 minutes of work. The price of a Hershey's chocolate bar has risen from 10 cents to 45 cents over the past 23 years; still its price in work time is a mere 2 minutes, one-tenth of what it cost at the turn of the century."

Another way to demonstrate the comparison is to consider the sticker shock if we still had to work as many hours today to buy things as we did in 1900. A pair of scissors would cost $67, a bicycle $2,200, and a telephone $1,200.

America's material standard of living is far higher than it is in other countries, and the U.S. lead in consumption is generally wider than our lead in income.

The High Cost of Living, 1897 Style

Item	1897 Sears Catalog Price	1997 Work-Equivalent Price
1-lb. box of baking soda	$0.06	$5.34
100 lb. 16d nails	$1.70	$151.39
Garden hoe	$0.28	$24.94
26" carpenter's saw	$0.50	$44.53
13" nail hammer	$0.42	$37.40
9" steel scissors	$0.75	$66.79
Aluminum bread pan	$0.37	$32.95
Ironing board	$0.60	$54.43
Telephone	$13.50	$1,202.23
Men's cowboy boots	$3.50	$311.69
Pair men's socks	$0.13	$11.58
Pair ladies' hose	$0.25	$22.26
200 yd spool of cotton thread	$0.02	$1.78
Webster's dictionary	$0.70	$62.34
One dozen pencils	$0.14	$12.47
250 manila envelopes	$0.35	$31.17
1 carat diamond ring	$74.00	$6,590.00
Upright piano	$125.00	$11,131.76
Bicycle	$24.95	$2,221.90
Baby carriage	$10.25	$912.80

SOURCE: Federal Reserve Bank of Dallas, 1997 Annual Report, *Time Well Spent: The Declining Real Cost of Living in America*, p. 3.

Note: Work-equivalent prices are in terms of how much a manufacturing employee would earn today working the same number of hours required to afford the item in 1897.

Personal Consumption Expenditures, 1998

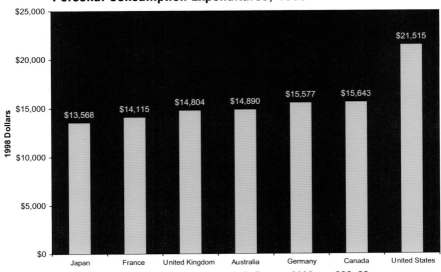

SOURCE: World Bank, *World Development Indicators 2000*, pp. 222–23.

37. Getting More Fun Out of Life: Recreational Spending

Poor societies spend almost all of their income on the necessities of life: food, clothing, and housing. But in the United States a shrinking share of the family budget is devoted to necessities. According to a recently released study by the Joint Economic Committee of the U.S. Congress, in 1900 Americans spent about two-thirds of their budgets on necessities, but now they spend just a bit over one-third of their budgets for food, clothing, and shelter.

Meanwhile, the single fastest-growing major expenditure for Americans (other than taxes) is for recreation. Today, the average American household spends about 10 times as much on recreation as it did in 1920 and about 5 times as much as it did in 1950.

In 1921 Americans spent $30 million for tickets to watch sporting events. That is less than it costs to buy 10 minutes of TV advertising during the Super Bowl ($32 million). Today, Americans spend $5 billion on admissions to sporting events.

Of course, today, because of innovations like ESPN, sports are available on TV 24 hours a day. Very few sporting events were broadcast on TV before 1960. At most, only a few million Americans ever had the chance to watch Babe Ruth, the greatest baseball player, during his entire career. In the 1990s a few million people were able to watch Michael Jordan, the greatest basketball player, every time he laced his shoes for a game.

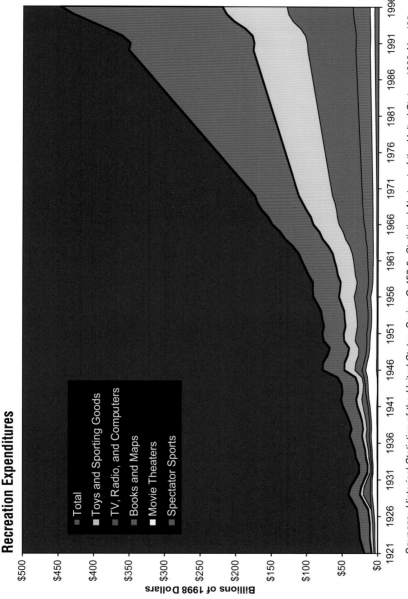

Recreation Expenditures

Billions of 1998 Dollars

- Total
- Toys and Sporting Goods
- TV, Radio, and Computers
- Books and Maps
- Movie Theaters
- Spectator Sports

1921 1926 1931 1936 1941 1946 1951 1956 1961 1966 1971 1976 1981 1986 1991 1996

$0 $50 $100 $150 $200 $250 $300 $350 $400 $450 $500

SOURCES: *Historical Statistics of the United States*, Series G 452-6; *Statistical Abstract of the United States: 1999*, No. 430; and Bureau of Economic Analysis, *Survey of Current Business*, various years.

111

38. Surviving the Heat

Although we hear a lot of gloomy talk about global warming nowadays, hot weather is much more tolerable today than it was 100 years ago. Climatologist Patrick J. Michaels of the University of Virginia points out that heat-related mortality is going down. "In 1995," Michaels notes, "Chicago saw several hundred deaths in a July heat wave. But there were 885 heat-related deaths in the Second City in 1955. Want to see true carnage? Go back to 1901 when 10,000 Americans perished in the heat. (The globe was 1 percent cooler then!)" What is the difference between now and then? Michaels says two words explain the reduction in deaths: air-conditioning.

In 1915 an article in *Ladies' Home Journal* titled "You Will Think This Is a Dream" first introduced Americans to the idea of cooled homes in the summer. Actually, that "dream" was still several decades away. Office buildings and apartment buildings, especially in the South, were steam baths in the summer. Supposedly, the United States Congress rarely convened in the summer months in Washington before the era of air conditioning. Today, people in the warm-climate states view air-conditioning as a near necessity. Almost all new homes feature central air conditioning. As of 1960 only about 1 in 10 American homes had air conditioning. Now more than two-thirds of all homes have air conditioning, and almost all new homes in warm climates are built with air conditioning.

Another summertime improvement has been the increased number of backyard swimming pools. Before the 1950s, in-ground swimming pools were a rarity owned by only the super-affluent. But between 1950 and 1982 the number of swimming pools rose from roughly 100,000 to 2 million—a 20-fold increase. Today, there are more than 7 million swimming pools in the United States.

Another invention of this century that has made summer more bearable and has contributed to a reduction in heat-related illnesses has been refrigeration. In 1900 almost no homes had refrigeration. Today, 99 percent of homes do and even more than 95 percent of poor households have refrigeration. In 1950 less than 10 percent of homes had freezers; today almost all homes do. And the quality has improved a lot too. Today's refrigerator/freezers have temperature control, ice makers, and even provide crushed ice with a push of a button.

Heat-Related Mortality in Chicago

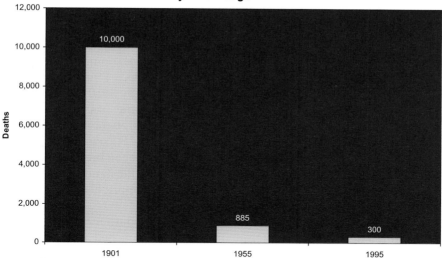

SOURCE: Patrick J. Michaels and Robert C. Balling, Jr., *The Satanic Gases: Clearing the Air about Global Warming* (Washington: Cato Institute, 2000), p. 174.

Keeping Cool

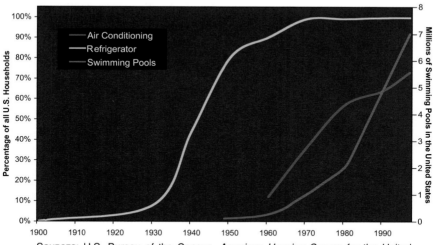

SOURCES: U.S. Bureau of the Census, *American Housing Survey for the United States in 1997*; and U.S. Bureau of the Census, "Housing Then and Now," www.census.gov/hhes/www/housing/census/histcensushsg.html.

39. Entertainment: Radio, Motion Pictures, and TV

One of the greatest inventions of the 20th century was the radio. In the 1920s radios first began to appear in homes—bringing instant news, entertainment, and music into U.S. living rooms. In 1925 only 20 percent of homes had a radio. By 1950 the average home had two radios. Now the average home has four to five radios. Historian Alan Brinkley describes this phenomenal rise in the spread of radio sales to vast numbers of U.S. consumers: "The first commercial radio station in America . . . began broadcasting in 1920. . . . By 1923 there were more than 500 radio stations, covering virtually every area of the country. (By 1929) more than 12 million families owned radio sets."

Motion pictures were perhaps the first modern means of entertainment. The motion picture industry was launched at the turn of the century and was so instantly popular that by 1930 Hollywood sold three tickets per week per household—an all-time peak. In the '60s, '70s, and '80s, movie ticket sales dropped dramatically.

The decline in movie attendance was due to the introduction of two more convenient and less expensive forms of recreation: the television in the 1950s and the VCR in the 1980s.

TV has become such an essential staple of American life these days that we often forget that it is a relatively recent invention. At just before the midpoint of this century, 1946, there were about 17,000 TV sets in the country. By 1960 there were more than 40 million TV sets in use. And those Zenith and Motorola TV sets were black and white. Today, 98 percent of American households own a color TV, 67 percent own two color TVs, 40 percent own three TVs, 74 percent have cable TV, 40 percent receive pay cable stations, 84 percent have a VCR, 32 percent have at least two VCRs, and 93 percent have a remote control clicker with their TV.

As recently as the late 1960s most TV shows were in black and white. Americans only had three or four channels to choose from. Reception, particularly in rural areas, was poor and fuzzy. Now most households have access to scores of channels suiting every imaginable viewing taste and several that provide 24-hour-a-day programming.

Cable TV has exploded as an industry and in its access to American homes. In the 1950s less than half a percent of American households had cable. By the late 1980s that figure had climbed to 45 percent. Most recent estimates indicate that almost 3 of 4 households have cable.

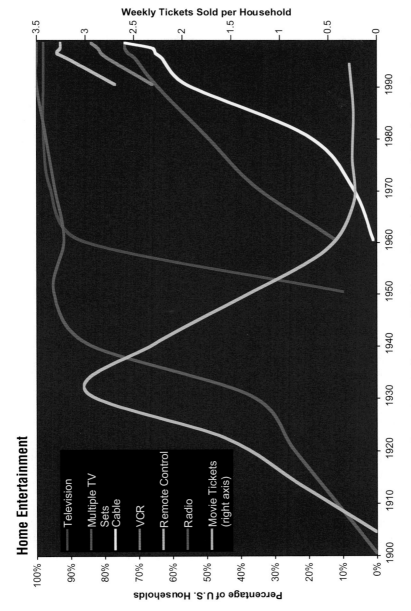

Home Entertainment

Weekly Tickets Sold per Household

Percentage of U.S. Households

Television
Multiple TV
Sets
Cable
VCR
Remote Control
Radio
Movie Tickets
(right axis)

SOURCES: Nielsen Media Research, *1998 Report on Television*, p. 15; Stanley Lebergott, *The American Economy: Income, Wealth, and Want* (Princeton, N.J.: Princeton University Press, 1976); *Historical Statistics of the United States*, Series H 522; and Motion Picture Association of America.

115

SECTION VIII. HOUSING

In recent years the rise in homelessness has heightened public concern about the adequacy and affordability of housing. However, it is beyond dispute that the vast majority of Americans today are much better housed than at any prior time in history. In 1900 the typical American city dweller lived in tenement housing; today most Americans live in homes that they own. Moreover, the homes today are of far superior quality: houses are bigger, less crowded, and are stocked with more modern conveniences— everything from garbage disposals to air conditioners to electric garage-door openers to cable television. Many of these household items are now considered "essentials" when just 30 years ago they were "conveniences" and 50 years ago they were "extravagances" available in only the most affluent homes.

40. Home Ownership: Pursuing the American Dream

To own one's home has historically been considered the equivalent to achieving the American dream. Despite recent news reports and books on the elusiveness of the American dream today, the rate of home ownership has been on a slow but steady rise for most of this century. In 1997 two-thirds of Americans owned their homes—the highest rate ever.

In 1900 about 50 percent of Americans owned their own homes. By 1950 that number had risen to about 55 percent. Today, about two-thirds of Americans own their own homes. Black home ownership has risen more rapidly: from just over 20 percent in 1900 to slightly more than 40 percent today. Almost as many poor Americans own their own homes today as all Americans did in 1900. The only period in the past half century when home ownership declined was in the late 1970s and early 1980s when loose monetary policy sent mortgage interest rates soaring to 18 to 20 percent.

A rising rate of home ownership has corollary societal benefits. According to Professor Nicholas Retsinas at Harvard's Joint Center for Housing Studies, "We are becoming a nation of home-owners: 66 percent of us own our own homes, an all-time high. . . . This home ownership surge is good news. Mortgages anchor owners in their neighborhoods, making them stakeholders in their communities. Homeownership correlates with family stability."

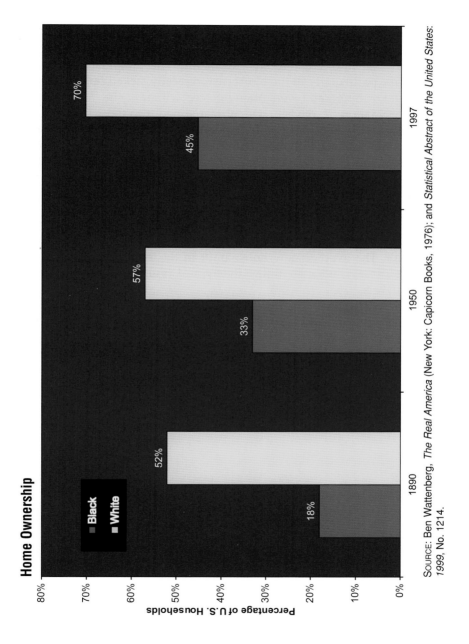

Home Ownership

Black
White

Percentage of U.S. Households

80%
70%
60%
50%
40%
30%
20%
10%
0%

1890 · 52% · 18%
1950 · 57% · 33%
1997 · 70% · 45%

SOURCE: Ben Wattenberg, *The Real America* (New York: Capicorn Books, 1976); and *Statistical Abstract of the United States: 1999*, No. 1214.

119

41. Bigger, Better, Less Crowded Houses

In 1890 Jacob Riis published in his famous book *How the Other Half Lives*, which described the horrid and unsanitary conditions of tenement slums. Families with three or four children were crowded into single-room apartments. The dilapidated housing units, particularly in the Northeast, typically lacked hot water and toilet facilities, and were often infested with rats.

No more. Today's houses are far superior to those squalid and cramped living quarters. In 1900 about 1 in 5 American families lived in housing with more than 3 persons per bedroom. Today only about 1 in 20 families live in such cramped housing conditions. The average house today has two to three times as many rooms per dweller as it had at the turn of the century.

In 1900 in the United States there was one housing unit for every five people, in 1950, for about four people; and currently, for less than three people. Furthermore, the houses are bigger and better built. The average new house built in the 1960s had about 1,400 square feet, whereas today the typical house has close to 2,100 square feet.

To appreciate the improved conditions and reduced crowding of U.S. housing, it is useful to compare housing space in the United States with other countries. The average U.S. house or apartment in the United States is two times larger than the average house or apartment in Japan and more than three times larger than the average house or apartment in Russia.

Less Crowded Homes

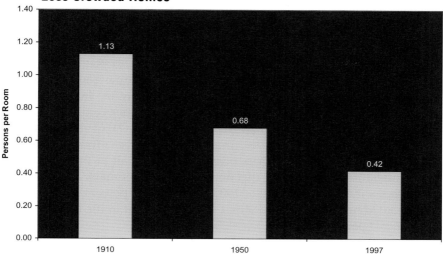

SOURCES: Stanley Lebergott, *The American Economy: Income, Wealth, and Want* (Princeton, N.J.: Princeton University Press, 1976), p. 258; and *American Housing Survey for the United States*, various years.

Housing Space, Square Feet per Person, 1995

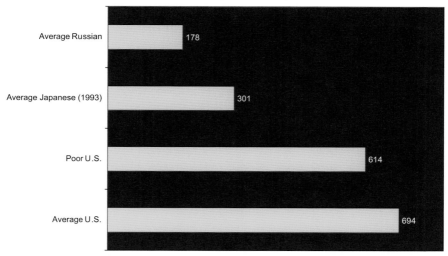

SOURCES: *American Housing Survey for the United States in 1995*; Japan Statistics Bureau; and Russian Statistical Agency.

42. The Modern Home Has Every Convenience

Homes are not just less crowded today. They have far more modern amenities as standard features—features that most young people do not even think much about these days. It is hard for us to imagine, for example, that in 1900 less than one in five homes had running water, flush toilets, a vacuum cleaner, or gas or electric heat. As of 1950 fewer than 20 percent of homes had air conditioning, a dishwasher, a dryer, or a microwave oven. Today, between 80 and 100 percent of American homes have all of these modern amenities. It is also true that homes are in better material condition today than they were 50 or 100 years ago. The percentage of dilapidated housing fell from about 15 to 20 percent in the late 1940s to 2 to 3 percent today.

Improvement in U.S. Housing

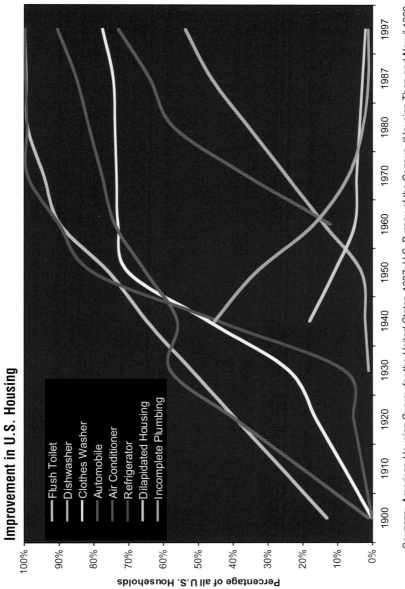

Legend:
- Flush Toilet
- Dishwasher
- Clothes Washer
- Automobile
- Air Conditioner
- Refrigerator
- Dilapidated Housing
- Incomplete Plumbing

Percentage of all U.S. Households

100% 90% 80% 70% 60% 50% 40% 30% 20% 10% 0%

1900 1910 1920 1930 1940 1950 1960 1970 1980 1987 1997

SOURCES: *American Housing Survey for the United States*, 1997; U.S. Bureau of the Census, "Housing Then and Now," 1999, www.census.gov/hhes/www/housing/census/histcensushsg.html; and Simon, p. 247.

123

43. Electrification of the Nation

The era of electricity dawned in the late 19th century and spawned a 50-year period economists have described as "the second industrial revolution." The new age of electricity modernized almost every aspect of U.S. industry and home life. Electricity replaced water and steam as a much more powerful and efficient source of industrial power. And, of course, the electrification of U.S. homes first brought light and then made possible the enormous revolution in household appliances: radios, TVs, refrigerators, vacuum cleaners, and washing machines. The rapid diffusion of electric power to U.S. households began in 1900.

In 1900, 2 percent of homes had electricity. In 1950, that percentage had increased to about 70 percent. By 1975, about 99 percent of American homes had electricity. The Westinghouse/Tesla AC distribution system, developed in 1887, that made electrification widespread.

Electric bills are much lower today than in the past. In 1900, the wage-indexed price of electricity was six times above its current level, and residential electricity costs were nearly 10 times higher than they are today. The Energy Information Agency describes the changes in this industry by noting, "From the opening of the first modern central generating station in 1882, the electric power industry has generally been marked by substantial growth in capacity and generation and dramatic declines in price. Technical efficiencies, economies of scale, consolidation within the industry, and consumer preferences for electricity all account for this growth and reduced price."

According to economist Jeremy Greenwood of the University of Rochester, the use of electric motors in industry began to explode in the second decade of the 20th century. In 1900 only about 5 percent of the power generation used in private industry came from electricity; by 1940 that percentage was 90 percent. Greenwood finds that this shift to the electric motor powered a tremendous productivity gain in manufacturing and paved the way for huge gains in factory output and worker incomes.

Electrification of U.S. Homes

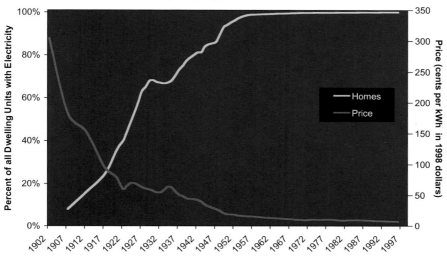

SOURCES: *Historical Statistics of the United States*, Series S 109, S 116; and *Statistical Abstract of the United States: 1998*, Table 959.

Electricity and Productivity

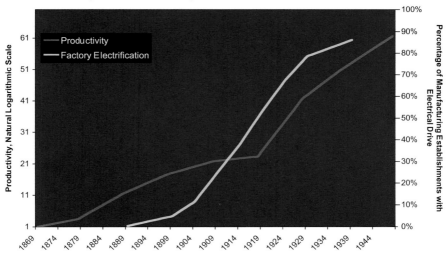

SOURCE: P. A. David, "Computer and Dynamo: The Modern Productivity Paradox in a Not-Too-Distant Mirror," in *Technology and Productivity: The Challenge for Economic Policy* (OECD: Paris, 1991), Tables 2 and 3.

44. Lighting Up the Nation

Americans take for granted today the ease of flicking a switch and having a light come on. Edison's light bulb was invented in the late 1800s, but it was not until the 1930s that most homes had electric lights. Now, of course, almost every home has electric lights. The light bulb is a case study in the innovation process that has so radically improved basic living conditions in the United States and across the globe in the 20th century. Since around 1900, the light produced by different light devices has increased more than 100-fold. And nowadays, GE makes lightbulbs that last for years.

The price has dropped too. According to economist William Nordhaus of Yale University, the price of a unit of light has fallen from 40 cents per 1,000 lumen hours to less than one-tenth of a cent today. That is a decline of more than 99.5 percent.

Bulb Life (hours)

Incandescent

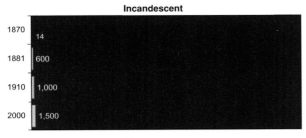

1870	14
1881	600
1910	1,000
2000	1,500

Fluorescent

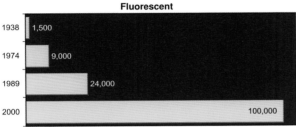

1938	1,500
1974	9,000
1989	24,000
2000	100,000

SOURCE: "Bulbs Last Longer," *USA Today*, March 9, 2000.

Let There Be More Light

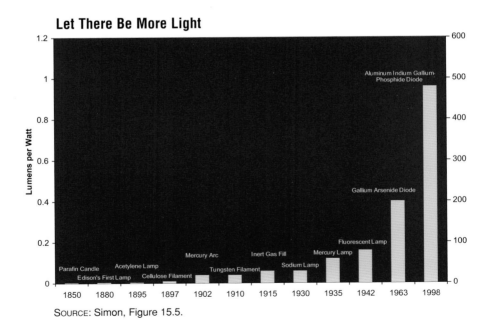

SOURCE: Simon, Figure 15.5.

SECTION IX. TRANSPORTATION AND COMMUNICATIONS

Ben Bagdikian, an expert on the history of communications at the University of California at Berkeley, describes the transition from the rudimentary telegraph to the telephone as follows: "In 1790 there was no telegraph, but by 1880, Western Union had 291 million miles of wire handling 32 million messages a year. Physically carrying pieces of paper by hand had been augmented by translating the words into electrical impulses, letter by letter, sent over wires to the destination where someone typed out the message and delivered it to the recipient in less time than it took the mail.

"By the mid-20th century something had happened to shrink the use of telegrams. In 1950 there were 179 million messages sent by telegram but by 1979 only 45 million. The spoken word transmitted directly from one person to another was faster. By 1978 at least 97 percent of homes had a phone and Americans were having phone conversations at the rate of 737 million a day."

Just as the telephone replaced the slow and cumbersome telegraph, the automobile and jet travel have replaced the horse and the railroad. Communications and transportation are not just faster, but substantially superior in quality and cheaper in price.

Perhaps an excerpt from a newspaper from the early part of the 20th century can demonstrate how far Americans have progressed in the past 100 years in transportation: "It was confidently predicted 100 years ago that in the century then coming (the 19th) man would learn to fly. But he has not made any striking advance in the pursuit of his hopes. . . . Possibly the 100 years of experiment teach us that we will never fly in the air as do the birds, or if we do so, it will be merely for the pleasure of the thing. Flying in so variable an element as the air can never, we think, be reduced to a science."

45. The Telephone: Reach Out and Touch Someone

A little more than 100 years ago Americans sent more telegrams than they made telephone calls. In 1900 few (about 5%) American households owned a phone. Fifty years ago telephones were still somewhat a luxury with only 60 percent of American households having phone service. Today, 99 percent of homes have a telephone but not too many of us ever send a telegram.

Telephones are far superior products to the devices Americans used to talk with each other 50 years ago. Making a person-to-person call in the 1940s and early 1950s often required operator assistance. Connections often got crossed and service was frequently disrupted or crackling with static. (Just watch an old Jimmy Stewart movie and you will see how prehistoric phone service was in that era.) One of the jobs that is becoming obsolete today due to technology in the United States is the telephone operator's.

Today, Americans do not just have phones in their homes. They have phones in their briefcases, their purses, and their cars. The corded phone is fast becoming obsolete because it does not travel well at all. Corded phone sales have been relatively flat in the 1990s. But sales of cordless and cellular phones have risen sharply. In 1997, for the first time ever, Americans bought more cordless than corded phones.

Phone service costs have plummeted over the past century. A 10-minute coast-to-coast phone call in 1915 cost about $65—at a time when the average worker earned less than $1 an hour in wages.

Similarly, the cost of international calls has fallen sharply since 1950. A three-minute transatlantic call from the United States to Europe has fallen in real terms by about 60 percent over the past four decades. Because of increased competition in telecommunications, monthly phone service charges have fallen about fivefold relative to wages since 1950.

An example of very recent modern technological innovation in telephone communications is the laying of transoceanic fiber-optic cables. As recently as the late 1980s none reached across the Atlantic or Pacific oceans. By 1995 there were about 20, and by 1999 there were about 100. The dawning of this new age of transoceanic fiber-optic cables promises to revolutionize and further reduce costs for communications in the next 20 years.

Three-Minute Call from New York to San Francisco

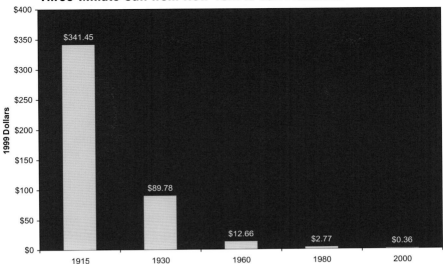

SOURCE: AT&T Corporate Archives, cited in Cox and Alm, 1997 Annual Report, Federal Reserve Bank of Dallas.

Modern Communication

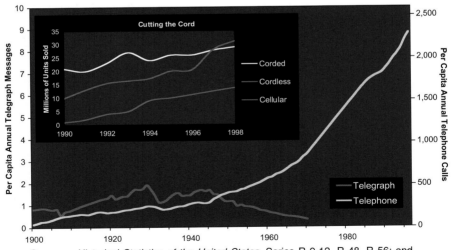

SOURCES: *Historical Statistics of the United States*, Series R 9-12, R 48, R 56; and *Statistical Abstract of the United States: 1998*, Table 915. Inset source: Consumer Electronics Association, cited in *Time*, March 23, 1998, p. 38.

Note: Cellular includes digital wireless phones.

46. From Horses to Horsepower

Author E. B. White once wrote that "everything we want in life is somewhere else, and we get there in a car." The automobile was the quintessential American invention—ideal for the wide-open frontiers of this spacious country. Next to the computer, the automobile is arguably the most liberating invention of the past 100 years. Cars were the first form of rapid-speed transportation that enabled Americans to go wherever they wanted, whenever they wanted. The automobile essentially replaced the horse as a means of popular transportation. In 1900 there were 20 horses for every 100 U.S. households and virtually no cars. By the end of the century about 85 of every 100 American households had a car and almost no one used a horse any longer for intra-city or intercity transportation.

Automobile production in the United States has surged since the time that Model Ts rolled off Henry Ford's assembly line. The automobile was an instant sensation with American households—at first a glitzy status symbol (like a private jet today), but soon an essential form of transportation for workers and families. In 1900 just 8,000 cars were registered in the United States. In 1910 sales of automobiles numbered around 180,000. But due primarily to Ford and the discovery of cheap oil in Texas, by 1916 the U.S. auto industry was rolling 1 million cars off the assembly line each year. By 1929 Americans bought 5 million cars. Today Americans own about 135 million cars with about 17 million new cars produced here every year.

The cost of a car has fallen three to four times relative to the hours of work needed to purchase one (4,700 in 1915 versus about 1,400 today). Even most of America's poor have a car today. The decline in automobile prices is especially impressive given the superiority of current cars to what was sold in the 1950s and before. Standard features, for example, of a new Ford Mustang today include a stereo (increasingly with a CD player), air conditioning, steel belted radial tires, power steering and brakes, antilock brakes, greater horsepower engine, and other features that were virtually unavailable 40 years ago. Today's car is a far superior machine to what was once produced in Detroit.

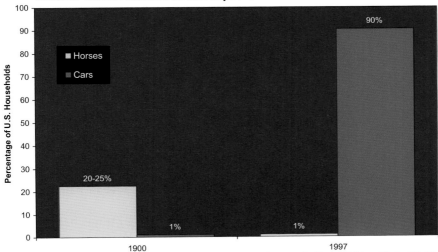

Ground Travel: Horses to Horsepower

SOURCE: Stanley Lebergott, *The Americans: An Economic Record* (New York: W. W. Norton, 1984).

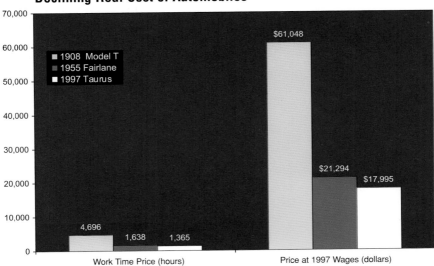

Declining Real Cost of Automobiles

SOURCE: Cox and Alm, 1997 Annual Report, Federal Reserve Bank of Dallas, p. 11.

47. Air Travel Makes the World a Smaller Place

Travel on commercial airlines has risen astonishingly over the past several decades. Even as recently as the early 1950s airplane travel was generally reserved for the wealthiest families and corporate travelers. Now air travel is a common form of transportation for middle-income and even lower-income family travelers.

Between 1960 and 1986 air travel grew by 350 percent. Plane miles traveled have risen from less than 100 per person per year to almost 1,000 per person in 1978 to 1,600 today.

Americans' preference for speed in travel is seen by tracing the trend away from rail and bus in intercity travel to plane during 1939 to 1978.

The primary explanation for the surge in air travel has been the rapid decline in the cost of plane tickets. The Federal Reserve Bank of Dallas has discovered that early plane travel for a 1,000-mile trip in 1920 would have cost the average American 220 work hours. Today, that same plane trip would only require about 11 work hours.

Another key factor behind lower airfares in the past 20 years was the deregulation of the airlines in the late 1970s, which substantially increased competition. Estimates from the Brookings Institution suggest that airline deregulation saves U.S. travelers more than $1 billion a year.

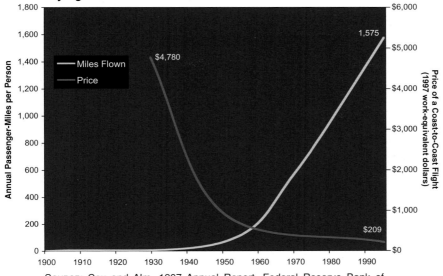

Flying More for Less

SOURCE: Cox and Alm, 1997 Annual Report, Federal Reserve Bank of Dallas, p. 13.

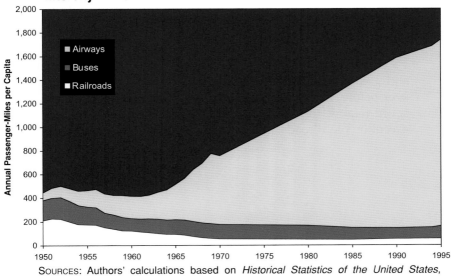

Intercity Travel

SOURCES: Authors' calculations based on *Historical Statistics of the United States*, Series Q 2, 4, 6, and 8; and *Current Population Survey*, various years.

135

48. The Accelerating Speed of Travel

At the start of the century it took weeks to cross the ocean on a cruise ship (the fastest mode of transatlantic travel). Now it takes only hours on a plane. Similarly, Americans have access to a much wider variety of choices in transportation than they did in earlier times when intra city travel was confined to railroad, stagecoach, or horse. The types of transportation modes available to Americans grew over the past 75 years.

The speed of travel has remarkably improved. Ground transportation speeds have increased about threefold in this century.

Consider travel times from New York to Boston. In the early 19th century a stagecoach took four days and three nights to make the trip. By the 1850s the railroads could make the trip in 9 to 10 hours. By the first half of the 20th century the trip by railroad or car took about 6 hours. By the 1960s the flight took a little more than an hour's time.

Airplane speeds have risen even more dramatically. At the turn of the century, when the Wright Brothers tested the first airplane, it traveled (briefly) at a top speed of 40 miles per hour. By the end of World War I planes had reached a top speed approaching 200 miles per hour. By the end of World War II planes were traveling at just over 500 miles per hour. Today, jets can travel over 2,500 miles per hour.

The average air flight time from Los Angeles to New York was about 12 hours in 1950. Today, the trip takes just over 5 hours.

The most positive impact of the reduced cost of transportation and greater speeds is that Americans travel far more often than ever before. For example, every type of vehicle has increased its speed relative to population size over the past 70 years with the exception of railroad cars.

Top Speeds of Ground Transport of Humans, 1784–1967

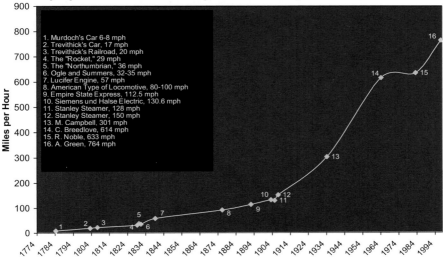

1. Murdoch's Car 6-8 mph
2. Trevithick's Car, 17 mph
3. Trevithick's Railroad, 20 mph
4. The "Rocket," 29 mph
5. The "Northumbrian," 36 mph
6. Ogle and Summers, 32-35 mph
7. Lucifer Engine, 57 mph
8. American Type of Locomotive, 80-100 mph
9. Empire State Express, 112.5 mph
10. Siemens und Halse Electric, 130.6 mph
11. Stanley Steamer, 128 mph
12. Stanley Steamer, 150 mph
13. M. Campbell, 301 mph
14. C. Breedlove, 614 mph
15. R. Noble, 633 mph
16. A. Green, 764 mph

SOURCES: Data from 1774 to 1964 from Jeremy Atack, "Long-Term Trends in Productivity," in Simon, p. 166. Data from 1965 to 1997 from Reuters Limited, "List of World Land Speed Record Holders," October 15, 1997.

Top Speeds of Air Transport of Humans, 1905–65 (excluding space travel)

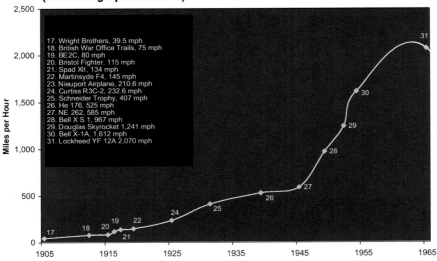

17. Wright Brothers, 39.5 mph
18. British War Office Trails, 75 mph
19. BE2C, 80 mph
20. Bristol Fighter, 115 mph
21. Spad XII, 134 mph
22. Martinsyde F4, 145 mph
23. Nieuport Airplane, 210.6 mph
24. Curtiss R3C-2, 232.6 mph
25. Schneider Trophy, 407 mph
26. He 176, 525 mph
27. NE 262, 585 mph
28. Bell X S 1, 967 mph
29. Douglas Skyrocket 1,241 mph
30. Bell X-1A, 1,612 mph
31. Lockheed YF 12A 2,070 mph

SOURCE: Jeremy Atack, "Trends in Productivity," in Simon, p. 167.

49. The Explosion of International Travel

Americans now travel to foreign countries in record numbers. As the previous discussion illustrates, before the airplane was invented, transportation to foreign countries was slow, expensive, and dangerous. Hence, in 1920 Americans embarked on only 300,000 trips abroad during the entire year. In 1970 Americans took more than 5 million trips to foreign countries. Now, Americans take more than 20 million overseas trips a year. Americans now take as many trips abroad in a week as they did in the year of 1950.

A roundtrip ticket to Europe on an ocean liner in 1900 cost about $750. Today, one can fly to Europe roundtrip with a discount airfare for around $400 (and this does not account for the inflation over the period). This explains why up until the second half of the 20th century most international travel was confined to the super-wealthy.

Although Charles Lindbergh's famous flight across the Atlantic occurred in 1927, it was not until the early 1950s that reliable and affordable international commercial flights were available. As recently as 1940, more overseas travel was done by ship than by air. Although sea travel might have been more luxurious, it was more expensive and much more time consuming. Today over 90 percent of international travel is by commercial airline.

Overseas Travel 1919–70

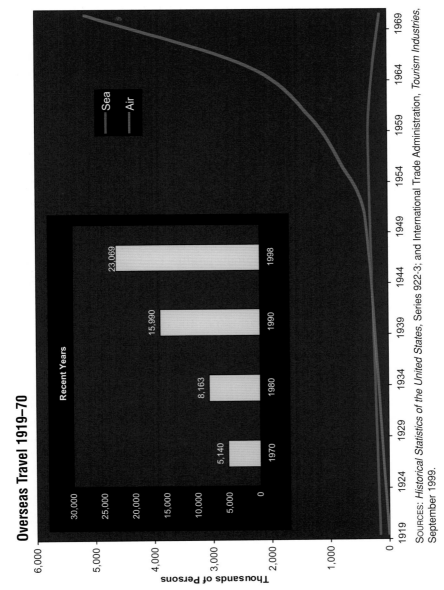

Thousands of Persons

Recent Years

	1970	1980	1990	1998
	5,140	8,163	15,990	23,069

SOURCES: *Historical Statistics of the United States*, Series 922-3; and International Trade Administration, *Tourism Industries*, September 1999.

Note: Overseas travel excludes Mexico and Canada.

139

50. Safer Highways and Airways

Travel safety in the modern age is far better than it ever was before, despite much higher volumes of traffic and congestion on the roads and in the air. Despite the Americans' fear of flying, air travel is now the safest form of transportation ever devised. In fact, in 1998 14 million commercial airline flights carried 615 million passengers. How many deaths? Zero. According to the research organization STATS, "Your odds of dying in a plane crash [based on recent experience from the early 1990s] and based on flying 100,000 miles a year on large commercial jets, are about 1 in 500,000." STATS also finds that if a preson flies just 2,000 miles a year, the odds of dying in a plane crash are roughly equivalent to those of being hit on the head by a falling plane. The death rate from flying on commercial airlines is at least four times lower per mile traveled than from driving a car.

One reason that Americans *think* that flying is dangerous is because major crashes occasionally kill several hundred people. Terrible airplane crashes naturally produce bold newspaper headlines. And, of course, 100 years ago there were no airplane crashes because there were no commercial airlines. Yet, despite the horrific and highly publicized crashes in recent years, the skies have never been safer. The rate of crashes per 100 million miles traveled has plummeted from 1.1 in 1950 to .8 in 1996, to zero in 1998.

Driving is not as safe as flying. In fact, the 40,000 to 50,000 lives lost yearly in car accidents makes driving one of the top 10 killers in America. That is not to say that driving is not safer today than at any time in the history of the automobile. Both 1997 and 1998 were the safest years ever recorded on the highways based on miles traveled. The current death rate of 1.6 deaths per 100 million miles traveled is about 3 times lower than it was 30 years ago and about 10 times safer than in the 1920s. On average, one automobile death occurs for every 1 million cross-country trips.

What accounts for the increased auto safety? Much safer cars—with antilock brakes, power steering, and other safety features—much better constructed roads and highways, improvements in people's driving, tough drunk-driving laws, and greater medical care to save the lives of those who are in accidents.

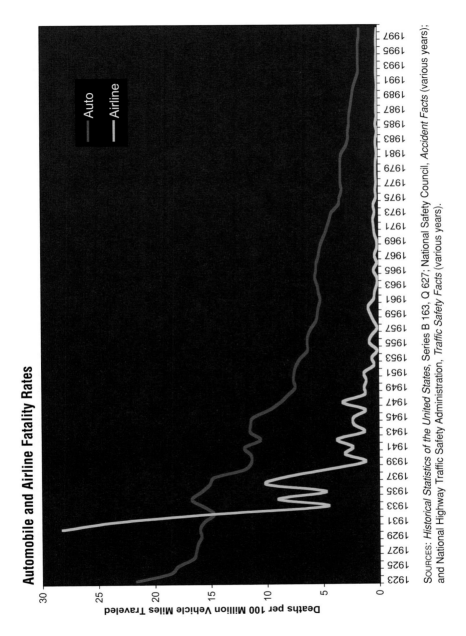

Automobile and Airline Fatality Rates

Deaths per 100 Million Vehicle Miles Traveled

Auto
Airline

SOURCES: *Historical Statistics of the United States*, Series B 163, Q 627; National Safety Council, *Accident Facts* (various years); and National Highway Traffic Safety Administration, *Traffic Safety Facts* (various years).

141

51. Exploring the Last Frontier: Space

One of the 20th century's most enduring symbols of scientific progress was the space flight in 1969 of Apollo 11, whose astronauts landed on the moon and planted the American flag there. This triumph of human intellect and imagination might have been thought of a century ago only as a Jules Verne science fiction. Despite myriad government bunglings, humankind has come a long way in space travel since the first liquid-fuel rocket was launched in 1926 by Dr. Robert Goddard. The table shows the chronology of major space exploration breakthroughs during the subsequent 75 years. One of the most significant recent milestones was the launching of Mars Pathfinder which, for the first time in history, landed on and explored the red planet's surface. One of the most important practical benefits of space exploration has been the birth of satellite communications. Today's shuttle, for example, can launch a 60,000-pound payload, some 300 times the size of Sputnik.

The latest exciting news in space travel is that private firms are beginning to develop a space tourism industry. The *Washington Post* recently reported a $12 million purchase of an eight-day round trip into space whose destination is an orbiting Soviet spacecraft. Of course, the cost of space travel will fall in coming decades as did the cost of every other form of transportation after its introduction in the 20th century.

Space Achievements

March 16, 1926	Dr. Robert Goddard launches the first liquid-fuel rocket.
October 4, 1957	The first artificial satellite is launched into orbit.
September 14, 1959	The first space probe, Luna 2, impacts on the moon.
April 1, 1960	The first weather satellite, Tiros, is placed in orbit around the earth.
April 12, 1961	The first man is launched into space.
July 10, 1962	The first private telecommunications satellite, Telstar, is placed in orbit around the Earth.
February 3, 1966	The first unnamed spaceship, Luna 9, lands on the moon.
December 24, 1968	The first men in the Apollo 8 spacecraft orbit the moon.
July 20, 1969	The first men in the Apollo 11 spacecraft land and walk on the moon.
December 15, 1970	The first spacecraft, Venera 7, lands on Venus.
March 29, 1974	The first robot probe, Mariner 10, flies by Mercury, photographing the planet.
July 20, 1976	The first spaceship, Viking 1, lands on Mars.
March 5, 1979	Robot probe, Voyager 1, flies past Jupiter, studying that planet and its moons.
November 12, 1980	Voyager 1 flies past Saturn.
January 24, 1986	Robot probe, Voyager 2, flies past Uranus.
August 25, 1989	Voyager 2 flies past Neptune.
July 4, 1997	The Mars Pathfinder lands on the Red Planet, and the first robot explores its surface.

SOURCE: Data collected by Ed Hudgins, Cato Institute.

143

SECTION X. INVENTION, INNOVATION, AND SCIENTIFIC PROGRESS

One of the most myopic predictions in American history was made by a patent office bureaucrat who claimed at the turn of the last century that "everything that can be invented already has been." The reality, of course, is that the era of great invention was only beginning as we entered the 20th century. As previous sections have already documented, the 20th century was an era of unprecedented innovation. From the automobile to the refrigerator, to the transistor, to the laser, to fiber optics, to modern medicines, the inventiveness and genius of Americans in this century is unquestionably the driving force behind the great gains in the living standards of Americans and all people worldwide over the past 100 years. Francis Bacon said it best: "The real and legitimate goal of the sciences is the endowment of human life with new inventions and riches."

52. Yankee Ingenuity: The Era of Invention

Probably the greatest inventor in history was Thomas A. Edison (1847–1931), whose light bulb, motion picture projector, phonograph, tape recorder, and roughly 1,000 other patents propelled the United States into the electronic age. Edison's giant footsteps have been followed by thousands of other American scientists and inventors whose brilliance and creativity are continually making our planet a richer place for everyone. The figure lists a chronology of the greatest inventions of the first half of the 20th century, including penicillin, the transistor, xerography, and jet propulsion. It taxes our imaginations to even conceive of what life must have been like before we had all of these modern discoveries.

The figure shows the history of patents granted since the U.S. patent office opened its doors in 1790. In 1900 roughly 25,000 patents were issued. By 1950 that number had jumped modestly to 43,000. But since 1950 there has been a tripling of the number of patents to nearly 150,000 in 1997.

Before the 20th century, even when inventions were discovered there were long waiting periods before their widespread practical application translated into improvements in industry or home life. The major inventions of the 19th century—for example, the locomotive, the telegraph, electricity production, and photography—took on average about 47 years before their widespread commercial use. The major inventions of most of the 20th century—refrigeration, aspirin, electric heating, the telephone, the electric railroad—took on average 33 years before their commercial use. Inventions of the past 25 years have become commercially viable and then have led to widespread ownership and usetypically within 20 years.

Another way to measure diffusion rates for inventions is to calculate how long it takes for a new product take to reach a sizable segment of the population. The best work on this subject has been completed by Michael Cox of the Dallas Federal Reserve Board. According to Cox, "It took 55 years to get the automobile to a quarter of the U.S. population. The telephone required 35 years; the television, 26. Now look at some recent innovations: a quarter of U.S. households owned a personal computer within 16 years of its introduction. For the cellular telephone the time shrank to 13 years. The Internet even faster."

146

Patents Granted by the United States

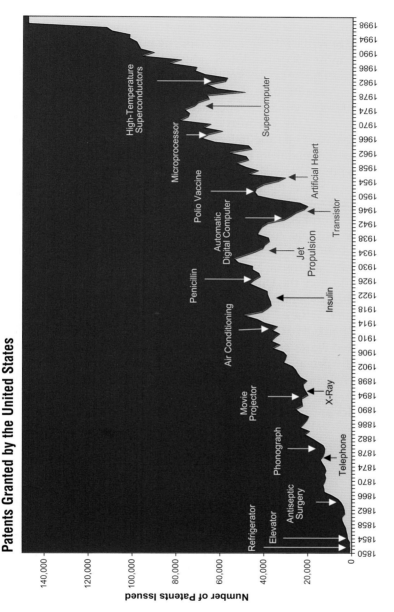

SOURCES: U.S. Patent and Trademark Office, *U.S. Patent Activity, 1790–1998* (Washington: Government Printing Office, 1999); and Louisiana State University, *Important Historical Inventions and Inventors*, www.lib.lsu.edu/sci/chem/patent/srs136.html.

53. Scientists Solve the Puzzles of Our Universe

Twentieth century scientists kept pushing the frontiers of knowledge of the physical universe. The human race has used this ever-expanding scientific know-how to tame, anticipate (i.e., climatology), and harness (i.e., splitting the atom) the awesome powers of nature. Scientific progress has made life on Earth more livable. A driving force behind the spectacular scientific breakthroughs in medicine, physics, chemistry, electronics, computer technology, and so on has been the increased number and quality of trained scientists and engineers exploring our universe.

Since the early years of this century, the number of engineers has grown more than fivefold relative to population. Another measure of our increasing scientific knowledge is the growth of scientific journals. In the late 19th century there were about 5,000 scientific journals, compared with the more than 60,000 that there are today. In 1900 there were about 10,000 physics and electrical engineering abstracts. Now there are more than 250,000.

In addition, the United States spends substantially more of its resources on scientific research today than it did before the turn of the century. In the early years of the 20th century, the U.S. spent less than 0.5 percent of GDP on research and development (R&D). Now the United States spends about 3 percent of GDP on R&D, mostly funded by private businesses and foundations.

In 1900 about 10 Ph.D.'s were awarded in physics each year. By the 1970s that total was up to more than 1,000. Today, 6,000 Ph.D.'s in physics are awarded each year.

The Number of U.S. Engineers, Scientists, and Scientific Journals

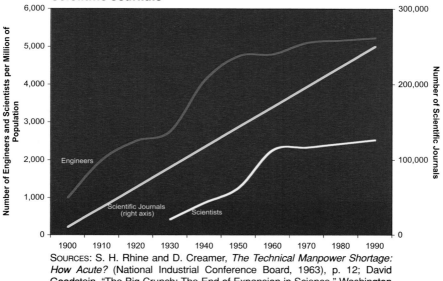

SOURCES: S. H. Rhine and D. Creamer, *The Technical Manpower Shortage: How Acute?* (National Industrial Conference Board, 1963), p. 12; David Goodstein, "The Big Crunch: The End of Expansion in Science," Washington Roundtable on Science and Public Policy, George C. Marshall Institute, Washington, p. 2; and *Statistical Abstract of the United States*.

Total Research and Development Spending by Source

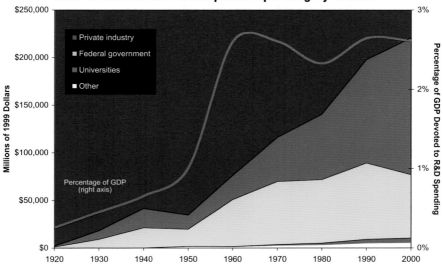

SOURCE: National Science Foundation, *National Patterns of R & D Resources*, various years.

SECTION XI. THE INFORMATION AGE

Just over 30 years ago D. H. Meadows and D. L. Meadows wrote the infamous *Limits to Growth*. They made one of the most outrageous predictions about the dreary outlook for the future of the planet: "The basic behavior mode of the world system is exponential growth of population and capital, followed by collapse. . . . When we introduce technological developments that successfully lift some restraint to growth or avoid some collapse, the system simply grows to another limit, temporarily surpasses it, and falls back."

What the *Limits to Growth* declinists never counted on was the microchip.

That the computer has revolutionized almost every aspect of life in modern-day America is a modern cliche. The central nervous system of the computer—the semiconductor—is clearly the most revolutionary invention of the past 50 years. With the possible exception of electric power, the computer chip may be the greatest wealth-producing invention in history. No single trend in this book can come close to matching the geometric rise in our capacity to transmit and compile information and knowledge. The curve is virtually vertical in shape. What these trends convey is that the most precious resource in the world, the stock of human knowledge, is available at virtually no cost. The trend also renders meaningless the *Limits to Growth* forecast of impending human tragedy from population growth. Yet, the really encouraging feature of the digital age is that it is still in its infancy in terms of vastly increasing the wealth of people.

Steve Jobs, the founder of Apple Computer, was extremely unsuccessful in trying to sell his invention of the personal computer in the mid-1970s. He was scoffed at. "Why," executives asked, "would anyone ever need a computer in their home?" Apple and other companies went on to make billions of dollars in retail sales of their products that supposedly no one would want and that almost half of all homes and almost all businesses and schools are stocked with.

54. The Microchip: The Greatest Invention Ever?

Texas Instruments introduced the first computer chip to the world in 1958. Since then the semiconductor has been doubling in capacity and speed almost every 18 months (Moore's Law). Today, the microchip contained in a single laptop computer contains more computing power than was available to all of the computers used in World War II combined. The power of the invention has been to launch a productivity revolution in America and across the globe by reducing the cost of just about every human and mechanical endeavor. The microchip has also been the brain for scores of cheap consumer items taken for granted today: answering machines, pacemakers, camcorders, digital cameras, PCs, radar detectors, VCRs, cordless phones, laser printers, microwave ovens, remote controls, CD players, entertainment centers, fax machines, Internet services, modern cash registers, traffic light signals, and so on.

Productivity expert Jeremy Atack of the National Bureau of Economic Research describes the recent historical trend in the computational capabilities of modern computers like this: "Early mainframe computers performed perhaps a million operations per second. The so-called super-computers perform two to four billion operations per second and up to 20 billion are claimed for NEC's [Nippon Electric Company] largest SX-3 machine."

The real cost of processing information and data that once might have cost hundreds of thousands, if not millions of dollars, is rapidly falling to zero. The IBM-370-168 mainframe circa 1975 sold for $3.4 million; a personal computer today with an Intel Pentium chip currently retails for around $1,000 and is at least 100 times faster. Thirty-five years ago, someone would have had to work an entire lifetime or more before he could pay for the calculating power that now rests in a handheld calculator.

According to an analysis by the Cato Institute, "If the automobile and aerospace technology had exploded at the same pace as computer and information technology, a new car would cost about $2 and go 600 miles on a thimble of gas. And you could buy a Boeing 747 for the cost of a pizza."

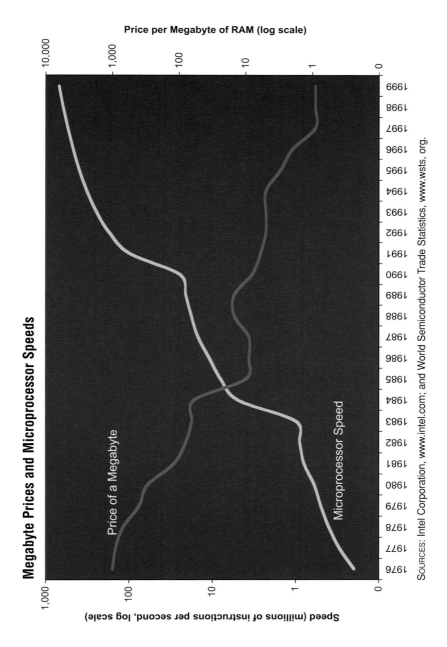

Megabyte Prices and Microprocessor Speeds

Price per Megabyte of RAM (log scale)

Price of a Megabyte

Microprocessor Speed

Speed (millions of instructions per second, log scale)

SOURCES: Intel Corporation, www.intel.com; and World Semiconductor Trade Statistics, www.wsts, org.

55. The Personal Computer Launches the Digital Revolution

The personal computer (PC) revolution was never predicted by anyone. In fact even after the invention of the computer in the early 1940s, people took years to recognize the significance of this new machine. Legend has it that in 1943 Thomas Watson, chairman of IBM, declared, "I think there is a world market for about five computers." A few years later in 1949, *Popular Mechanics* prophesied hopefully that "where a calculator on the ENIAC computer is equipped with 18,000 vacuum tubes and weighs 30 tons, computers in the future may have only 1,000 vacuum tubes and perhaps only weigh 1 1/2 tons."

Due to the rapid fall in the price of PCs, the rise of computer sales today to Americans through the mass retail market is resembling the sales pattern of radios in the 1930s and television sets in the 1950s.

In 1975 there were no personal computers. By 1983 there were about 4 million PCs. Now there are more than 50 million PCs in American homes.

Some social scientists and politicians have begun to worry about an "information underclass" in the United States. According to these skeptics, Americans are splintering into a digitally divided society of computer-haves and computer have-nots. The trends in computer sales and Internet usage portray just the opposite phenomenon: the computer is one of the most democratic inventions in history, spreading information into the homes of more and more low-income Americans. The largest growth market of personal computers is to middle- and lower-income Americans. In 1995, about one-fifth of computer-owning homes had incomes of $30,000 or less. That's a 30 percent increase in one year.

American Households in the Information Age

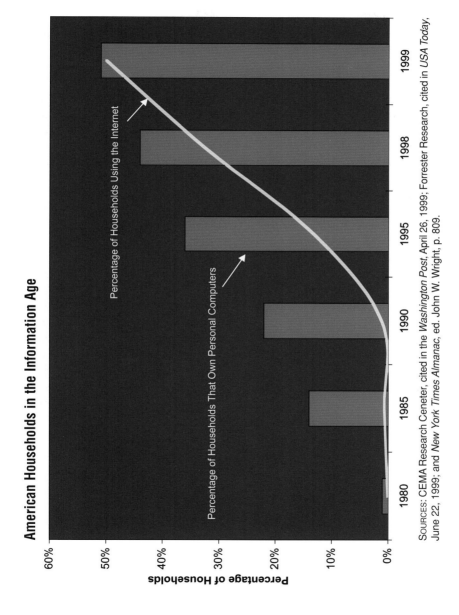

Percentage of Households Using the Internet

Percentage of Households That Own Personal Computers

SOURCES: CEMA Research Ceneter, cited in the *Washington Post*, April 26, 1999; Forrester Research, cited in *USA Today*, June 22, 1999; and *New York Times Almanac*, ed. John W. Wright, p. 809.

Percentage of Households

60% 50% 40% 30% 20% 10% 0%

1980 1985 1990 1995 1998 1999

155

56. From the Pony Express to the Internet Generation

The speed of communications in this century has been breath-taking. In the 19th century a letter sent from New York to San Francisco could take weeks because mail was delivered by the Post Office on slow rambling trains or horseback. With the invention of the automobile, that travel time was cut to a week or so. With planes, the delivery of that letter was sped up to a few days. The facsimile (fax) machine accelerated the process to a few minutes. And now E-mail has shrunk the travel time of a letter to seconds.

The Internet has become a ubiquitous tool for communicating cheaply and efficiently with people around the globe, for gathering knowledge, and for storehousing information. Because of personal computers and the Internet, at least 50 million Americans across the country are now connected to an information source right at their fingertips (requiring just a double-click) that is greater than all of the books in the Library of Congress. As recently as 1990 only 1 million Americans had ready access to the Internet.

In 1989 there were fewer than 1 million Internet hosts. Ten years later that number had grown more than 30-fold.

Almost one-fifth of today's Internet households have incomes below $30,000 a year.

Eric Schmidt, CEO of Novell, predicts: "At the current rate of growth of the Internet, every man, woman, and child in the United States will be connected to the Internet by 2007."

Growth in the Number of Internet Hosts

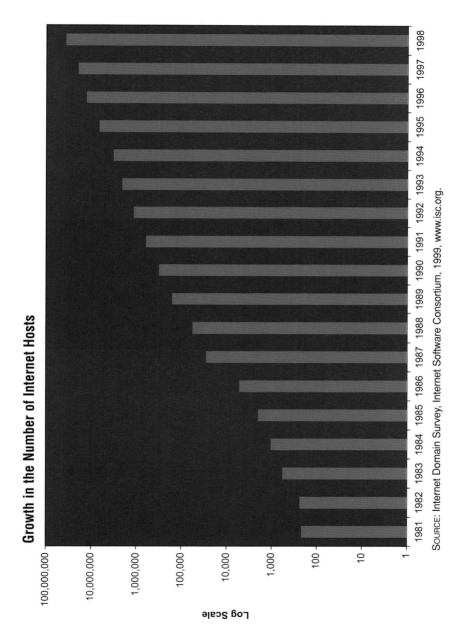

Log Scale

SOURCE: Internet Domain Survey, Internet Software Consortium, 1999, www.isc.org.

157

SECTION XII. EDUCATION

In the United States, we are stretching the human mind by attaining ever greater levels of education. In fact, one of the most encouraging trends in the United States over the past century has been the steep and nearly uninterrupted increase in the educational attainment of the American people. Today, the percentage of Americans graduating from college is higher than the percentage of Americans graduating from high school 100 years ago. And the percentage receiving advanced degrees is higher today than the percentage receiving a college degree at the start of the 20th century. In fact, today the United States has the most educated labor force in the history of the world.

This increased quantity of schooling has been a vital component of economic success in this century for several reasons. First, Americans' educational attainment over time closely tracks the increased lifetime earnings of the U.S. workforce. Clearly, if the United States is to continue to compete and succeed in the global economy of the 21st century, the country will need to retain its status as the world's most highly skilled and educated population. Second, high levels of education are a precondition to the kind of scientific and technological progress of the past century and the one to come. Third, as James Madison often wrote, self-government "presupposes an enlightened citizenry to a higher degree than any other form of government."

So it is good news indeed that every measure of the amount of schooling received is high as is the amount of resources we devote to it. What is less clear is whether the quality of education is high today, relative to earlier periods. Many achievement measures indicate a decline over the past 30 years. One particularly heartening sign of improvement, however, has been the rise in literacy rates.

57. The Most Educated People in History

There has been a steady rise in the amount of education received by this country's youths. The median years of schooling have increased from 8 to 12 since 1920 for whites and from 6 to 12 for blacks. The percentage of Americans aged 5 to 17 enrolled in school has risen from about one in two in 1900 to about two in three in 1950 to about nine in ten today.

High school enrollment and graduation rates have soared in this century. Only about 20 percent of Americans aged 20 to 29 had no higher than a high school diploma in 1920. By 1950 that graduation rate had risen to about 50 percent. Today, it is just under 90 percent. Again, the gains have been most rapid for minorities.

In addition, quantity of education has risen dramatically worldwide over the past 150 years. In 1850 the average amount of formal education was just 2 years. By 1900 that was up to about 4 years and by 1980 the average was roughly 8 years.

School Enrollment

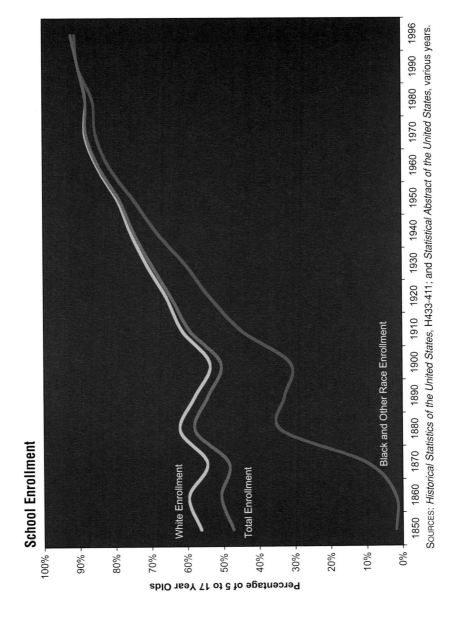

Percentage of 5 to 17 Year Olds

White Enrollment

Total Enrollment

Black and Other Race Enrollment

1850 1860 1870 1880 1890 1900 1910 1920 1930 1940 1950 1960 1970 1980 1990 1996

SOURCES: *Historical Statistics of the United States*, H433-411; and *Statistical Abstract of the United States*, various years.

161

58. Fewer School Dropouts

The school dropout rate has been on a steady, rapid decline. The percentage of Americans without a high school diploma has plummeted fivefold from about 60 percent in 1940 to about 10 percent in 1997, according to the official statistics of the U.S. Department of Education.

About 3 of every 4 American children born in 1900 did not receive a high school diploma. But only about 1 in 10 children born 1960 did not receive a high school diploma. Even more encouraging is that a child born in 1900 had a 60 percent chance of not completing grade school, compared with just 4 percent today.

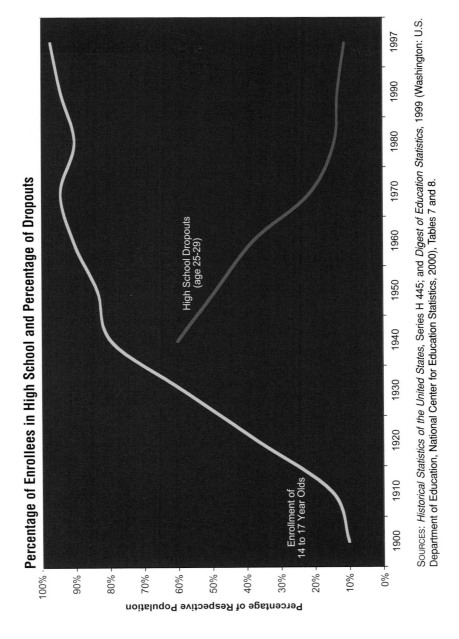

Percentage of Enrollees in High School and Percentage of Dropouts

High School Dropouts
(age 25-29)

Enrollment of
14 to 17 Year Olds

Percentage of Respective Population

100% 90% 80% 70% 60% 50% 40% 30% 20% 10% 0%

1900 1910 1920 1930 1940 1950 1960 1970 1980 1990 1997

SOURCES: *Historical Statistics of the United States*, Series H 445; and *Digest of Education Statistics, 1999* (Washington: U.S. Department of Education, National Center for Education Statistics, 2000), Tables 7 and 8.

163

59. College: No Longer Just for the Elite

College used to be reserved for only the wealthiest, the smartest, or the most privileged students. But over the past century, opportunities to attend college have rapidly escalated. About 1 of 20 children born in 1900 received a college degree, compared with 1 in 9 children born in 1930, and more than 1 in 4 born in 1960. Only 1 in 10 of the birth group in 1900 received any college education, versus well over half today.

The United Negro College Fund ads proclaim: "A mind is a terrible thing to waste." The good news is that college opportunities are vast today for blacks compared to the first half of the century. Before the 1920s a college degree for a black American was extremely rare—about 1 percent. Now almost 20 percent of adult blacks have a college degree, and that percentage continues to rise.

Moreover, before the 1950s, options for blacks were extremely limited due to segregation. About half of the universities were essentially closed to minorities, which meant that those blacks who went to college at all went mostly to segregated colleges, which had more limited resources and opportunities than the majority of the colleges that whites attended. Nowadays, virtually all universities, even in the deep South, are open to minorities.

American high school graduates now have a vast array of universities, colleges, and junior colleges to choose from. In 1900 there were fewer than 1,000 colleges in the United States. By 1930 that number had grown to 1,400. Today there are more than 3,500.

Since the late 1960s, the number of higher education degrees conferred has skyrocketed. In 1968 there were 550,000 bachelor's, master's, and doctor's degrees awarded; today that figure has risen to 1.2 million. Despite all of our school woes, Americans are a highly educated people.

Percentage of Adults Who Completed High School or College

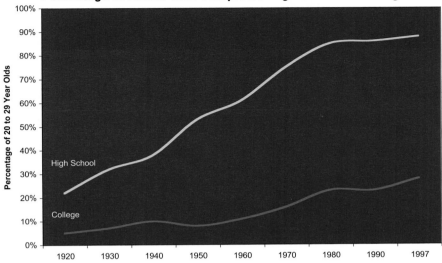

SOURCE: *Digest of Education Statistics*, 1998, Table 8.

Distribution of Highest Level of Educational Attainment for the 1886–1905, 1916–35, and 1944–63 Birth Cohorts

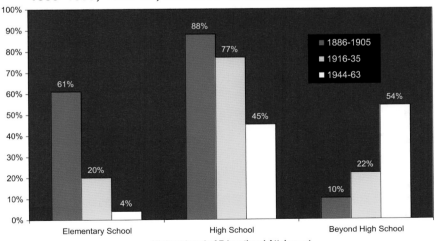

SOURCE: Bureau of the Census data cited in *Special Report*, Washington Research Council, July 22, 1999.

60. Fighting Global Illiteracy

In the late 19th century, about 20 percent of Americans could not read or write. About two-thirds of blacks were illiterate. By 1950 the illiteracy rate had plummeted to less than 10 percent and then declined slightly in the next few decades.

Recent disturbing signs show that illiteracy is on the rise again in the United States, due mainly to the deteriorating quality of the public school system. A 1995 National Adult Literacy Survey found that half of the U.S. adult population scored in the lowest two levels for reading and writing, a level educators call "well below what American workers need to be competitive in the global economy." Despite this indictment of the public school system, there still can be no doubt that literacy rose throughout the 20th century in the United States.

Dramatic literacy gains have also been recorded around the world. UNESCO reports that the global adult illiteracy rate worldwide was about 75 percent for those born before 1926 and was still about 52 percent for those born in 1948, but for those born in 1970 global illiteracy fell to around 20 percent.

Literacy is a key component to achieving economic growth. A 1988 Heritage Foundation study found that the female literacy rate is 21 percent in nations with per capita incomes of $200 per year or less, 60 percent in nations with incomes of $800, and 88 percent in nations with per capita incomes of $2,000 or more.

Percentage of Illiteracy in the Population by Race

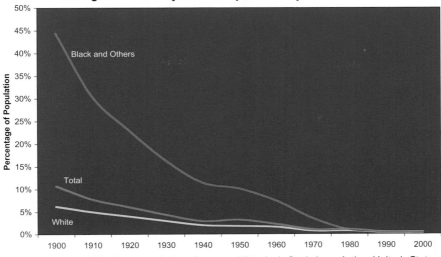

SOURCES: U.S. Bureau of the Census, *Historical Statistics of the United States*, Series H 664-668; and Current Population Survey, various years.

Adult Illiteracy in Developing Countries by Birth Year

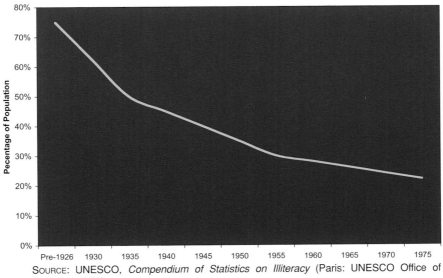

SOURCE: UNESCO, *Compendium of Statistics on Illiteracy* (Paris: UNESCO Office of Statistics, 1990).

61. Investing in Quality Education

The public school system in the United States has been described as the last great monopoly enterprise. The monopoly structure of the public schools, particularly in the inner cities, deprives poor families of choice in selecting the schools they prefer and inhibits the healthy impact of competition in education. For this reason, we believe that one of the most promising educational trends in the country today is the wider range of choices in schools and the rush toward quality improvements to retain and attract students. These are very recent innovations but are already showing great promise.

One highly encouraging development is the increased amount of private investment in school scholarship programs. Between 1991 and 1998 private investment in alternative schools rose from $400,000 to $16.5 million.

The number of privately funded school choice programs has risen from 1 in 1991 to more than 40 in 1998. Enrollment in the CEO program has risen from 1,000 to 16,000.

Finally, public charter schools, which are schools with alternative curriculum and teaching environments formed by parents and educators, have risen from 1 in 1991 to almost 1,200 by 1999. The Center for Education Reform estimates that there will be as many as 3,000 charter schools by 2001.

Private Investment in Alternative Schools

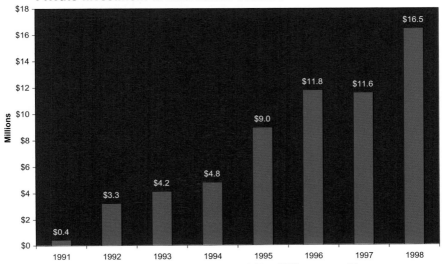

SOURCE: CEO America, *1999 Annual Report*, ed. Tony Williamson, p. 16.

Growth of CEO America Programs

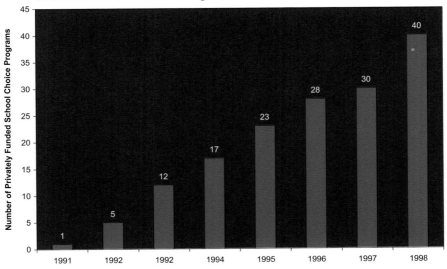

SOURCE: CEO America, *1999 Annual Report*, p. 9.

SECTION XIII. SAFETY

A recent CNN/*USA Today* public opinion poll finds that these days Americans worry about strange things. More than 50 percent of Americans say that successful cloning is one of the things they most dread in the 21st century. But what is shocking is that many Americans seem to fear technology generally. This is unfortunate, because technology saves lives, it does not destroy them.

A sign of how safe these times are is that people have shifted their fears to obscure and distant threats like global climate change, alien invasions, cloning, the amount of fat in breakfast cereals, and secondhand smoke. Most of the threats that were really risky and frightening in the earlier parts of this century—like tuberculosis and polio—are no longer worries at all.

Many people worry that life is riskier today than a century ago because modern technologies, such as nuclear weapons, make it easier for a catastrophic occurrence to wipe out entire cities or even whole populations. But even here we tend to romanticize the past. Our ancestors lived in mortal peril of seeing their civilizations wiped out by invaders like William the Conqueror, who may not have had weapons of mass destruction but were certainly capable of mass destruction. The Asians and Europeans did not build giant walls around cities and countries for nothing. Nevertheless, the facts show that larger percentages of the population died from catastrophic occurrences (fires, hurricanes, floods, famines, explosions, etc.) 100, 200, or 1,000 years ago than they do today. The Black Plague destroyed 40 percent of Europe, for example, in just a few years' time.

Studies show that one of the causes, if not the leading cause, of death in America and around the world today is poverty. Wealthier is healthier. The best way to continue to reduce the risk of early death and injury is to promote economic growth and rising living standards through free-market capitalism.

62. A Safer World: Fewer Fatal Accidents

Anyone who reads the newspaper headlines or watches the six o'clock evening news might believe that these are mighty dangerous times we live in. It seems that the number of murders, shootings, thefts, airplane crashes, highway fatalities, acts of terrorism, accidents from unsafe foods and products, and fatal sports injuries have soared to unprecedented levels. Here is some surprisingly good news: the rate of deaths from accidents has fallen by half since the early 1900s.

The most dramatic improvement has occurred in recent years. In the 1980s the death rate from accidents fell by 20 percent and in the 1990s it fell by another 3 percent.

Accidental death rates have fallen steadily for every age group. The biggest improvements have been in the rate of accidents for infants (down 88 percent since 1900) and for seniors (down 72 percent).

Fatal accidents in the home are also rarer than ever—again a reflection of improved technology. In the 1920s and 1930s roughly 25 Americans out of 100,000 died in home accidents—fires, falls, accidental shootings, smothering—versus about 20 such deaths in 1950, and now roughly about 15. Incredibly, even in absolute numbers, despite a doubling of the population, deaths from home accidents have declined from 29,000 in 1950 to 26,500 in 1996.

As mentioned earlier, travel-related deaths have also hit record lows. In addition, airline and highway fatalities are at an all-time low per mile traveled. Peter Spencer of *Consumers' Research* magazine estimates that if an individual were to take a random flight every day, on average 20,000 years would pass before the person perished in a fatal crash.

Accidental Injury Death Rates (per 100,000 population), 1905–98

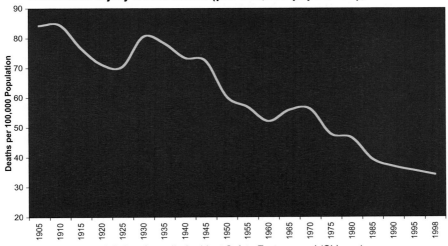

SOURCE: National Safety Council, *Accident Safety Facts*, annual (Chicago).

Percentage of Decline in Accidental Death Rates by Age since 1912

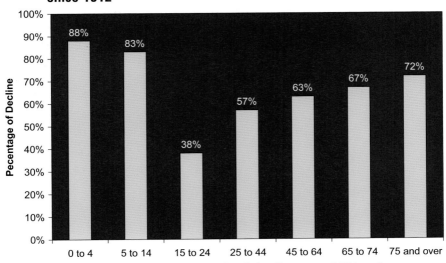

SOURCE: National Safety Council, *Accident Safety Facts*, annual (Chicago).

173

63. Safety on the Job

Americans are now employed in occupations that are far safer than in the past. The accidental death rate at work has plummeted from about 38 per 100,000 workers in 1930 to about 28 in 1950 to about about 4 per 100,000 today. This sevenfold reduction in job-related deaths is due to several factors: first, fewer Americans work in risky occupations, such as in unsafe factories and coal mines; second, for those who do work in risky occupations, safety measures are vastly improved; and finally, for those who do become injured, improved medical care saves more lives. The figure also shows that government regulatory agencies, such as OSHA, have had almost no impact on the trend toward greater safety.)

The rate of occupational injuries have also fallen sharply—at least over the past 25 years. The figure shows an average of under 15 workplace injuries and illnesses per 100 workers in 1973, versus about 4 in 1995.

Workers Fatally Injured on the Job

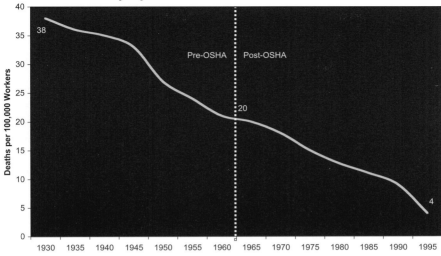

SOURCES: National Safety Council, *Accident Safety Facts*, annual (Chicago); and Charles Murray, *What It Means to Be a Libertarian* (New York: Broadway Books, 1997).

Occupational Injury and Illness Rates per 100 Full-Time Workers

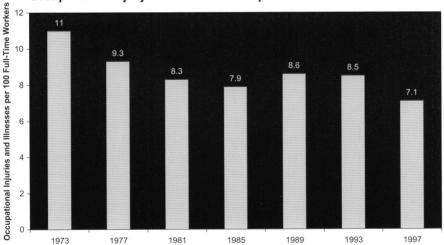

SOURCES: *Statistical Abstract of the United States: 1998*, No. 708; and U.S. Bureau of Labor Statistics, *Occupational Injuries and Illnesses in the United States by Industry*, various years.

175

64. Natural Disasters: Living with Mother Nature

There are always understandable fears about the safety of our natural environment. Today, people worry about earthquakes (especially Californians), floods, volcanic eruptions, hurricanes, and other such acts of nature that often leave in their wake a terrible toll of thousands or more of lives lost and untold property damage. No doubt the release of a new Hollywood movie depicting the death and carnage from some horrific natural disaster (with ever more spectacular special effects)—has raised public concerns about "the big one." The reality is not quite as depressing as what Steven Spielberg may have us believe. For at least the past 50 years the likelihood of dying from an act of nature has declined steadily.

Almost all of the worst natural disasters in modern times—in terms of total fatalities from floods, hurricanes, earthquakes, tornadoes, mine accidents, and fires—happened in the late 1800s or the first half of the 20th century.

The worst flood in American history was in Galveston, Texas, in 1900 when 6,000 people drowned in a tidal wave. Now waterbreaks make Galveston far less prone to this kind of life-threatening natural disaster. Two terrible earthquakes of recent years were in San Francisco in 1989 and in Northridge, California, in 1994. Both earthquakes caused billions of dollars of property damage, but because of improved preparedness, neither of these quakes caused a large loss of lives.

The death rate from tornadoes fluctuates widely from one year to the next but, as the figure shows, the trend line is clearly lower over the past century.

The fewer deaths are not a result of fewer earthquakes, tornadoes, or floods, but rather of improved methods of preparing for such events. For example, these days buildings, bridges, homes, and other structures are sturdier and able to withstand quakes that in earlier times might have caused facilities to crumble. Better and more accurate weather reporting is available, thus preparing people for natural disasters. Firefighting equipment is much more sophisticated and effective than it was 50 or 100 years ago. We may not have tamed Mother Nature, but we have a much better capacity to cope with her nowadays.

Death Rates from Tornadoes, Hurricanes, and Floods

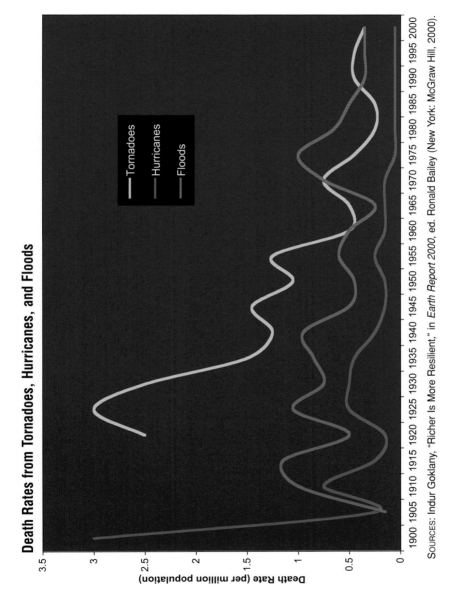

SOURCES: Indur Goklany, "Richer Is More Resilient," in *Earth Report 2000*, ed. Ronald Bailey (New York: McGraw Hill, 2000).

65. The Reduced Risk of Catastrophic Events

Food poisoning. Radiation. Airplane crashes. Terrorist bombings. Nuclear accidents. These are the kinds of random manmade disasters that seem commonplace these days. Such catastrophes can destroy untold numbers of people in an instant. Many of the most terrible accidents are permanently imbedded in our memories. The TWA flight 800 explosion. The Three Mile Island nuclear accident. The bombings of the World Trade Center, and Oklahoma City Federal center. The Exxon Valdez oil spill. In this modern age we seem more exposed to such catastrophic risks than ever before. The evidence provides compelling evidence that we are not.

There is a high cost in dollars and our psychological well-being to worrying about small risks. According to the statistical organization STATS, "One of the most substantial risks we run is simply fear itself. According to the journal Psychological Science, people (especially males) who see bad things that happen to them as a part of a global pattern of evil and pain have an increased risk of dying before age 65. Such individuals who catastrophize their experiences suffer from poor decisionmaking, and are more likely to be perpetually in the wrong place at the wrong time."

Over the past 50 years the rate of death from catastrophic accidents (accidents killing at least five people) has fallen by about fourfold.

Today, the likelihood of dying in a catastrophic accident, such as a terrorist attack or an earthquake, in any year is just one in 400,000.

Acts of terrorism terrify the public because these indiscriminate acts could victimize anyone at any time. Fortunately, the risk of dying from a terrorist incident is miniscule. Less than 1,000 Americans die from terrorist attacks every year, which accounts for far fewer deaths than from falling off a ladder at home or from riding a bicycle.

Death Rates from Catastrophic Accidents (deaths per 100,000 persons, annualized)

SOURCES: Metropolitan Life Insurance Company; and *Statistical Abstract of the United States.*

179

66. The Diminished Threat of Nuclear Disaster

Ever since the first atom bomb was dropped on Hiroshima in 1945, humankind has been in a collective panic over the specter of nuclear annihilation. It is difficult to assess the risks of such an Armageddon-type event. However, according to the U.S. Department of Energy monitoring project, the number of nuclear weapons tests has fallen from a high of more than 150 in the early 1960s to less than 4 in 1998.

Meanwhile, ever since the Three Mile Island disaster, Americans have also been terrified about the safety of nuclear energy. The facts do not justify this degree of fear. The chance of getting cancer from the radiation of a nuclear power plant—even for those who live closest to it for an entire lifetime—is about 1 in 70,000. This is 1 percent of the chance of contracting cancer from exposure to natural radiation in the environment. In fact, there has not been a single accident from a nuclear power plant in 25 years. The risk of lost life from a nuclear power accident is then compared with the risks of smoking, obesity, motorcycle driving, drowning, and even bike riding.

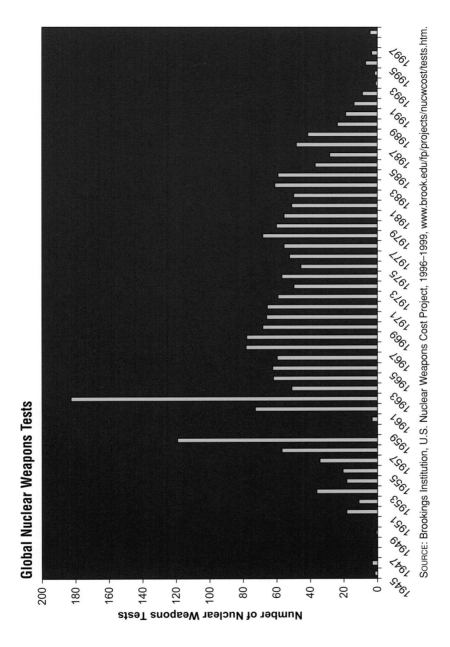

Global Nuclear Weapons Tests

SOURCE: Brookings Institution, U.S. Nuclear Weapons Cost Project, 1996–1999, www.brook.edu/fp/projects/nucwcost/tests.htm.

SECTION XIV. ENVIRONMENTAL PROTECTION

There is almost no issue of modern times in which Americans' general beliefs about the state of affairs contradicts objective reality like the issue of the environment. Most Americans are influenced by doomsday academicians and journalists, who tend to portray environmental conditions as dire. They believe that because of industrialization, population growth, and mass consumption, our air and water are deteriorating and that our access to natural resources will soon run dry. Stories about global warming, ozone depletion, and the paving over of the planet imply that the environment must have been cleaner and purer many decades ago. In a recent poll, when Americans were asked what they thought some of the worst problems would be over the next 50 years, the top two responses dealt with the environment. More than four of five said they feared "severe water pollution" and "severe air pollution."

The fact is that one of the greatest trends of the past 100 years has been the astonishing rate of progress in reducing almost every form of pollution.

The major pollutions of the late 19th century caused death and severe diseases like typhoid and bronchitis. Those pollutions have been eradicated almost entirely. Eradicating the pollutions has enabled us to concentrate clean-up efforts on reducing other types of pollutions like smog that are unpleasant but generally not life threatening. The good news is that cities like Los Angeles have seen dramatic declines in smog levels over the past 25 years.

The major driving forces behind an improved environment are affluence and technology. Technological improvements and new inventions have helped combat the worst kinds of pollution. The computer, for example, is arguably the most environment friendly invention in world history. It produces enormous amounts of output with virtually no environmental costs. The automobile, although it emits carbon monoxide into the air, replaced a far more polluting form of transportation: the horse, which left huge piles of dung on the roads. As economists William Baumol and Wallace Oates have noted, from an environmental standpoint, the automobile is "certainly an improvement from the incredibly filthy streets and waterways of medieval and Renaissance cities."

67. Breathing Clean Air

Has the stunning economic progress of the past century and the increased material well-being of Americans come at the expense of degrading our natural environment? Economist John Kenneth Galbraith voiced the prevalent attitude in the 1960s and 1970s about economic growth and the environment in his book *The Affluent Society*: "The penultimate Western man, stalled in the ultimate traffic jam and slowly succumbing to carbon monoxide, will not be cheered to hear from the last survivor that the gross national product went up by a record amount." Vice President Al Gore agrees; his book *Earth in the Balance*, argues that we have been mortgaging our environmental future through our mindless pursuit of economic growth. The surprisingly good news is that the economic progress of the last century has not come at the expense of clean air. Rather, economic growth has generally corresponded with improvements in the natural environment.

The national picture on air quality shows improvement for almost every type of pollution—with particularly dramatic declines in carbon monoxide, sulfur, and lead. Lead concentrations have fallen precipitously, by more than 90 percent since 1976. The total volume of lead emissions was lower in 1990 than it was in 1940 (the furthest back for which we have reliable data) and was lower in every intervening year.

Ambient air pollution levels have been decreasing steadily since the 1970s. Between 1976 and 1997, levels of all six major air pollutants decreased significantly: sulfur dioxide levels decreased 58 percent, nitrogen dioxides decreased 27 percent, ozone decreased 30 percent, carbon monoxide decreased 61 percent, and lead decreased an overwhelming 97 percent.

An incredible success story is the decline in pollution per unit of output. From 1940 to 1990 air pollution emissions fell by 3 percent per year relative to output—suggesting that America has become far more environmentally efficient in recent decades. In fact, we now produce about six times more output per ton of emission of air pollution than we did before 1920.

Equally impressive is that emissions per capita have fallen by almost half over the past 50 years even though we produce and consume far more today than in the 1940s.

National Ambient Air Quality

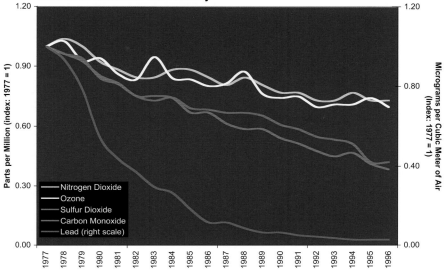

SOURCE: Environmental Protection Agency, Office of Air Quality, Planning and Standards, *National Air Quality and Emissions Trends Report* (Research Triangle Park, N.C.: EPA, OAQPS, 1996).

Emissions per Unit of GDP

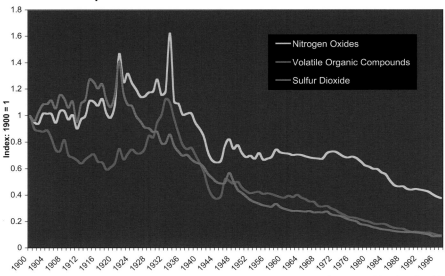

SOURCE: Environmental Protection Agency data as cited in Indur Goklany, *Clearing the Air*, pp. 67–86.

185

68. Reducing Smog in Cities

In 1968 doomsayer Paul Ehrlich wrote in *The Population Bomb*, that "smog disasters" might kill 200,000 people in New York and Los Angeles by 1973. The reality is that air pollution in American cities has been falling for at least the past three decades. Since the 1950s, air pollution in major cities has dramatically declined. For example, the air pollution rate (or soot) over Manhattan has fallen by two-thirds since the end of World War II.

The air pollution over Chicago has declined by more than half since the late 1960s. Long-term improvements have also been recorded in Pittsburgh, Cincinnati, and Detroit. The average number of days of poor air quality in these cities fell by about half from 1978 to 1992. Some, but not all, of the improvement in air quality has occurred since the passage of the 1972 Clean Air Act regulations.

Perhaps the most gratifying environmental success story in recent years has been the rapid reduction in smog levels over Los Angeles in just the past decade. From 1985 to 1995 the number of days in the year of unhealthy air quality has fallen by half—from about 160 to about 80.

Pittsburgh's air quality improvements over the past 40 years have been even more spectacular. In the 1920s, 30s, 40s, and 50s, as the steel mills smoke stacks belched out black soot, there were typically more than 300 "smoky" days a year. Since the late 1960s, that number has fallen to about 60 smoky days a year. There are now fewer smoky days in Pittsburgh than there were in 1900.

These favorable urban air quality trends have not been confined to just a handful of industrial cities. Over the 25-year period 1962 to 1987, smog levels fell by more than half using an index of all urban areas.

Air Quality Trends in Major Urban Areas

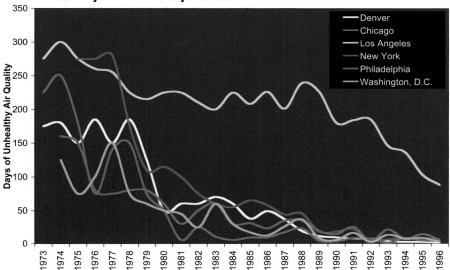

SOURCES: Council on Environmental Quality, *Annual Report* (Washington: Government Printing Office, various years); and Environmental Protection Agency, Office of Air Quality Planning and Standards, *National Air Quality and Emissions Trends Report*, 1996, Table A-17.

Smoky Days in Pittsburgh

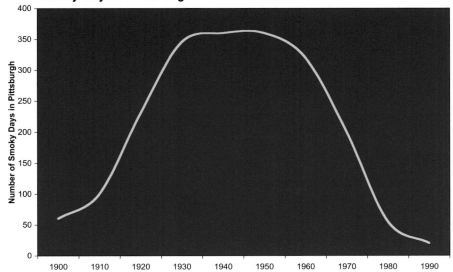

SOURCES: Cliff I. Davidson, "Air Pollution in Pittsburgh: A Historical Perspective," *Journal of the Air Pollution Control Association* 29 (1979): 1035–41; and Council on Environmental Quality, *Annual Report*, various years.

187

69. Cleaner Lakes, Rivers, and Streams

At the start of the century, many disorders, such as diarrhea, were a result of Americans' drinking and using impure water. Today, because of improved technology in water purification, drinking water is much cleaner and safer than in any earlier times, as measured by the reduction in illnesses caused by bacteria in the water. No reliable long-term data on the pollution levels of American lakes and rivers are available, but anecdotal evidence indicates that many of the waterways were filthy. Official data beginning in 1970 come from the Environmental Protection Agency, shortly before the Clean Water Act was signed into law. U.S. lakes, rivers, and streams have been much less polluted over the past quarter century, and the trend is toward continued improvement. Since 1970 an estimated $500 billion has been spent on water cleanup.

The safety of drinking water is most important to Americans. The percentage of water sources that were judged by the Council on Environmental Quality to be poor or severe fell from 30 percent in 1961 (the furthest back in time for which we have good data) to 17 percent in 1974 to less than 5 percent today.

Huge progress has been made in purifying industrial and municipal waste before it is emitted into streams, rivers, and lakes. In 1960 only 40 million Americans—22 percent of the population–were served by wastewater treatment plants. By 1996 that number had risen to 190 million Americans, or 70 percent of the population.

According to the Pacific Research Institute's *Index of Leading Environmental Indicators,* industrial water pollution has plummeted since 1980. Organic wastes have fallen by 46 percent, toxic organics by 99 percent, and toxic metals by 98 percent.

In 1994, 86 percent of U.S. rivers and streams were usable for fishing and swimming as were 91 percent of U.S. lakes, up from 36 percent in 1972.

Since the 1960s (in 1969 a part of Lake Erie was on fire in downtown Cleveland) the water quality of the Great Lakes has improved dramatically. In fact, in recent years Lake Erie, which was considered "dead" in the 1970s, has been yielding record fish catches and is routinely used for recreational purposes. Similarly, the salmon catch on Lake Ontario is thriving again after several decades of decline.

Percentage of Streams Usable for Fishing and Swimming

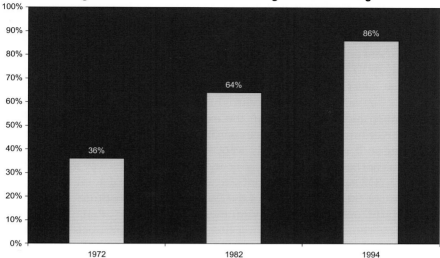

SOURCE: Council on Environmental Quality, *Annual Report* (various years).

Service by Municipal Wastewater Treatment

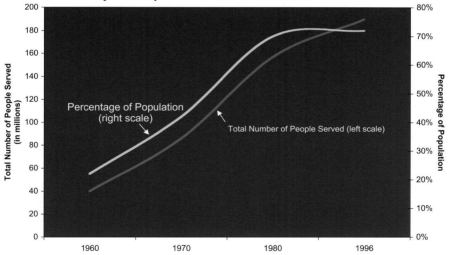

SOURCES: *Statistical Abstract of the United States: 1998*, No. 397; and U.S. Environmental Protection Agency, Office of Wastewater Management, *Clean Water Needs Survey Report*.

70. Fewer Oil Spills

Almost all Americans can remember vividly the scenes from the Exxon Valdez oil spill in 1989. Fish and birds were washed ashore enwrapped in black tar. The good news is that the trend in oil spills by volume has been falling from 1973 to 1993. Moreover, the latest news from Prince William Sound in Alaska where the Exxon Valdez accident occurred is that fish and wildlife are proving much more resilient than the experts predicted. Stan Senner, the government's chief science coordinator for monitoring the impact of the spill, declared in early 1999, "Although full ecological recovery has not been achieved . . . the ecosystem is well on its way to recovery."

Oil spills also account for a tiny amount of total petroleum waste. Steven Hayward of the Pacific Research Institute notes in his study on "Leading Environmental Indicators" that "American households pour 1.3 billion liters of oil-based products down the drain each year. In comparison, the Exxon Valdez spilled just over 41 million liters of crude oil into Prince William Sound."

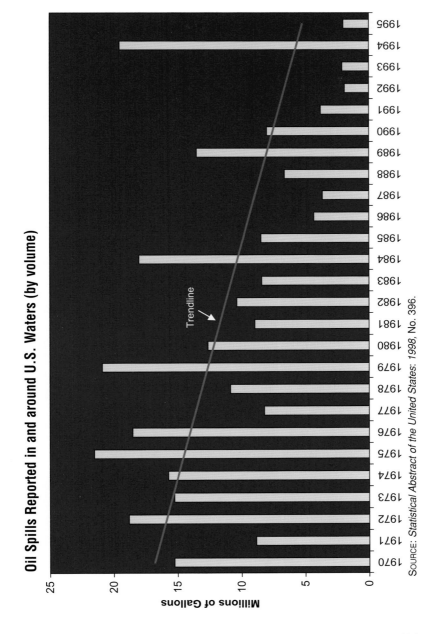

Oil Spills Reported in and around U.S. Waters (by volume)

Millions of Gallons

Trendline

1970 1971 1972 1973 1974 1975 1976 1977 1978 1979 1980 1981 1982 1983 1984 1985 1986 1987 1988 1989 1990 1991 1992 1993 1994 1995

SOURCE: *Statistical Abstract of the United States: 1998*, No. 396.

71. The Energy-Efficient Society

The United States today may well be the most energy-efficient society in human history. According to calculations by the National Center for Policy Analysis, "the amount of energy needed to produce a dollar of GNP (in real terms) has been steadily declining at a rate of 1 percent per year since 1929. By 1989, the amount of energy needed to produce a dollar of GNP was almost half of what it was 60 years earlier." Energy efficiency continued to surge so much in the 1990s that today almost twice as much output is produced per unit of energy as was produced in the first half of the century. One often-overlooked benefit of the digital and the information age is the huge gains registered in energy efficiency in the world economy.

Economic development and free markets are the keys to increasing energy efficiency. In 1986, a few years before the collapse of the Berlin Wall, the United States and other developed countries used less than half the amount of energy per dollar of GDP growth than did the socialist economies. Communist North Korea still uses three times as much energy to produce a dollar output as does South Korea.

Because of inventions like the catalytic converter, unleaded gasoline, and other technologies cars pollute much less nowadays, are lighter, and are much more fuel efficient. The Clean Air Act has also played an important role. (However, the recent popularity of sports utility vehicles has started to reverse the trend of lighter cars.) The fuel efficiency of new cars has risen from about 15 miles per gallon in 1940 to about 18 miles per gallon by 1985, to 21 today.

The amount of energy recovery through incineration skyrocketed by 800 percent between 1960 and 1990.

In recent decades, our modern society has also become much more efficient in waste disposal. Solid waste in the United States slightly more than doubled from 1960 to 1990. Yet over this same period the amount of recycling rose by 96 percent. About 70 percent, a record high, of physical waste now generated in America is biodegradable.

U.S. Energy Consumption per $1,000 of GDP

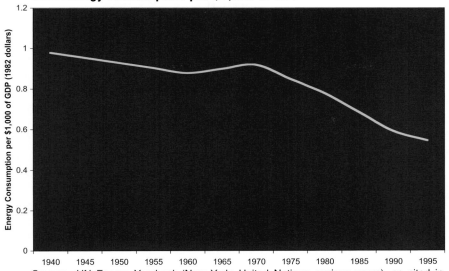

SOURCE: *UN Energy Yearbook* (New York: United Nations, various years), as cited in Simon, p. 506.

Fuel Economy for Autos

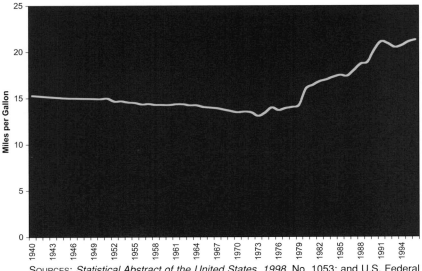

SOURCES: *Statistical Abstract of the United States, 1998,* No. 1053; and U.S. Federal Highway Administration, *Highway Statistics*, various years.

SECTION XV. NATURAL RESOURCES: AN AGE OF ABUNDANCE

Contrary to the doom-and-gloom reports of the 1960s and 1970s, including the Club of Rome's 1972 *Limits to Growth* and the Carter Administration's 1980 *Global 2000* Report, we are not running out of energy, food, forests, or minerals. The data clearly show that natural resource scarcity—as measured by cost or price—has been decreasing rather than increasing in the long run for all raw materials, energy, and food, with only temporary exceptions from time to time. That is, resources have become more abundant, not less so. In fact, due to improvements in technology and know-how, the 20th century is noted for the very rapid reduction in resource scarcity. The availability of natural resources is less a constraint on growth than ever before.

Even the U.S. government now apparently recognizes the errors of its judgments in the past. Reversing the forecasts of studies such as *Global 2000* the Office of Technology Assessment has concluded, "The nation's future has probably never been less constrained by the cost of natural resources."

The experience of the 1970s, however, demonstrates that declining prices of natural resources are not inevitable. Unwise government intervention into the marketplace for natural resources can often have economically and ecologically debilitating consequences. For example, most economists today agree that a rash of new energy regulations introduced in the mid-1970s after the OPEC embargoes worsened the disruptions to the oil market in the ensuing years and produced severe hardships for Americans as lines at the gasoline pump lengthened, home-heating bills skyrocketed, and the pace of industrial production slowed to a crawl. However, the deregulation of oil and natural gas prices under President Reagan created a wave of innovation in the area of energy exploration and helped generate today's low prices.

72. The Green Revolution Proves Malthus Wrong

Previous sections highlighted the reduction in hunger in America and the spectacular productivity gains by American farmers. This section discusses the third magnificent trend in agriculture: the declining scarcity of food.

Just about 200 years ago British economist Thomas Malthus issued his dreary and world-famous prediction that food supplies would run out because "the power of population is infinitely greater than the power of the earth to produce subsistence for man." What Malthus never envisioned was the coming green revolution that caused a meteoric rise in food production—particularly in the United States. Over the past 50 years food production has grown an astounding 40 percent, despite a doubling of the planet's population.

One sign of rising food supplies is their falling prices. Since at least the turn of the century, virtually every agricultural commodity—corn, wheat, milk, and eggs—is substantially more affordable today (relative to wages) than at any time in the past. For instance, in the year 1900, barley, corn, cotton, oats, and wheat were 10 times more affordable than today, when adjusting for wages. Currently, they are about three times cheaper than in 1950. The figure shows an index of food scarcity. On average the cost of agricultural commodities fell by more than 40 percent in the 1980s to an all-time low in the early 1990s.

The green revolution has not just been restricted to the United States. The world food yield per acre has about doubled since 1950. Meanwhile, world food prices fell amazingly by half from 1960 to 1995.

Scientists now estimate that the world could feed another 1 billion people with existing know-how and farm capacity. In fact, enough food is available to provide more than 4 pounds of food per person per day worldwide.

World Food Production vs. World Population Growth

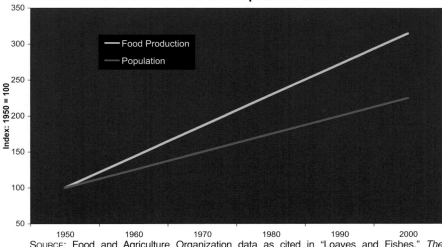

SOURCE: Food and Agriculture Organization data as cited in "Loaves and Fishes," *The Economist*, March 21, 1998.

Total Food Commodity Price Index, World

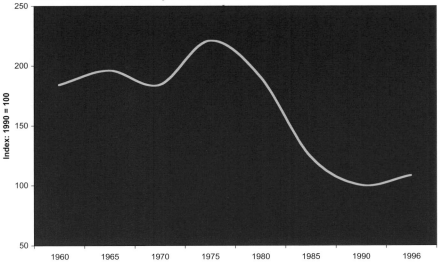

SOURCES: World Resources Institute, UN Environmental Programme, UN Development Program; and World Bank, *World Resources 1998–1999: A Guide to the Global Environment* (New York: Oxford University Press, 1998), Table 6.3, as cited in Ronald Bailey, *Earth Report 2000*.

73. Minerals and Metals: The End of Scarcity

The United States is often criticized for consuming between 20 and 40 percent of Earth's natural resources even though Americans account for only 5 percent of the world's population. Of greater concern is the potential exhaustion of nonrenewable resources—for example, fossil fuels, copper, zinc, aluminum, and electricity. The good news is that the long-term price trends relative to wages—or how long we have to work to purchase these resources—show decreasing scarcity for almost all minerals and metals. The figure shows the price trend for copper since 1800. Minerals become less scarce over time for several reasons. First, excavation technology continues to improve markedly, thus creating ever-larger retrievable supplies. Second, cheap substitutes for minerals are constantly being developed, thus lowering expected demand. A standard example is substituting satellites and fiber optics for copper wires for telephonic and data transmission. The essential point is that Americans are not resource destroyers but resource creators, who will leave future generations with a greater abundance of nature's bounty.

The cost of a ton of copper is only about a tenth now of what it was 200 years ago. Copper prices have continued to fall for a very long time.

In the 18th century B.C.E. in Babylonia under Hammurabi—almost 4,000 years ago—the price of copper was about a thousand times its price in the United States now relative to wages. During the Roman Empire the price was about a hundred times the present price. The lowering price trends of copper are indicative of the lowering price trends for virtually all other natural resources. Today, relative to wages—that is, the time we have to work to purchase the things we want—natural resources are half as costly as they were in 1950 and one-fifth as costly as they were in 1900. Americans have to work less and less all the time to obtain minerals like copper and silver.

Commodity Prices (real dollars)

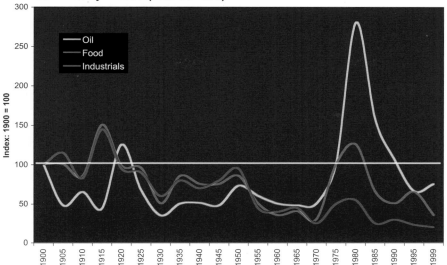

SOURCE: Data from BP Amoco as cited in "Shortage? What Shortage?" *The Economist*, September 11, 1999, p. 31.

Copper

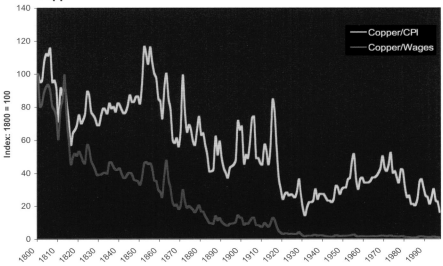

SOURCE: U.S. Geological Survey, *Commodity Statistics*, various years.

199

74. The Age of Cheap and Abundant Energy

In the early years of the 20th century there was a panic scare over the scarcity of oil. In the 1920s many geologists predicted that the United States faced certain depletion within 50 years. That never happened. But the gloomy prognostications continued. In late 1977—in the midst of the OPEC-created energy crisis—President Jimmy Carter announced, "We could use up all of the proven reserves of oil in the entire world by the end of the next decade." The Club of Rome had predicted a few years earlier that oil prices would skyrocket upward to $100 a barrel. That never happened either. Energy prices plummeted in the 1980s and 1990s following a long-term trend of greater affordability of oil, gas, and other fuels. Why? Because the world is not running out of energy. Today, oil sells far below the $100 a barrel predicted in the 1970s.

Energy prices in the United States have fluctuated substantially since 1900. But the trend has been one of greater affordability. Adjusted for wage growth, oil today is about five times cheaper than it was in 1900 and roughly the same price as it was in 1950, notwithstanding the huge and temporary spike in the world price in the 1970s. As noted earlier, electricity prices, have fallen more than eightfold since 1900. Coal was almost seven times more expensive.

Before the 1950s it was almost unthinkable that oil could be drilled and extracted from the bottom of the sea. In 1965 one of the first offshore oil rigs drilled oil from 600 feet deep off the coast of California. By the late 1980s the record for offshore oil drilling reached 10,000 feet. It has been precisely this kind of innovation that has confounded the doomsayers who in the 1960s and 1970s predicted global oil shortages and even depletion.

Gasoline prices paid at the pump have been on a steady rate of decline since the 1920s, with the obvious exception of the 1970s. In 1920, the real price of gas (excluding taxes) was twice as high as today. If the cost of gasoline relative to wages cost what it did 75 years ago, we would be paying almost $10 a gallon at the pump.

Index of Energy Prices Relative to Wages

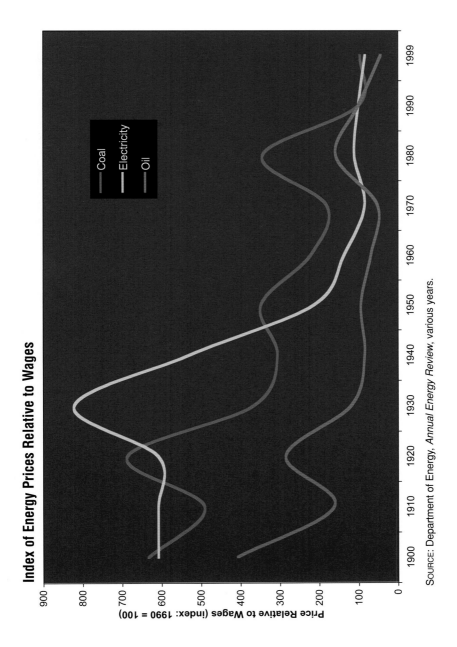

Source: Department of Energy, *Annual Energy Review*, various years.

75. Gaining Ground: The False Threat of Lost Land

We sometimes hear it said that economic progress in the United States has come at the expense of one of our most treasured national assets: our land. Suburbanization and increasing population is said to be imperiling our ability to feed ourselves in the future as we pave hundreds of thousands of additional acres in concrete every year. From 1960 to 1990 the number of acres classified as "urban land" has more than doubled from 25 million to 56 million. Yet the percentage of land in the United States that is devoted to urban/suburban use is only about 3 percent of the total land area of the continent. The rate at which land is being converted to suburban development is about 0.0006 percent per year, which is hardly a worrisome trend. In fact, lands protected from development have outpaced urban land conversion over recent decades. According to the Pacific Research Institute, "the ratio of protected lands to urban and agricultural lands rose from 6.4 percent to 22.9 percent from 1959–1987."

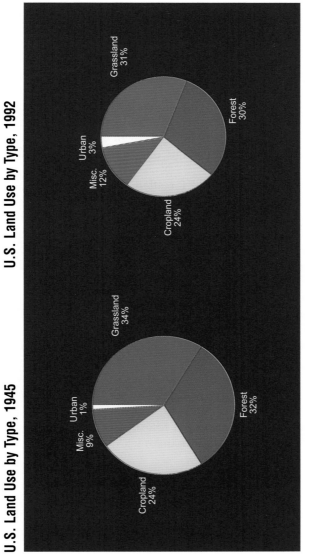

U.S. Land Use by Type, 1945

U.S. Land Use by Type, 1992

Grassland 34%

Urban 1%

Misc. 9%

Cropland 24%

Forest 32%

Grassland 31%

Urban 3%

Misc. 12%

Cropland 24%

Forest 30%

SOURCE: Council on Environmental Quality, *Annual Report*, various years.

76. More Trees and Forests

By some estimates, there are more trees in North America today than there were the day Columbus arrived on this continent some 500 years ago. Although there may be some cause for concern about preserving tropical rain forests in Brazil and other developing nations, the U.S. forests are not shrinking. Currently, the Forest Service reports that the United States is growing about 22 million net new cubic feet of wood a year and harvesting only 16.5 million—a net increase of 36 percent per year. This contrasts with the situation in the early years of this century, when about twice as many trees were cut as were planted.

In this century, despite a fivefold increase in population, the percentage of land space that is covered by forest has remained remarkably constant at about one-third of the land area of the United States.

The amount of world forestland has held remarkably steady over the course of the past 50 years. There are now roughly 4 billion hectares of forestland on the globe, up from about 3.6 billion in the late 1940s. Nor are rain forests disappearing at an alarming rate.

The price data for forest products over the past decade confirm this good news. Lumber prices relative to wages are about one-third the level of 1950 and about one-sixth the level in 1900. There is no timber famine.

Economists Roger A. Sedjo and Marion Clawson of Resources for the Future have documented the long-term improvement in the inventory of U.S. forests: "As a result of dramatically higher wood growth in the United States, and as a result of timber harvest at a rate less than growth, inventories of standing timber have increased significantly since 1920. The popular view is that the United States is consuming its wood faster than it is growing and that we are denuding our forests. In fact, exactly the reverse is happening—we are building them up."

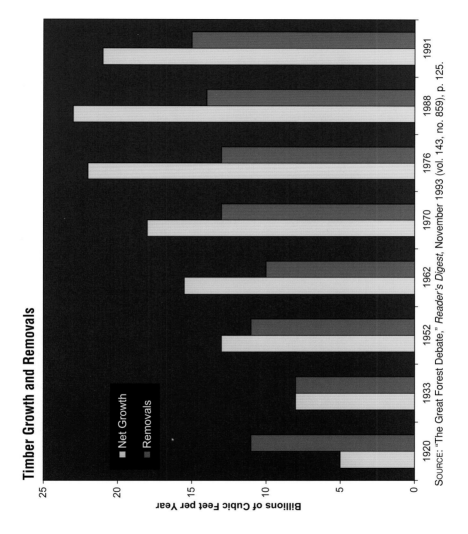

Timber Growth and Removals

Net Growth
Removals

Billions of Cubic Feet per Year

25   20   15   10   5   0

1920   1933   1952   1962   1970   1976   1988   1991

SOURCE: "The Great Forest Debate," *Reader's Digest*, November 1993 (vol. 143, no. 859), p. 125.

SECTION XVI. SOCIAL AND CULTURAL INDICATORS

Almost all of the data here up until now have dealt with economic and material well-being. What about the social and cultural health of the nation?

For at least the past two decades a growing chorus of conservatives have complained that the United States is experiencing a social/cultural retrenchment. These warnings of social decline in an era of growing material prosperity were loudest in the early 1990s. Pat Buchanan proclaimed "a cultural war in America" during his prime-time speech at the Republican National Convention in 1992. That message was reinforced in William Bennett's 1994 book *The Index of Leading Cultural Indicators.*

"Over the past 30 years almost all social statistics have gotten worse," Bennett wrote. His conclusion could not have been more dire: "Unless these exploding social pathologies are reversed, they will lead to the decline and perhaps even to the fall of the American Republic."

Bennett was largely right. The 1960s and 1970s were years of social regression. Between 1960 and 1990 the violent crime rate quadrupled; illegitimate births, single-parent households, and teen suicides tripled. Divorces doubled and the rate of marriage fell by almost half.

Over the past decade a fairly remarkable turnabout has occurred. With few exceptions, the very same social statistics that showed decline in the 1960s, 1970s, and early 1980s have shown improvement or at least plateaued. Since 1990, the abortion rate has fallen, illegitimacy has declined, welfare use has dropped precipitously, as have crime and drug use.

What has been missing from the debate over America's social condition has been a sense of historical perspective. Yes, there are many areas of our social life in which things have gotten worse— crime and family breakup, for instance. But many of the serious social problems in our communities that we combat today were worse in earlier eras of our history. Race relations, for example, were much worse 50 and 100 years ago than they are today. Alcohol abuse and smoking are both on a long-run decline. The income distribution was more unequal 100 years ago than today.

77. Thank You for Not Smoking: Americans Quit the Habit

Cigarette smoking became widespread in the 20th century. Through the first half of the 20th century the rate of cigarette consumption soared. Partly this reflected the rise in Americans' incomes and the commensurate increased affordability of smoking. The adverse health consequences of smoking became well documented and widely known only in the latter half of the century. Since 1960 cigarette consumption has been on a steady decline. Cigarette use has fallen by about 50 percent since the Surgeon General's report on smoking was released in 1964. Even with these impressive declines, smoking still is responsible for about 400,000 deaths a year—mostly due to cancer.

In 1900 the number of cigarettes smoked per adult per year was about 50. At its peak just before the Surgeon General's report, Americans were smoking 4,500 cigarettes a year per capita. The latest statistics indicate that Americans smoke fewer than 2,700 cigarettes a year.

In 1960 about 40 percent of American adults smoked. Today, less than 25 percent do. This decline is attributable to the increased education on the impact of smoking on one's health, the steadily rising tax on a package of cigarettes, and on the increased negative social stigma attached to smoking.

Record numbers of Americans have quit smoking. In 1965 less than 30 percent of smokers had quit. Today, that number above 40 percent. New products on the market, such as patches, have made it easier for smokers to quit the habit in recent years.

In the 1990s, cigarette sales fell by 20 percent. In 1990, 525 billion packages were sold; in 1999, an estimated 420 million were.

In 1989 about 20 percent of pregnant women smoked. Now only about 14 percent do. Smoking during pregnancy can cause low birth-rate babies and health abnormalities in newborns.

U.S. Cigarette Consumption per Capita by Persons 18 Years and Older

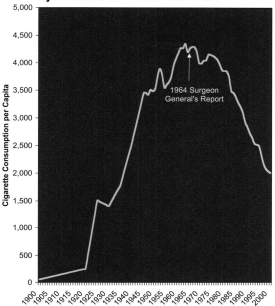

SOURCES: U.S. Department of Agriculture, *Tobacco Situation and Outlook Report*, various years.

Number of Cigarette Smokers and Smoker/Quit Ratio

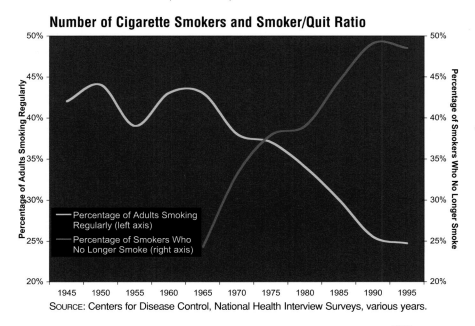

SOURCE: Centers for Disease Control, National Health Interview Surveys, various years.

209

78. Alcohol Abuse on the Wane

Consumption of alcohol is a leisure activity enjoyed by tens of millions of Americans. In moderation, drinking is pleasurable and even healthy. Drinking has deleterious social consequences in only a small percentage of cases. According to Professor James Roberts of Duke University, "It can be argued that alcohol consumption is generally a product of growing prosperity, not an index of social misery." Professor Dwight B. Heath, an anthropologist at Brown University, has found that "although about two-thirds of American adults drink, only about 10 percent of drinkers suffer in any respect from drinking. It is a truism that the root of most alcohol problems lie with the drinker, not the beverage." On balance, although Americans draw enjoyment from recreational drinking, we view an individual-choice decline in overall levels of alcohol consumption as a favorable social trend.

Although liquor sales rose after 1900, alcohol consumption fell when comparing the 20th century with the 19th. The rate of alcohol consumption in the United States was about 20 to 25 percent higher in the 19th century than in the 20th century. Alcohol consumption was at least 25 percent higher in the first half of the 19th century than the latter part of the 20th century. Before the Temperance Movement of the 1840s and 1850s, public drunkenness and intoxication at work were widespread social problems in America. The alcohol abuse problem today in no way rivals the near epidemic levels of excessive drinking in that era.

The percentage of Americans who say that alcohol has been a source of trouble in their families has declined from more than 1 in 3 in 1950 to less than 1 in 6 half a century later.

Consumption of hard liquor has been on a long-term downward slide, whereas beer and wine consumption has been rising. Clearly, hard liquor has more destructive social effects and is more hazardous to individual health than beer and wine.

Drunk drivers kill 15,000 to 20,000 Americans every year. The good news is that the long-term trend in fatalities due to drunk driving is downward and has declined by 20 percent just since 1980.

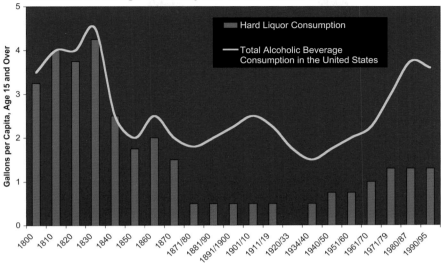

Alcoholic Beverage Consumption in the United States

SOURCES: *Statistical Abstract of the United States: 1998*, No. 249; and Simon, Table 11.1.

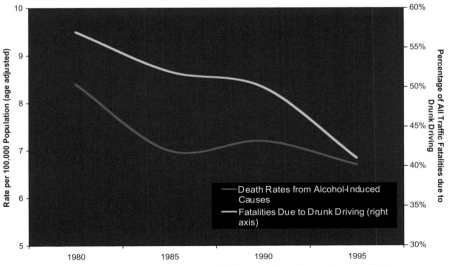

Death Rates from Alcohol-Induced Causes

SOURCES: *Statistical Abstract of the United States: 1998*, No. 154; and National Highway Safety Administration, *Traffic Safety Facts*, various years.

211

79. Volunteerism in America

Some 150 years ago Alexis de Tocqueville remarked with admiration about the generosity of the American people and their propensity to voluntarily provide aid and relief to those in need. Volunteerism has always been a hallmark of the American character. But today we hear about the "me generation," the "greed decade," and the decline of a sense of community and altruism in America. The fact is that most statistics illustrate increased donations of time and resources to those in need—especially in recent decades.

Everett Carl Ladd, the director of the Roper Center for Public Opinion Research, has compiled data on volunteerism in America since 1977. The figure shows the steady climb of personal involvement of time in serving the needs of other people. Twice as many American adults volunteer today as they did 20 years ago. More than four of five Americans now say they volunteer at least once a month for social service or civic activities.

"When study after study shows the same pattern, and trend-lines are clearly etched," concludes Ladd, "we should sit up and take notice. The levels of volunteering that Americans are now reporting are substantially higher than those reported a decade or two ago."

Percentage of Citizens Involved in Voluntary Charitable or Social Service Activity

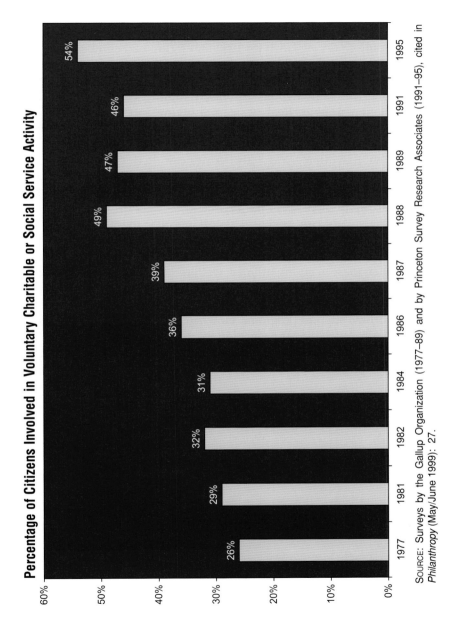

SOURCE: Surveys by the Gallup Organization (1977–89) and by Princeton Survey Research Associates (1991–95), cited in *Philanthropy* (May/June 1999): 27.

80. The Most Generous Society Ever

Americans are contributing their money, not just their time, to charitable causes in record amounts. In 1955 Americans contributed about $40 billion (in 1997 dollars) to private charities, according to *Giving USA*. By 1980 that figure had climbed to nearly $85 billion. By 1997 total charitable gifts had nearly doubled again to almost $160 billion.

Charitable giving has increased rapidly even adjusting for population growth. Real per capita giving rose from more than $250 per person in 1955 to about $450 per person in 1980 to more than $550 per capita by 1996.

The Salvation Army, the American Red Cross, and U.S. Catholic Charities receive the largest charitable contributions. Charitable giving as a share of GDP rose from 1.7 percent in 1960 to 2.2 percent of incomes in the 1990s.

The steady rise in charitable giving over the past 40 years is especially remarkable given that government spending to help the poor has also risen dramatically since the early 1960s—though whether these well-intentioned welfare programs help or hinder the recipients is a matter of some dispute. Today, governments in the United States spend nearly a third of a trillion dollars on low-income support programs. However, this aid has not completely supplanted private giving, though no doubt private charitable activity might be higher if it were not for the mandatory contributions Americans give to the poor through taxes.

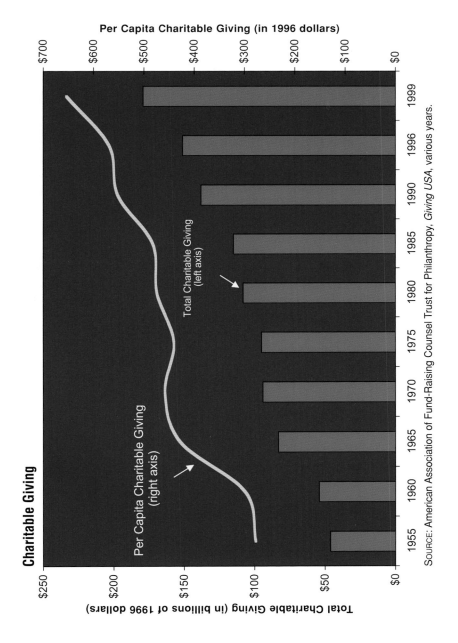

Charitable Giving

Per Capita Charitable Giving (in 1996 dollars)

Total Charitable Giving (in billions of 1996 dollars)

Total Charitable Giving (left axis)

Per Capita Charitable Giving (right axis)

81. A Symphony of Music

The 20th century—particularly the second 50 years— brought music into our lives as no other period before did. Because of the radio, the phonograph, and then the stereo and the CD players, our days are filled with music—whatever we want to hear, whenever we want to hear it.

Starting in the late 1950s, jazz, soul, country and western, and classical music gave way to one of the most innovative musical eras in history: rock 'n' roll. A litany of spectacular songwriters, singers, and musicians flourished in this era, including Elvis, the Beatles, the Rolling Stones, and the Motown Sound. It is quite possible that 500 years from now people will still be listening to artists like Frank Sinatra and Lennon-McCartney in much the same way that we still appreciate Bach and Beethoven today.

In 1982 only 19 percent of Americans listened to classical music on the radio at least occasionally. Now 41 percent do.

Americans have far more classical music selections to choose from than ever before. According to an analysis by Professor Tyler Cowen of George Mason University, "A small Tower Records outlet will offer at least 10,000 classical music titles, and the largest Tower branch in Manhattan has over 20,000 titles."

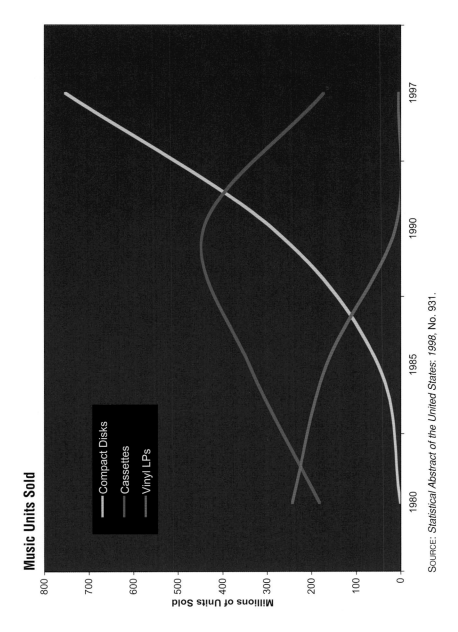

Music Units Sold

Millions of Units Sold

Compact Disks
Cassettes
Vinyl LPs

1980   1985   1990   1997

800 700 600 500 400 300 200 100 0

SOURCE: *Statistical Abstract of the United States: 1998*, No. 931.

82. America's Cultural Resurgence

Edmund Burke once described culture as "all of those qualities which raise life above mere survival and infuse it with elegance, dignity and high purpose." By that definition, America is certainly experiencing a cultural renaissance. For example, the past 50 years have almost certainly been the era of the greatest Broadway hits since Shakespeare was writing plays. From *My Fair Lady* to *The Sound of Music* to *The Phantom of the Opera* to *Death of a Salesman* to *Grease*, the box office hits have just kept on coming. Even off-Broadway theater has grown at a prodigious pace over this period. In 1965 there were only 60 nonprofit professional theater companies in the United States. Today, according to the Theater Communications Group in New York, there are more than 800.

Sales for live theater entertainment (plays, concerts, and operas) rose from $80 million in 1920 to $180 million in 1950 to $9 billion in 1990.

One cultural highbrow activity that is still as popular as ever is opera. Opera attendance in 1997 was an all-time high of 7.5 million. This figure was up 34 percent since 1980 and triple the 2.5 million attendance in 1970.

Between 1965 and 1990 museum attendance rose from 200 million to 500 million.

The private philanthropic sector contributed more than $1 billion to the arts in 1990, up from $22 million in 1967—roughly a tenfold increase after adjusting for inflation.

Classical music is also flourishing again. According to the American Symphony Orchestra League, between 1950 and 1995 the number of symphony orchestras in the United States nearly doubled—from 900 to about 1,700.

Number of Symphony Orchestras

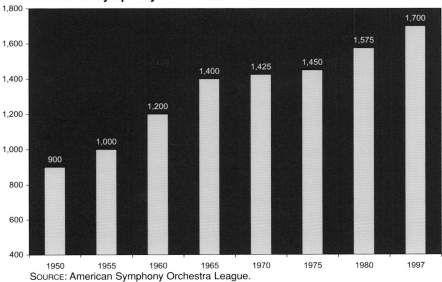

SOURCE: American Symphony Orchestra League.

Sales for Live Theater Entertainment

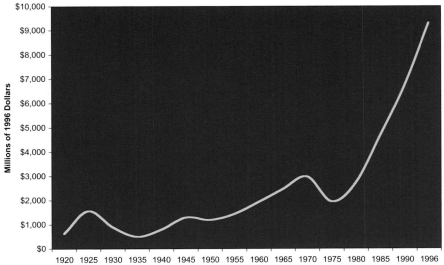

SOURCE: *Historical Statistics of the United States*; and *Statistical Abstract of the United States: 1998,* No. 425.

219

83. A Century of Reading

Despite concerns from the cultural elite that Johnny will not—or, worse, cannot—read, book sales have never been greater. In 1975, 1.4 billion books were sold. In 1997 that number had risen by 50 percent to 2.1 billion due in part to the explosion of discount booksellers in the 1980s and the advent of on-line book sellers like Amazon.com in the 1990s.

The long-term trend in book publishing shows a substantial, though bumpy, rise in this century. In 1900 6,400 books were published. By 1950 that number was about 11,000. By 1985 that number had grown to 50,000. And now the figure stands at over 65,000 new titles published a year. On a per household basis, book publishing fell rather sharply through 1960, due to the emergence of three major entertainment competitors: motion pictures, radio, and then TV. But since 1960 the book publishing business has blossomed. Currently, well more than twice as many books per capita are published as were published in 1950. And the average American buys twice as many books today as in 1950 and 50 percent more than in 1900.

Americans also spend more on books than ever before—even though books are significantly cheaper to publish and print today than in earlier eras. In 1920 Americans spent roughly $2 billion on books. In 1950 that had risen to about $5 billion. By 1999 Americans were spending $24 billion a year on books.

There are 10 times as many book stores today as there were in 1950, and this does not even include the spectacular rise of on-line book stores.

Magazine publishing has experienced a jolty trend in this century similar to that of book publishing. Beginning about 1950 many general circulation magazines found themselves in severe financial difficulty. In the 1980s and 1990s the magazine industry rejuvenated itself by specializing in trade publications and highly specific and even obscure hobby and interests periodicals. Thus we have seen the proliferation of profitable magazines, ranging from *The Wine Spectator* to *Yachting* to the computer magazine *Byte*.

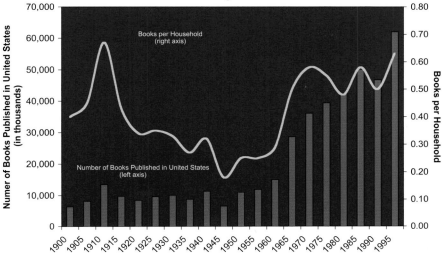

The Growth of Book Printing

SOURCES: *Historical Statistics of the United States*, Series R 192; and *Statistical Abstract of the United States: 1998,* No. 428.

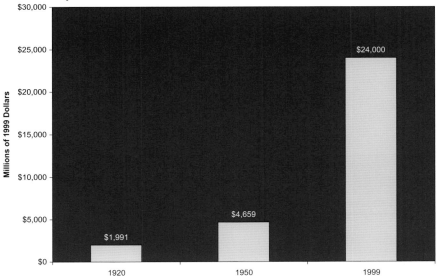

Expenditures on Books

SOURCES: *Historical Statistics of the United States*, Series H 890; and *New York Times Almanac 2000* (New York: Penguin, 1999), p. 406.

221

SECTION XVII. HUMAN ACHIEVEMENT IN SPORTS

Human achievement and the improvement in our physical health and conditioning over the past century can be measured by examining the trends in sports records. How fast can a human run a mile? Swim 800 meters? How high and how long can humans jump? How much weight can they lift? The constant shattering of virtually every sports record over the course of the 20th century, including perhaps the most famous sports record of them all, Roger Maris's 61 home runs in 1961 broken by Mark McGwire's 70 home runs in 1998—indicates that people are bigger, stronger, and more physically fit than 100 years ago.

84. Faster: The 4-Minute Mile and Other Milestones

The table shows the frequency in the 20th century that athletes broke the world record for major running events. In 1900 the fastest time in the mile was held by Thomas Conneff, who ran the race in 4:16. In 1954 Roger Bannister broke the once-believed-unattainable goal: the 4-minute mile. In 1966 American Jim Ryan ran the mile in 3:51. Today, the fastest recorded time in the mile is less than 3:50. Incredibly, today the fastest miler can run the race just about a full minute ahead of the world-record time in the mid-19th century. Even mediocre high school track runners can run the mile faster than the world's fastest man 150 years ago.

Virtually every track and field event follows a pattern similar to the running of the mile: records once deemed unattainable have been broken time and again. For example, the pole vault record in 1900 was 11 feet, 10.5 inches. In 1951 the world record was 15 feet, 7.5 inches. Today, it is just under twice the 1900 mark at 20 feet, 14 inches.

Evolution of Sports Records in the 20th Century

	Start of the Century - 1901	Middle of the Century - 1951	Present-Day Record
Greatest weight lift	4,133 pounds	4,133 pounds	6,270 pounds
Fastest 100 meters	10.6 secs	10.2 secs	9.79 secs
Fastest one mile	4 min, 12.8 secs	4 min, 1.3 secs	3 min, 43 secs
One hour running	11 miles, 932 yards	12 miles, 29 yards	13 miles, 11 yards,
Highest high jump	6 feet, 5 inches	6 feet, 11 inches	8 feet
Highest pole vault	11 feet, 10.5 inches	15 feet, 7.5 inches	20 feet, 14 inches
Long jump	24 feet, 7.5 inches	26 feet, 8.25 inches	29 feet, 36 inches
Longest shot put	48 feet, 2 inches	58 feet, 10.25 inches	75 feet, 83 inches
Longest discus throw	122 feet, 3.5 inches	186 feet, 11 inches	242 feet, 98 inches
Longest hammer throw	169 feet, 4 inches	196 feet, 5 inches	284 feet, 51 inches

SOURCE: *New York Times Almanac, 2000* (New York: Penguin Reference Books, 1999).

85. Female Athletes Shatter Sports Records

The proud and magical moment for Americans in 1999 when Mia Hamm and the United States women's soccer team won the World Cup against China could not have been possible 50 years ago. Very few women were able to play organized sports. The World Cup is just one tiny reminder of how far women have come in this century—reversing thousands of years of second-class citizenship. Because of the increased participation in athletics by women in the past quarter century, women are now trouncing sports records at a faster clip than men are.

In recent decades, women have shown stunning gains in their running times. The Boston Marathon is a case in point. Twenty-five years ago the top women runners crossed the tape about 30 to 40 minutes behind the men in the marathon: now the female winner is only about 15 minutes behind the male winner. Although the Boston Marathon has been run for more than 100 years, it was not until 1966 that women were permitted to run the race.

Winning Times in the Boston Marathon for Men and Women

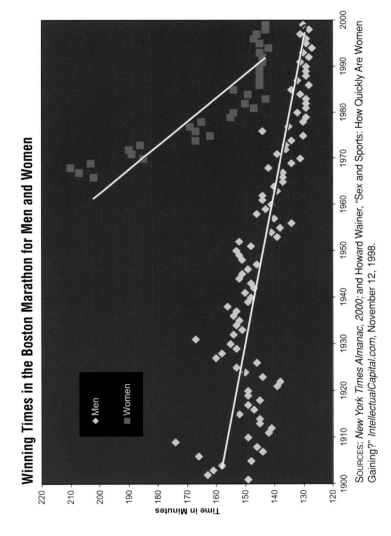

SOURCES: *New York Times Almanac, 2000;* and Howard Wainer, "Sex and Sports: How Quickly Are Women Gaining?" *IntellectualCapital.com,* November 12, 1998.

227

86. The Sporting, Physically Fit Society

One reason Americans are shattering sports records is that as a society Americans are bigger, stronger, and in better physical condition than their ancestors. Americans are devoting an increasing amount of their free time to playing sports and to physical fitness. Since 1965 the amount of time that Americans spend on fitness and sports has roughly tripled. Physical fitness has become a passion for a growing number of Americans, as the proliferation of health clubs, joggers, and sales of Jane Fonda's workout tapes can attest. The percentage of Americans who exercise daily has risen from 24 to 60 percent since 1960.

Participation in sports has also flourished. American society has become more affluent and therefore has more money and time for leisure activities. For example, the *Wall Street Journal* reported on April 13, 2000, that "only 3.5 percent of golf in the 1960s. Today, 11.7 percent play. . . . The number of women golfers 24 percent in the last decade to 5.7 million. The number of African-American golfers doubled to 870,000." Participation in many other sports showed similar gains.

According to scholar John Robinson of the University of Maryland, women now spend more than three times as many hours a week engaged in sports/outdoor activities as they did as recently as 1965.

Do You Do Anything Daily That Helps You Keep Physically Fit?

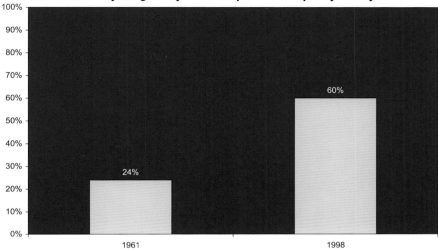

Percentage of Respondants Who Said Yes

SOURCE: *USA Today*, "How We've Changed," December 31, 1999.

Sports Participation

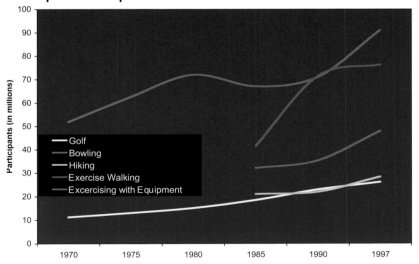

SOURCE: *Wall Street Journal Almanac 1999* (New York: Ballantine Books, 1998), p. 825.

229

SECTION XVIII. THE REMARKABLE GAINS BY WOMEN

Throughout this book we have tended to concentrate our attention on absolute gains for Americans rather than relative gains for one group versus another. It is more important, in our opinion, to measure whether groups are doing better in absolute terms than in the past, rather than whether some groups are advancing faster than others. John Tierney of the *New York Times* expressed a frustration that matches our own when he recently wrote, "No matter how much wealthier and healthier everyone becomes, we always read about a 'gap' between one group or another."

Two groups in particular have been historically discriminated against in American society: women and blacks. So in the next two sections we present data on the absolute and relative gains of these groups, because to the extent that disparities are declining, it is a sign of another important trend in America—the decline in sexism and bigotry.

To appreciate the gains made by women over the past 100 years, consider the following prediction by columnist Gertrude Thayer back in 1899 regarding the gains she hoped women would make in the coming century at the start of the last century: "By the end of the 20th century, she is going to vote. She is going to insist that she is paid the same wages as men for an equal amount of work. She will be able to go alone to the theatre or a restaurant without the painful necessity of dragging a man with her. She will hold any or every office. In fact, should matters become too bad, she wouldn't mind becoming president of the United States."

The 20th century's spectacular improvements in living standards and economic opportunities were particularly remarkable for women. Almost every objective measure we could find shows that women made giant strides both in absolute terms and relative to men. The march to equal rights for women is visibly evident in almost every area of routine life: government (in 1900 women still did not have the right to vote), occupations (like medicine, law, and the sciences), sports, opportunities in the arts and entertainment, and so on. In the 1960s and 1970s many women wore famous buttons that read: "59 cents." This was said to be the amount that a woman earned for every dollar a man earned. By 2000, equality of pay had nearly been fully attained for women.

87. Liberating Women from Housework

Probably the single greatest area of improvement in the everyday life of American women has been in their gradual emancipation from the drudgery of housework from sunup to sun-down. The typical married woman was virtually a slave to the backbreaking toil of household chores before the 20th century—unless she lived in a very wealthy family and had servants working for her. Here is a statistic that we suspect women would find joyful: the amount of time that women have been chained to domestic housework—washing clothes and dishes, cleaning a house, preparing and cooking meals, and so forth—has shrank in the 20th century by almost half.

American housewives (and nowadays househusbands) spend about 40 hours a week less on housework than a century ago. The reduction in housework is a result of three factors: (1) the inventions of household appliances like washing machines, vacuum cleaners, dishwashers, electric disposals, and so on; (2) the increase in family income; and (3) the increased share of the workload now borne by husbands.

Almost all of the modern appliances that have eased the burden of housework had not been invented before 1900 and most were not widely available until the 1950s. Futurologist H. G. Wells had imagined an electric dishwasher in his writings at the turn of the century, but it was not until the 1960s that this machine started to become a standard feature in homes. Similarly, refrigerators and freezers, vacuum cleaners, garbage disposals, washing machines and dryers, self-cleaning ovens, and microwave ovens are virtually universal among American households today, though before the middle of the 20th century they were still novelty household items.

Equality between the sexes in sharing household chores is also on the rise (though women may have a hard time believing this). According to a 1997 report by the National Bureau of Economic Research entitled "Trends in the Well-Being of American Women, 1970–95," there has been "a small but notable reallocation of housework between husbands and wives." In 1950 only 62 percent of husbands helped with housework. Now 85 percent do.

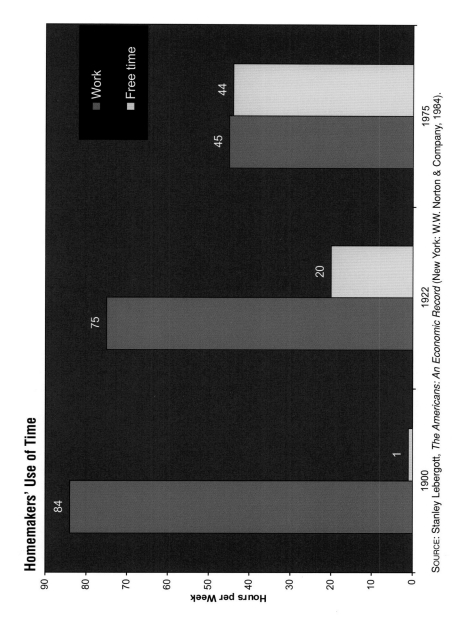

Homemakers' Use of Time

Hours per Week

Work
Free time

84   1   75   20   45   44

1900   1922   1975

SOURCE: Stanley Lebergott, *The Americans: An Economic Record* (New York: W.W. Norton & Company, 1984).

88. Economic Equality in the Workplace

Perhaps the best single measure of women's economic condition is their earnings. The figure shows that the average real income of women since 1950 has doubled.

The long-term data provide a real appreciation for the advances made by women toward the goal of pay equity. Before 1850 women earned about 40 cents for every dollar men earned in the same professions. By 1900 that pay gap had closed to about 55 cents earned by women for every dollar earned by men. By 1950 the gap was about 35 cents. Today, young women are closing in on parity in pay. Women in all professions now earn about 72 cents for every dollar men earn, but for women between the ages of 16 to 29, women earn about 92 cents for every dollar men earned.

According to former Congressional Budget Office director June O'Neill, "When earning comparisons are restricted to women and men more similar in their experience and life situations, the wage differentials are quite small." O'Neill estimates that when men and women are similar in all work-relevant characteristics, women earn 98 cents for every dollar men do, which is close to wage parity.

Black Women as Domestic Servants

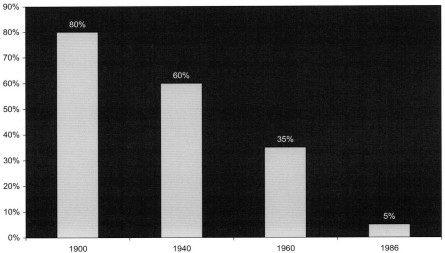

SOURCES: Stephan and Abigail Thernstrom, *America in Black and White* (New York: Simon and Schuster, 1997), p. 81; and authors' calculations.

234

Gains in Real Median Income for Women

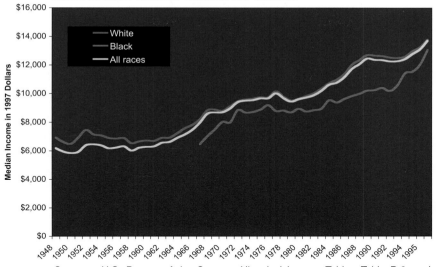

SOURCES: U.S. Bureau of the Census, *Historical Income Tables*, Table P-2; and *Current Population Survey*, various years.

Ratio of Female to Male Earnings

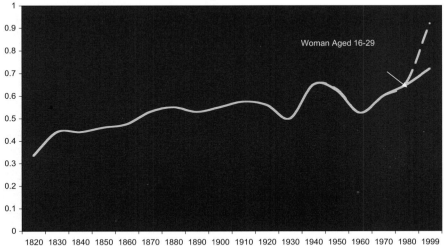

SOURCES: *Journal of Economic Literature*, vol. 29 (September 1991): 34; and Diana Furchtgott-Roth and Christine Stolba, *Women's Figures* (Washington : American Enterprise Institute, 1999), Table A2-2, p. 83.

89. The Rise of the Female Entrepreneur and CEO

American women are starting businesses at record rates today. Between 1972 and 1997 the number of women-owned businesses increased from 1 million to 8.5 million. The 8.5 million women-owned businesses employ nearly 24 million workers and generate about $3 trillion in sales, according to an American Enterprise Institute report, *Women's Figures*.

The old boys' network is breaking down in corporate America as well. More than 80 percent of Fortune 500 firms now have women on their boards. In 1999, Carly Fiorina became the first female CEO of a Fortune 100 company (Hewlett-Packard). The number of female vice presidents of major companies doubled over the decade 1985–95.

In the 1970s a popular bumper sticker read: "A WOMAN'S PLACE IS IN THE HOUSE—AND THE SENATE." Women have made huge strides in the number of elected offices they hold. In 1920, for example, there was 1 female member of Congress. In 1950, there were 10. Today, there are 65. It is also worth noting that women did not generally have the right to vote before 1920.

Number of Women-Owned Businesses

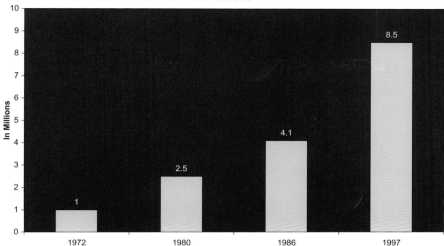

SOURCES: U.S. Bureau of the Census, *Economic Census*, "Women-Owned Businesses," U.S. Small Business Administration, Office of Advocacy, *Women in Business*, October 1998, as cited in Diana Furchgott-Roth and Christine Stolba, *Women's Figures*, (Washington: American Enterprise Institute, 1999).

Number of Women in Congress

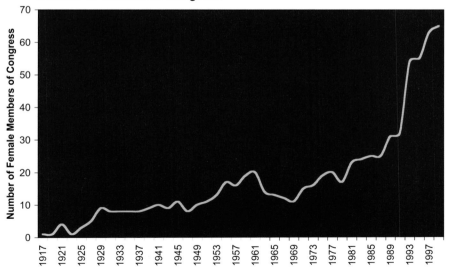

SOURCE: Center for the American Woman and Politics, Eagleton Institute of Politics, Rutgers University.

90. The Educated Woman

At the start of the 20th century almost no women went to college. Almost all of the elite, well-funded colleges were exclusively male. Today, women are more likely to attend college than men are. Not only are women more likely to earn advanced degrees, but the degrees are increasingly in areas once virtually closed to women: law, business management, engineering, and medicine, to name a few. These ongoing gains in educational attainment suggest that in the future wage differences between men and women will narrow still further. In 1950 only half of American female workers had a high school degree. Now 90 percent do.

Percentage of Degrees Awarded to Women

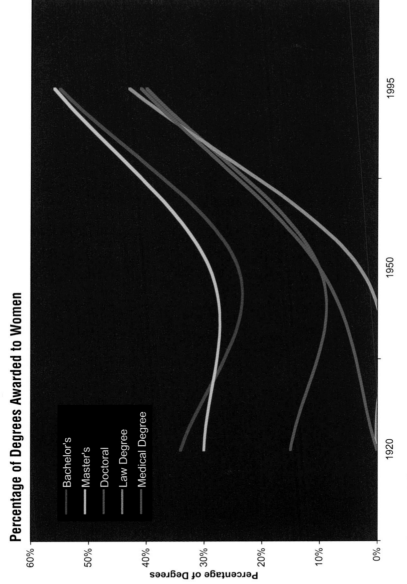

Legend:
- Bachelor's
- Master's
- Doctoral
- Law Degree
- Medical Degree

Y-axis: Percentage of Degrees (0% to 60%)

X-axis: 1920, 1950, 1995

SOURCE: U.S. Department of Education, National Center for Education Statistics, Integrated Postsecondary Education Data Systems, *Completions*, Washington, various years.

SECTION XIX. THE DECLINE OF RACISM

Slavery and racism have been two of the greatest stains on American society since the Declaration of Independence. Racial discrimination manifested in so many ways—from slavery to lynchings to the Ku Klux Klan to Jim Crow laws to segregation—has undermined the American ideal of "all men are created equal." In fact, as recently as 1968 the Kerner Commission on race, appointed after the riots in Watts, Detroit, and other cities, concluded glumly that "Our nation is moving toward two societies, one black, one white—separate and unequal."

The Kerner Commission was fantastically wrong.

Racism has been on a long-term decline for a century. Almost without exception, black Americans have made gains in living standards and social conditions. Not only did black Americans make substantial material gains in the 20th century, but they made remarkable relative gains compared with whites as well. This is true of black incomes, poverty rates, educational status, health, home ownership, and wealth.

No, racism has not disappeared from the American landscape. But all objective evidence suggests that the amount of bigotry against minorities fell sharply during the century, particularly since the civil rights era of the 1960s. The wage gap, for example, between comparably skilled blacks and whites and men and women has narrowed by at least half since 1950. Throughout the century color lines increasingly dissappeared in the United States. We all are familiar with the famous story in the 1950s of Branch Rickey hiring Jackie Robinson, the first black American to play baseball in the major leagues. But less celebrated color lines have been crossed in almost every area of life. Almost every occupation is open to minorities today. We are not yet a colorblind society, but we should recognize that black progress was fairly steady throughout the entire century.

91. No More Racial Terrorism

In 1990 Supreme Court nominee Clarence Thomas complained of a "high-tech lynching" against his character. One hundred years ago real lynchings were all too common in the United States—used as a terrorist tactic to keep blacks and other minorities "in their place." This form of mob violence and vigilante justice was a symbol of the blacks' second-class citizen status. Lynching became an all-too-common substitute for the rule of law, often used by the Ku Klux Klan in the deep South to terrorize blacks and immigrants. In the late 19th century there were hundreds of lynchings every year. By the 1930s that number had dwindled to a few dozen. In recent decades, there have been virtually no lynchings—save for the occasional "high-tech" variety.

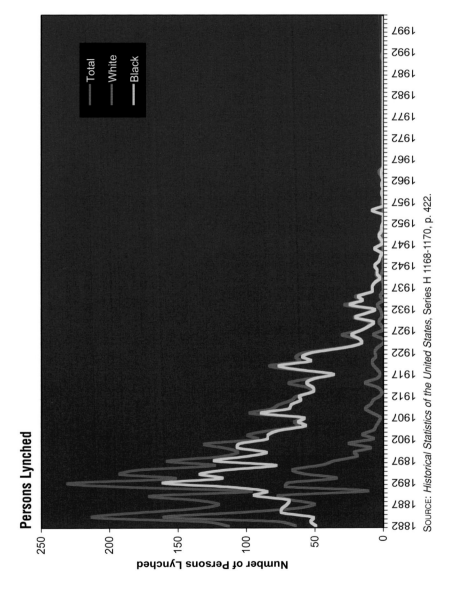

Persons Lynched

Number of Persons Lynched

SOURCE: *Historical Statistics of the United States, Series H 1168-1170, p. 422.*

243

92. Huge Economic Gains for Black Americans

Here is how scholars Abigail and Stephan Thernstrom describe the economic status of black Americans in the first half of the 20th century: "On the eve of World War II, a mere 5 percent of black men were engaged in white-collar work of any kind. The majority eked out a bare existence, predominantly in agriculture. Six out of 10 African–American women were household servants, who often worked 12-hour days, often for pathetically low wages." Today economic opportunities for blacks—women and men—have improved substantially. The single best indication of the economic progress of black Americans is to track their income growth.

Black incomes surged in the 20th century, contrary to conventional belief. In 1900 the per capita income for black Americans was below $1,500. At century's end that figure had risen to above $9,000. That is a sixfold real increase in per person income.

The percentage of blacks in white-collar jobs has multiplied several times over since the 1930s. In 1940 5 percent of black men were in white-collar occupations. By 1970 that had leaped to 22 percent. Today it is roughly 33 percent. For black women the progress has been even more impressive. In 1940 only 6 percent were in the higher paying white-collar jobs. By 1970 that number had increased to 36 percent. Now, almost half of black women work in such jobs.

The poverty rate among blacks was estimated at about 80 percent before the 1940s. By 1950 the black poverty rate was still above 50 percent. Today, about 25 percent of blacks are in poverty.

In 1900 only about one in four blacks owned their own home. Most lived in Jim Crow–style segregated housing owned by absent (mostly white) landlords. By 1950 the home-ownership rate had increased to about one in three. Today, nearly one-half of all black families are home owners.

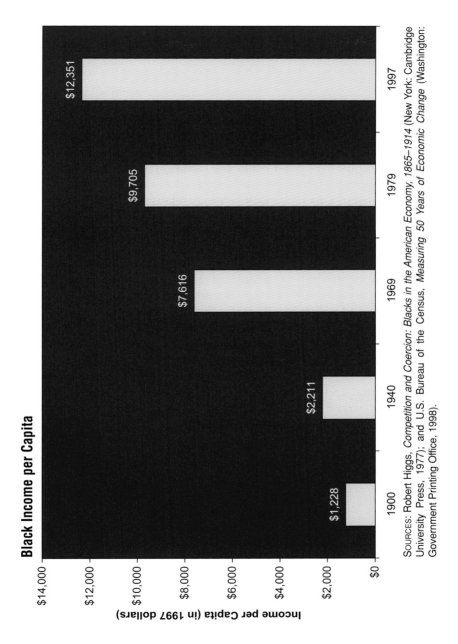

Black Income per Capita

SOURCES: Robert Higgs, *Competition and Coercion: Blacks in the American Economy, 1865–1914* (New York: Cambridge University Press, 1977); and U.S. Bureau of the Census, *Measuring 50 Years of Economic Change* (Washington: Government Printing Office, 1998).

245

93. Moving toward a Colorblind Society

Again, we do not generally concentrate on the relative gains of one group versus another in this book. But in our quest to end racism and discrimination, which have been such a scourge on our society for the past 350 years, it makes sense to examine how blacks are doing compared with whites. In our judgment the comparative status of blacks is the most objective way to gauge whether discrimination is increasing or decreasing in the United States. The 20th century was one in which blacks, in a gradual but almost uninterrupted process, engaged in "catching up" to whites in almost all social and economic measures.

Contrary to popular belief, the racial gap in incomes is not getting wider, it is shrinking—although not as rapidly and thoroughly as it should. In 1900 black earnings relative to whites' was only about 35 percent. This percentage rose to around 50 percent by 1950 and today it stands at about 75 percent. Much closing of the gap still needs to be achieved, but the direction is very positive, not negative, suggesting that employment discrimination is falling.

The income gap on the basis of race has also fallen very sharply in this century. Economists Robert Higgs of the Independent Institute and Robert Margo of Vanderbilt University have calculated that "over the long run average black income increased much faster than average white income: black income rose from about 24 percent to nearly 60 percent of white income [from 1900 to 1990]."

A recent study by the U.S. Census Bureau tracks the gains for black men and women over 30 years. In 1967 the average black woman earned 79 percent of what a white woman earned; today that ratio is up to 95 percent. For men the racial gap is larger, but is closing faster. In 1967 black male earnings were 57 percent of white male earnings. Thirty years later that gap had shrunk by 21 percent to 69 percent.

Black/White Income Ratio

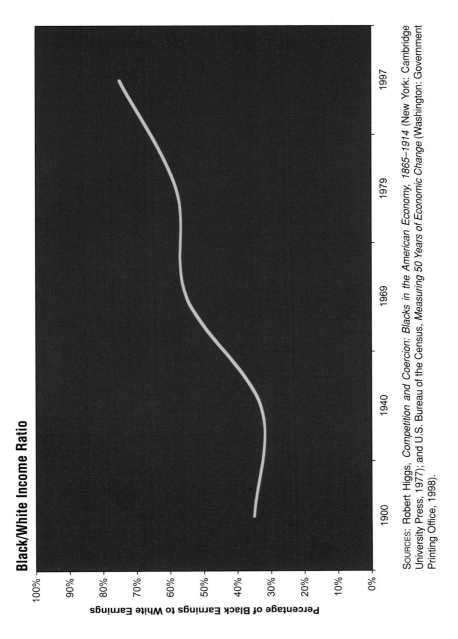

Percentage of Black Earnings to White Earnings

100% 90% 80% 70% 60% 50% 40% 30% 20% 10% 0%

1900   1940   1969   1979   1997

Sources: Robert Higgs, *Competition and Coercion: Blacks in the American Economy, 1865–1914* (New York: Cambridge University Press, 1977); and U.S. Bureau of the Census, *Measuring 50 Years of Economic Change* (Washington: Government Printing Office, 1998).

94. Getting Along with Each Other: Race Relations

At the turn of the 20th century W.E.B. Du Bois wrote that America would struggle for years to overcome its homespun system of legal apartheid. "The problem of the 20th century," he lamented, "is the problem of the color line—the relation of the darker to the lighter races of men." In recent decades, however, race relations have seen vast improvements by various measures. One indication of improved racial harmony has been the steady decline in the number of race riots in the United States in the past two decades. Another sign is the gradual increase in interracial dating and interracial marriages. (Note the stinging and near-universal rebuke that Governor George W. Bush received during the 2000 presidential primaries for giving a speech at Bob Jones University, where interracial dating was forbidden.) Stephan and Abigail Thernstrom of the Manhattan Institute report on public opinion data that "in 1975 21 percent of blacks and 9 percent of whites had a 'good friend' of the other race; but by 1994 the proportion was 78 percent of blacks and 73 percent of whites."

Finally, for all the international criticism that the United States receives for poor racial relations, the level of bigotry is lower in the country than in many nations that are supposedly racially tolerant. The Europeans are particularly hypocritical on the issue of ethnic harmony.

Race Riots

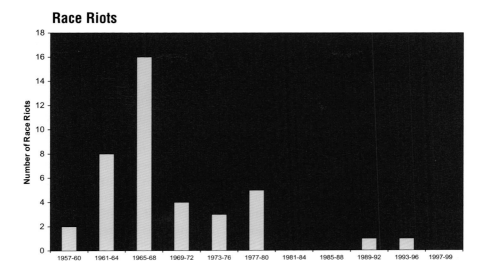

SOURCE: Data from *The Encyclopedia of American Facts and Dates*, as printed in "America! America! God Shed His Grace on Thee," Laffer Associates, December 29, 1998.

Percentage of the Population with an Unfavorable View of National Minorities, 1991

Country	Minority Group	Percentage Disliking
East Germany	Poles	54%
Czechoslovakia	Hungarians	49%
West Germany	Turks	45%
Russia	Azerbaijanis	44%
France	North Africans	42%
Poland	Ukranians	42%
Hungary	Romanians	40%
Spain	Catalans	22%
Great Britain	Irish	21%
United States	African Americans	13%

SOURCE: Times Mirror Center, *The Pulse of Europe*, 1991, as printed in *American Enterprise*, November/December 1998, p. 18.

95. Minority Gains in Health and Education

Virtually all of the health gains discussed in the first section of this book have been more impressive for blacks than for whites. For example, though black life expectancy is substantially lower than for whites, the gap is narrowing. The same is true of infant mortality, heart disease, AIDS, access to quality health care, and other measures of medical care. (See figure on infant mortality in Section I.)

The good news is that college opportunities are vast today for blacks compared with the first half of the 20th century. Before the 1920s a college degree for a black American was extremely rare—about 1 percent. Now almost 20 percent of adult blacks have earned a college degree, and that percentage is still rapidly rising.

Before the 1950s, about half of the universities were essentially closed to minorities, which meant that for those blacks who went to college at all, most went to black colleges, which had more limited resources and opportunities than the major colleges whites attended.

Since 1920 the median years of schooling for all 25 to 29 year-olds has risen from 8 years to 12. The rise has been all the more astonishing for blacks. In 1920 the median years of schooling for blacks was under 6 years; it doubled in the past 75 years to almost 12 years at century's end.

High school graduation rates by race are approaching parity (90 percent for whites and 84.5 percent for blacks). College, however, is still almost twice as common for whites as blacks, but even here the disparity has narrowed—just more slowly than other measures of educational gains.

Median Years of School Completed, 25 to 29 Year Olds

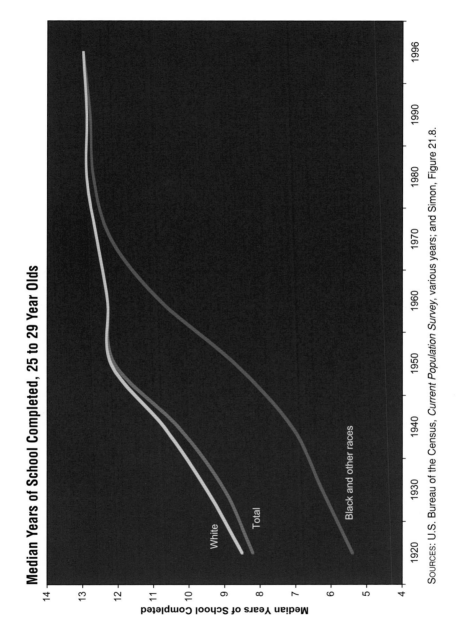

SOURCES: U.S. Bureau of the Census, *Current Population Survey*, various years; and Simon, Figure 21.8.

251

SECTION XX. FREEDOM AND DEMOCRACY

The 20th century was punctuated by two terrible world wars and numerous horrid episodes of genocide. At least 200 million people perished as a consequence of the brutality. Still the century ended with far greater freedom for a far greater percentage of the world's population than ever before in recorded history. According to the Freedom House *Freedom of the World Index*, "The proportion of the world's population living in freedom is the highest in the history of the survey." There is also far more democracy, economic liberty, and free trade than there was in previous centuries.

96. The Relentless March toward Freedom

A larger percentage of the world's inhabitants are freer than ever before in history. Economic historian Stanley Engerman has noted that as recently as the late 18th century, "The bulk of mankind, over 95 percent, were miserable slaves or despotic tyrants." Adam Smith estimated in 1762 that "slavery is entirely abolished at this time . . . in only a small part of Europe"—which was the most respectful part of the world in terms of human rights during that era. Slavery was still common as recently as the early 19th century in the British Empire, the French and Danish colonies, the United States, Brazil, Africa, and Asia. Legal slavery was officially outlawed throughout the world when slaves were emancipated in 1970 in the Arabian nations. The figure shows the decline of slavery from 1750 through the end of the 20th century.

Totalitarianism was another kind of suppression of freedom that emerged after World War II. That dehumanizing political system has also been all but eradicated from the globe as of 2000. In 1950 more than one third of the world's population lived under Marxist-Leninist regimes compared with 2 to 3 percent today. There is much truth to the adage that virtually the only Marxist-Leninists left in the world teach at American universities.

Percentage of Slaves or Serfs in the World

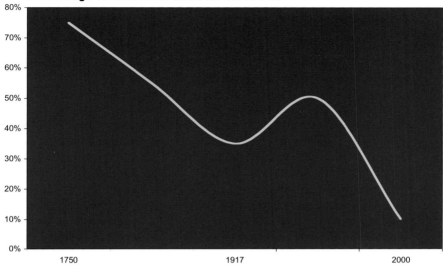

SOURCES: Simon, pp. 171–77; and authors' calculations.

Percentage of World Population under Totalitarian Rule

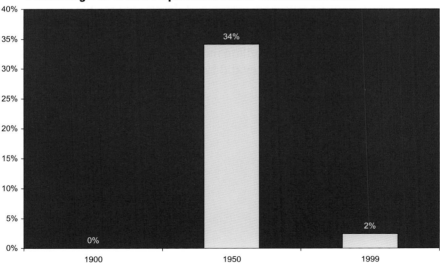

SOURCE: Freedom House.

97. The Diffusion of Democracy and Human Rights

A democratic government is one in which self-rule and self-determination are exercised through free elections. An autocratic government is one that does not allow free and open elections. Democratic rule is not a guarantee of freedom and free enterprise for all citizens, and indeed democratic nations can and do use majority rule at the ballot box to suppress rights of minorities. But, on balance, the spread of democracy is a positive development because it is simply superior to almost all of the alternatives that have been tried.

We agree wholeheartedly with the conclusion of the editors of *The Economist* magazine who wrote approvingly of the spread of democratic governments by observing, "Democracy now exerts a powerful appeal, less because of what it can do than because of what people hope it will stop, namely, the horrific calamities associated with unaccountable authority." The figure shows that democracy has spread from 12 percent of the world population in 1900 to 63 percent today.

The annual Freedom House survey measures political rights and freedoms and civil liberties in nations. This survey has been conducted every year since 1981. It finds that the number of people who live in nations that are free or partly free has risen from 58 to 67 percent. Almost 1.5 billion more people live in free or partly free countries today than they did two decades ago.

Percentage of World Population under Democracies

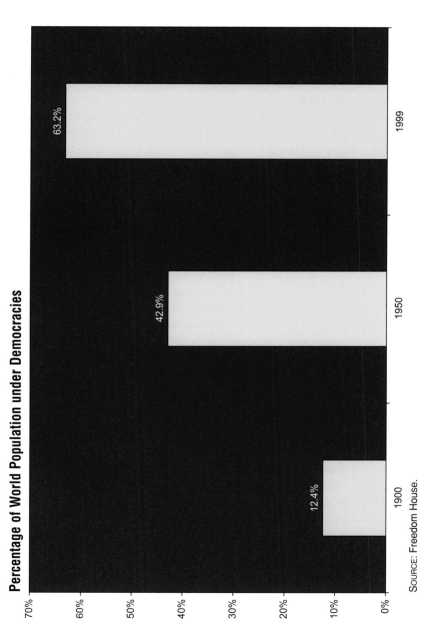

63.2%

42.9%

12.4%

1999

1950

1900

70%

60%

50%

40%

30%

20%

10%

0%

SOURCE: Freedom House.

98. The Expansion of Free Trade Promotes Prosperity

The move to free trade is a wholesome development for two reasons: first, because free trade generally promotes economic growth; and second and more important, because free trade is an indication of the level of economic freedom in a society.

Up until the 20th century the United States was generally a protectionist economy—with its markets closed to foreign competition. In the 20th century the country gradually moved toward an economic philosophy of generally open and free trade—though to be sure, there still are left standing many trade barriers. In 1911 the value of total U.S. exports and imports equaled just $4 billion. By 1950 that amount of trade had accelerated to $200 billion. The real explosion of trade has occurred since 1960. Today annual U.S. exports and imports have an annual price tag of almost $2 trillion.

One trend toward greater freedom and free markets is the decline in average tariffs over time. The average tariff on imports fell from between 40 and 50 percent throughout the early part of the 19th century to about 20 percent in 1900 and to less than 5 percent at the end of the century. Almost all industrial nations have reduced their trade barriers over the past half-century—some even more so than the United States. Since tariffs are a form of taxation on consumers, the reduction of trade restrictions increases the sovereignty of citizens.

The only period in the past century when free trade was curtailed and protectionist walls heightened was during the Great Depression. In 1929 the United States engaged in $10 billion of trade. By 1935 after duties had risen on many imports to more than 50 percent, the volume of trade had dropped by 35 percent to $6.5 billion. In his famous book *The Way the World Works*, former *Wall Street Journal* reporter Jude Wanniski documents that the wave of protectionism in 1929 was an instigator to the great stock market crash.

Clearly, free trade has not had the negative consequences that some Americans fear. Worker incomes grew, they did not fall, and working conditions improved, rather than deteriorated over the course of the 20th century even as restraints on trade loosened. Especially since the early 1980s, U.S. manufacturing companies have thrived, and key industries like computers and microchips gained market share even as foreign competition grew more intense.

U.S. Imports and Exports

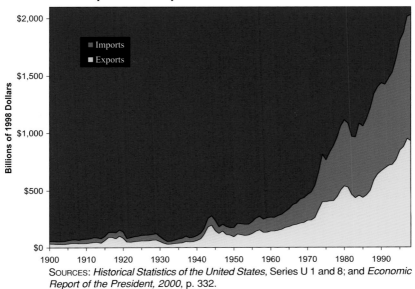

SOURCES: *Historical Statistics of the United States*, Series U 1 and 8; and *Economic Report of the President, 2000*, p. 332.

Ratio of Import Duties to Imports in the United States

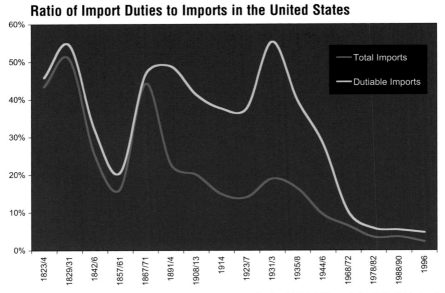

SOURCES: *Historical Statistics of the United States*, Series U211-212, and *Statistical Abstract of the United States*, No. 1325.

SECTION XXI. THE AMERICAN PEOPLE: THE WORLD'S GREATEST RESOURCE

America is a great country recording giant strides in social, economic, and cultural progress because the American people have greatness residing inside of them. Without trying to sound excessively patriotic, we agree with historian Paul Johnson who ends his epic study, *A History of the American People*, by noting that the Americans are "the first, best hope of the human race." If people are a country's ultimate resource, then the American people in this century have indeed proven themselves to be the ultimate, ultimate resource. It is for this reason that no book on the great trends of the 20th century can be complete without addressing the demographic changes in the United States over the past 100 years—almost all of which we regard as extremely positive.

One of those demographic trends that we take special note of is immigration. Franklin Delano Roosevelt once opened a speech by saying, "My fellow immigrants." And the great immigration historian Oscar Handlin once correctly noted about the United States: "Immigrants are the history of America." Through immigration, the United States gains energetic, talented, motivated, freedom-loving, hard-working, and often brilliant human beings. We skim the cream from the rest of the world, people who are human assets, net contributors both culturally and economically to our ethnically diverse society.

99. A Nation of Immigrants: The Melting Pot Still Works

In the 20th century the United States opened its gates for some 40 to 50 million immigrants. Most people reading this book are immigrants, the children of immigrants, or the grandchildren of immigrants. It seems appropriate that the two greatest waves of immigration marked the start and the close of the century—as if tying a bow around this hundred years of progress. The first decade of the 20th century saw about 1 million immigrants (mostly Europeans) enter the United States. This was the great Ellis Island wave of immigration. In the 1980s and 1990s the United States admitted roughly 15 million immigrants—with a much larger contingent from Asia and Latin America. The early waves of immigrants provided the brawn to help power the industrialization of America. The latest wave of immigrants provides essential brainpower for our information age economy.

The economic contributions of immigrants to this country in the 20th century have been considerate. In fact, a 1990 poll of 40 of the most prominent economists in the country—Nobel prizewinners, members of the President's Council of Economic Advisers, and past presidents of the American Economic Association—found that 90 percent believed that immigration has had "a substantial positive impact on U.S. economic growth in this century."

The new immigrants are contributing just as the former immigrants did. A comprehensive National Research Council study recently concluded that immigrants add about $10 billion each year to the size of the economy.

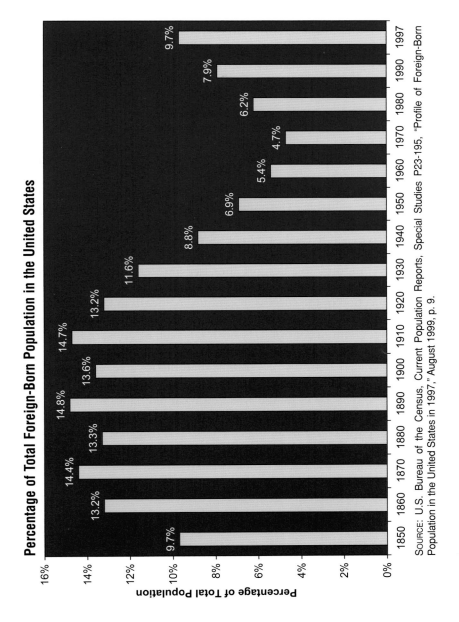

Percentage of Total Foreign-Born Population in the United States

SOURCE: U.S. Bureau of the Census, Current Population Reports, Special Studies P23-195, "Profile of Foreign-Born Population in the United States in 1997," August 1999, p. 9.

263

100. The Greatest Trend of All: 270 Million Americans and Growing

A central message of this book is that the fruits of a free society are prosperity and wealth. All of the evidence in this book documents that in every material way, life in the United States is much better today with 270 million people than it was in 1900 with 70 million people. Moreover, as we documented earlier, the American people are net resource creators, not resource depleters—protectors of the environment, not destroyers. Each generation leaves the ecological fate of the planet and our continent in better condition for future generations. Thus, the growth of the American population, which is healthy and wealthy, is a trend to celebrate, not to bemoan.

Taking a long-term historical perspective on population growth is valuable. Throughout history, human population was curtailed by war, famine, and disease. But the 20th century saw fewer lives lost to the last two of these disasters and to war as well. There are 200 million more Americans than 100 years ago mainly due to compounding, because they live longer, healthier, safer, and more prosperous lives than their ancestors did. A larger population is a reflection of the success in conquering death in this country.

The evidence does not support the contention that population is growing out of control. U.S. birth rates fell for most of the century and are now at or near replacement level. Prosperity tends to beget smaller family sizes—rather than the reverse. Fertility rates are falling all over the world. In fact, the average fertility rate in India today is lower than it was in the United States in the 1950s.

Yes, some areas of the country are getting crowded and congested, particularly booming cities like Los Angeles, Houston, and Denver. But we are hardly running out of space in this country. According to an analysis by the Population Research Institute, even if every family in the United States were all to move to Texas, there would still be enough room for every household to have about five acres of land—and the rest of the nation would be deserted.

So the best trend of all is shown in the final figure. There are now, at the cusp of a new century, more Americans than ever before, living in greater affluence than ever before. We hope and predict that in the 21st century millions more Americans and non-Americans too will live long, healthy, happy lives.

Resident U.S. Population

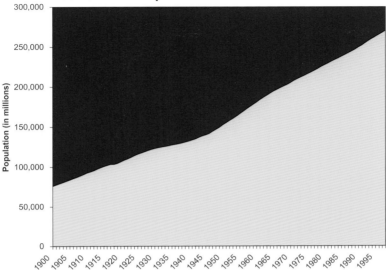

SOURCES: *Historical Statistics of the United States,* Series A 23; and *Statistical Abstract of the United States: 1998,* No. 2.

Fertility Rates

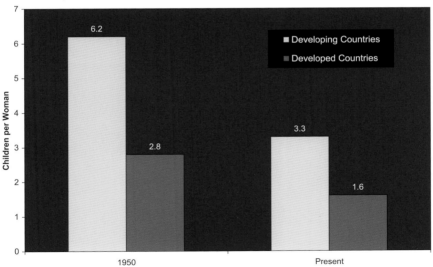

SOURCE: National Geographic Society.

Notes

Introduction

New York Times quote from "Living in the American Century: 1900–1910," *Washington Post*, September 20, 1999, pp. C1, C8–9.

Quote from Friedman in Thomas L. Friedman, *The Lexus and the Olive Tree* (New York: Farrar, Straus & Giroux, 1999).

Story on pet obesity from David Crary, "America's Pets Becoming Fat Cats," Associated Press, February 20, 2000.

Automobile as pro-environment invention from "Freedom's Journey: A Survey of the 20th Century," *The Economist*, September 11, 1999, p. 7.

Adam Smith quote from Robert L. Heilbronner, *The Worldly Philosophers* (New York: Touchstone, 1999).

Speed of information during the Middle Ages from *Newsweek* story on the millennium, January 1, 2000.

Historical per capita income estimates from Joyce Burnett and Joel Mokyr, "The Standard of Living through the Ages," in *The State of Humanity*, ed. Julian Simon (Cambridge, Mass.: Blackwell, 1995), pp. 135–46.

Queen Elizabeth quote from Heilbronner, *The Worldly Philosophers*, 1999.

Jon Carroll quote from Jon Carroll, "What It Means to Be Dead," *San Francisco Chronicle*, August 6, 1998.

Depiction of early 20th-century life in America from "Living in the American Century: 1900–1910," *Washington Post*, September 20, 1999, pp. C1, C8–9.

Information on influenza pandemic from Gina Bari Kolata, *Flu: The Story of the Great Influenza Pandemic and the Search for the Virus That Caused It* (New York: Farrar, Straus & Giroux, 1999).

Theodore Dalrymple quote from "Taking Good Health for Granted," *Wall Street Journal*, March 31, 1999, p. A-22.

Oliver Wendell Holmes quote from ibid.

H. G. Wells quote from John Tierney, "The Optimists Are Right," *New York Times Magazine*, September 29, 1996, p. 92.

New York Times warning about light bulbs causing blindness from ibid., p. 95.

Henry Sigerist quote from *Civilization and Disease* (Chicago: University of Chicago Press, 1942), p. 176.

Comparison of the material well-being of the poor today versus the rich 100 years ago, from Robert Rector, "How Poor Are America's Poor?" in *The State of Humanity*, ed. Julian Simon, pp. 241–52.

The power of the microchip and computing power from Howard Rheingold, "The Underside of Moore's Law," *IntellectualCapital.com*, May 20, 1999; and Bob Kolasky, "The Era of the Cheap PC," same publication and date.

Declining agricultural prices throughout the past 200 years from Julian L. Simon, *The Ultimate Resource II* (Princeton, N.J.: Princeton University Press, 1991).

Robert Samuelson quote on child labor from "An Ageless Society," *Washington Post*, September 15, 1999, p. A25.

Angus Maddison quote on lack of economic progress throughout the ages from *Phases of Capitalist Development* (Oxford University Press, 1982).

Black poverty throughout 20th century from Stephan Thernstrom and Abigail Thernstrom, "We Have Overcome," *New Republic*, October 13, 1997.

Declining workweek from W. Michael Cox and Richard Alm, *Myths of Rich and Poor* (New York: Basic Books, 1999).

Increased recreational time available to Americans from John P. Robinson, "Trends in Free Time," in *The State of Humanity*, pp. 224–30.

Declining poverty and improved living standards of the poor, see Rector, op. cit.

Miles of paved roads in 1900 from "Living in the American Century: 1900–1910," *Washington Post*, September 20, 1999, pp. C1, C8–9.

Safety of flying from Peter Spencer, "Smart Talk: What to Make of a Deadly Plane

Crash," *IntellectualCapital.com*, May 1, 1997.

R. Stanley Williams quote on power of original computers from "Computing in the 21st Century," *Phil. Trans. R. Soc.* London, 1998, vol. 356, p. 2.

Fifty percent computer ownership from Cox and Alm, "The New Paradigm," Federal Reserve Bank of Dallas, *1999 Annual Report.*

Figures on education quantity from Julian L. Simon and Rebecca Boggs, "Trends in the Quantity of Education," in Simon, *The State of Humanity*, pp. 208–18.

Environment and improved clean air from Ronald Bailey, *Earth Report 2000* (McGraw-Hill, 1999), pp. 290–310.

Trends in natural resource availability from Julian L. Simon, *Ultimate Resource II*, op. cit.

Falling production cost of oil from Peter Huber, "Running Strong," *National Review*, April 17, 2000, p. 24.

Booker T. Washington quote from "Predictions from a Century Ago," *USA Today*, December 31, 1999, p. 31A.

Black wages relative to white wages from Robert Higgs and Robert A. Margo, "Black Americans," in Simon, *The State of Humanity*, pp. 178–87.

The Economist quote on American leadership in 20th century from "Freedom's Journey: A Survey of the 20th Century," *The Economist*, September 11, 1999, p. 11.

U.S. income versus other nations, Joint Economic Committee of Congress, "The U.S. Economy at the Beginning and End of the 20th Century," Washington, December 1999.

Benefits of immigration from Julian Simon, *The Economic Consequences of Immigration* (Cambridge, Mass.: Blackwell, 1989).

Freedom and economic growth from James Gwartney, Robert Lawson, and Dexter Samida, *Economic Freedom of the World, 2000 Annual Report* (Vancouver, B.C.: Fraser Institute, 1999).

David Corn from "History Learned," *The Nation*, December 29, 1999, p. 11.

OSHA impact on work safety from Charles Murray, *What It Means to Be a Libertarian* (New York: Broadway Books, 1998).

Friedman on Food and Drug Administration costing lives, National Public Radio debate with James Tobin, 1997.

Amartya Sen quote from *Development as Freedom* (New York: Anchor Books, 2000).

Henry George quote on chickens and hawks from John Tierney, "Betting the Planet," *New York Times Magazine*, December 2, 1990, p. 58.

Spread of quality of life improvements to all segments of population from Robert Rector in *The State of Humanity*.

Size of government in 20th century from "The Thing That Won't Go Away," *The Economist*, July 31, 1999, p. 8.

Negative social trends from William Bennett, *Index of Leading Cultural Indicators*.

Educational declines from Stephen Moore, *Government: America's #1 Growth Industry* (Lewisville, Tex.: Institute for Policy Innovation, 1995).

Crime rates from *Historical Statistics of the United States* (Washington: U.S. Bureau of the Census, 1975), Series H-972; and *Health, United States, 1999* (Hyattsville, Md.: National Center for Health Statistics, 1999), Table 46.

Suicide rates historically from Jean-Claud Chesnais, "Worldwide Historical Trends in Homicide and Suicide," in *The State of Humanity*, pp. 91–99.

Global 2000 quote from Fay Willey and William J. Cook, "A Grim Year 2000," *Newsweek*, August 4, 1980, p. 38.

Simon bet with Ehrlich from John Tierney, "Betting the Planet," *New York Times Magazine*, op. cit., pp. 52–78.

Paul Ehrlich quote on England from *The Population Bomb*, reprint (New York: Bucaneer Books, 1997).

Paul Ehrlich quote that the battle to feed humanity is over from ibid.

Jackie Gleason quoted in Syliva Nasar, "The Economy," *Fortune Magazine*, September 14, 1997, p. 39.

False scare about DDT from Roger Meiners, "The Green Scare," *The Freeman*, May 1999, pp. 18–19.

No airline crashes in 1998 from Alan Levin, "615 Million People, 0 Crash Deaths in '98 on U.S. Airlines," *USA Today*, January 7, 1999, p. A-2.

Michael Prowse quote from Michael Prowse, "A Deep Debt of Gratitude," *Financial Times*, November 25, 1996, p. 20.

Churchill quote from Simon, *Ultimate Resource II*.

Will Rogers quote in *This I Believe*, ed. Edward R. Murrow (New York: Simon and Schuster, 1954).

Section I: Health

Summary

Death rates from infectious diseases, cited in *Historical Statistics of the United States* and *Health, United States* (1999).

Quote from Cathy Popescu and the American Council on Science and Health in "The Good News About America's Health," October 1988.

1. Lengthening Human Life

Quote from John Tierney in "This Way to the Future," *New York Times Magazine*, September 29, 1996, p. 94.

Quote from Samuel H. Preston in "Human Mortality throughout History and Prehistory," *The State of Humanity*, p. 31.

Life expectancy at birth by race and sex, U.S. National Center for Health and Statistics, *Monthly Vital Statistics Report*, various years.

Increased male life expectancy from "The Changing Pattern of American Mortality Decline," *Population and Development Review*, June 1981, p. 250.

Life expectancy in less developed countries from "Population and Resources," *National Geographic Society*, August 1998.

2. Reducing Infant Death

Infant mortality rates from *Health, United States, 1998*.

Decreasing infant mortality rates in more developed countries from *Simon*, p. 37.

Infant mortality rates by race, *Health, United States, 1998*.

Child mortality rates in India, "Child Mortality," *The Economist*, October 10, 1998, p. 110.

3. Fewer Mothers Die Giving Birth

Maternal death rate from *Historical Statistics of the United States*, Series B145, p. 57, and *Health, United States*, 1998.

Prenatal care from Elizabeth Whelan, "The Good News about America's Health," American Council of Science and Health, 1988.

Prenatal care for live births from *Health, United States, 1998*.

Crude death rates for Americans, *Historical Statistics of the United States*, Series B181, p. 60, and *Health, United States*, 1999.

Decline in American child mortality rates from Eileen Crimmins, "The Changing Pattern of American Mortality Decline and Its Implications for the Future," *Population and Development Review*, vol. 7, no. 2, June 1981, p. 242.

Quote from Dr. Alan Fisher from "The Good News about America's Health," October 1988, p. 6.

5. Eradicating the Killer Diseases throughout the Ages

Leading causes of death from CDC, *Morbidity and Mortality Weekly Report*, 1998, p. 48.

AIDS statistics from *HIV/AIDS Surveillance Report*, U.S. Department of Health and Human Services, December 1997, vol. 9, no. 2.

Quote from Dr. Judith Wasserheit from "Syphilis May Be on Its Way Out in U.S.," *Los Angeles* Times, January 14, 1999, p. 3.

6. Vaccines and Drugs: The Miracle Cures

Quote from Gina Kolata, *Flu: The Story of the Great Influenza Pandemic of 1918 and the Search for the Virus that Caused It* (New York: Farrar, Straus & Giroux, 1999).

Increased life expectancy through improved vaccines from *The State of Humanity*, p. 58.

Vaccine success, *Historical Statistics of the United States*, 1912–1970, Series B149-166, p. 58, and *Health, United States, 1998*.

7. Winning the Race for the Cancer Cure

Cancer and heart disease death rates from CDC, *Morbidity and Mortality Weekly Report*, 1998, p. 48.

Female death rates from R. Doll and R. Peto, *The Causes of Cancer* (New York: New York University Press, 1981), and Centers for Disease Control, "New Report of Declining Cancer Incidence and Death Rates," March 12, 1998.

Cancer survival rates from *Health, United States, 1998.*

8. Surviving Heart Disease

Heart attack survival rates from "U.S. Heart Attack Trend Less Severe," *Washington Post*, March 25, 1999, p. A18.

Heart disease death rates from *Health, United States, 1998.*

Death rates for stroke and hypertension from American Heart Association, *1988 Heart Facts.*

9. Better Dental Care, More Teeth

Statistics on teeth from Cathy Popescu and the American Council on Science and Health, "The Good News about America's Health," October 1988.

Quote from ibid.

10. A Future Free of Ailments and Disease

Quote from Laura Johannes in "Tailor-Made Vaccines against Cancer Show Promise in Early Trials," *Wall Street Journal*, May 14, 1999, p. A1.

Biotechnology from Bob Kolasky, "Issue of the Week: Unlocking Life," *Intellectual Capital.com*, July 10, 1997.

Decoding and sequencing human genes, Tim Friend, "The Race through Our Genes Nears End," *USA Today*, October 21, 1999, p. D1.

11. Better Hygiene

Hygiene habits from "How We've Changed," *USA Today*, December 31, 1999.

Section II. Diets and Nutrition

Summary

Quote from Michael Fumento from "Unpopular Science," *American Outlook*, The Hudson Institute, Summer 1999, p. 24.

12. Getting Enough to Eat

Calorie intake from Stanley Lebergott, *The State of Humanity*, p. 154.

Consumption changes from ibid, p. 155.

Sugar consumption from *Historical Statistics of the United States*, Series G911, p. 331.

Ice cream consumption from *Historical Statistics of the United States*, Series G908, p. 331, and *Statistical Abstract of the United States: 1998.*

13. The Declining Cost of Food

Quote from Stanley Lebergott, op. cit., regarding decline in food costs.

Food purchases in terms of time worked from Federal Reserve Bank of Dallas, *1997 Annual Report: Time Well Spent.*

14. Bigger, Taller, Stronger Americans

Quote from Robert Fogle from *The State of Humanity*, p. 65.

Height of Americans from American Council on Science and Health, "The Good News about America's Health," October 1988.

Quote from a Heritage Foundation study regarding the increased size in Americans.

Rising height of Europeans from *The State of Humanity*, p. 65.

Underweight Americans from *Health, United States, 1999*, Table 170.

Section III. Wealth

Summary

U.S. per capita output from Angus Maddison, *Dynamic Forces in Capitalist Development* (New York: Oxford University, 1991), Figure 13.8.

15. Expanding Economic Output

U.S. GDP growth from U.S. Bureau of Economic Analysis.

U.S. GDP growth outpacing population growth and inflation from Joint Economic Committee, *Monitoring the World Economy 1820–1992*, p. 3.

Quote from Angus Maddison regarding large 20th-century economic growth from *The State of Humanity*, p. 136.

Paraphrase from Edward Denison regarding post–World War II economic growth, John Naisbitt, *Megatrends: Ten New Directions Transforming Our Lives* (1982), p. 17.

16. The United States Emerges as an Economic Superpower

U.S. emergence as the richest country in the world during the 20th century from Angus Maddison, *Dynamic Forces in Capitalist Development* (New York: Oxford University, 1991).

U.S. per capita GDP growth rate between 19th and 20th centuries from *The State of Humanity*, p. 139.

Comparison between the size of the United States and its influence on world output from John Naisbitt, *Megatrends: Ten New Directions for the 1990s* (New York: Warner Books, 1990), p. 33.

U.S. high economic status will continue to grow from Joint Economic Committee, *Chartbook*, 1999, p. 4.

17. The Rising Affluence of the Middle Class

Quote from Barbara Ehrenreich regarding the economic turmoil of the middle class from "Is the Middle Class Doomed?" *New York Times Magazine*, September 7, 1986, p. 42.

Increase in middle-class family income from U.S. Census Bureau, "Measuring 50 Years of Economic Change," 1997.

Proper income adjustments for inflation from Michael Boskin et al., *Toward a More Accurate Measure of the Cost of Living*, Final Report to the Senate Finance Committee, December 4, 1996.

Decrease in average family size and increase in middle-class family size from U.S. Census Bureau, "Measuring 50 Years of Economic Change," 1997.

18. The Millionaire Next Door

Middle-class workers rising into ranks of asset millionaires from Thomas J. Stanley and William D. Danko, *The Millionaire Next Door* (New York: Pocket Books, 1998).

Example pertaining to Theodore R. Johnson, United Parcel Service worker from "Ex-UPS Worker Parlays Earnings into $70 Million," Associated Press article printed in *Chicago Tribune*, October 15, 1991, p. 3.

19. The Great Bull Market of the 20th Century

Rising rate of return in the stock market from Jeremy Siegel, *Stocks for the Long Run*, (New York: McGraw Hill, 1998).

Compound interest gains from Savers & Investors League, www.savers.org, 1998.

20. The Wealthiest Society

Increasing value of Americans' financial wealth from Federal Reserve Board (FRB), *Flow of Funds Accounts of the United States*, various years.

Rising value of Americans' assets from FRB, *Flow of Funds Accounts of the United States*, various years.

Far more wealthy Americans today than 15 years ago from "Philanthropy in America," *The Economist*, May 30, 1998, pp. 19–20.

Rise in median household net worth from Federal Reserve Board of Governors, *Survey of Consumer Finances*, 1962, 1983, 1989, 1992, 1995, 1998.

21. A Nation of Owners

Rising American ownership in stock from Peter Hart Associates.

Increasing value and investment in mutual funds from Anne Kates Smith, "The Golden Years," *US News and World Report*, April 5, 1999, p. 69.

Section IV. The State of Poor Americans

Summary

    Increased spending on poverty still leading to failure of the welfare state from Robert Rector and the Heritage Foundation.

    Quote from poverty expert Rebecca Blank regarding the feeling that poverty indexes based on consumption show a greater decline in need from *The State of Humanity*, p. 237.

22. *Abating Poverty*

    Fluctuating poverty rates over the course of the 20th century from www.census.gov/income/histpov/hstpov2.txt., Table 2.

    Declining rate of blacks living in poverty in the last half of the 20th century from www.census.gov/income/histpov/hstpov2.txt., Table 2.

    Quote from sociologist James Q. Wilson giving three keys to avoiding poverty from James Q. Wilson, Francis Boyer Lecture, American Enterprise Institute, December 4, 1997.

    Poverty can be measured on the basis of the actual consumption levels of poor households from Daniel Slesnick, "Gaining Ground: Poverty in the Postwar United States," *Journal of Political Economy* (1993), vol. 101, no. 1.

23. *Rising Living Standards for the Poor*

    Quote from Adam Smith defining poverty as the lack of necessities needed to live from Megan Gallagher and Gregory Acs, "Snapshots of America's Families," *Assessing the New Federalism* (Washington: Urban Institute, 1999).

    U.S. poverty level would be considered wealthy in most countries of the world today from World Bank, http://www.worldbank.org/data/databytopic/GNPPC.pdf.

    Poor Americans faring much better today than they did in the past from "The Heritage Foundation Backgrounder," September 18, 1998, no. 1221, p. 5, Table 1.

    Much higher percentage of poor Americans owning dishwashers and refrigerators today than in the past from *American Housing Survey for the United States in 1997*; U.S. Bureau of the Census, *Housing Then and Now*, p. 246; and *Historical Statistics of the United States*, Series Q 175.

24. *The World's First Universal Opportunity Society*

    Remarkable income mobility in America today from Alexis de Tocqueville Institute.

Section V. The State of Children and Teens

Summary

    Most child abuse reports get dismissed from Douglas Besharov, *Child Abuse and Media Coverage* (Washington: American Enterprise Institute, 1998).

    Children are less likely to die before age 12 today than in the past from *Historical Statistics of the United States*, Series B 182–84, p. 60, and CDC: *Health, United States, 1999*.

25. *Reducing Child Poverty*

    Rate of children living in poverty is declining from U.S. Census Bureau.

    Children more likely to live in poverty if they are in a one-parent household from Megan Gallagher and Sheila Zedlewski, "Snapshots on American Families: Poverty among Children" (Washington: Urban Institute, 1999).

    Quote from Robert J. Samuelson describing the condition of children during the 19th century from "An Ageless Society," *Washington Post*, April 18, 1998, editorial page.

26. *The Toy Culture*

    Toy production and sales have surged over the course of the 20th century from *Historical Statistics of the United States*, Series P 332, p. 700; Series H 879–880, p. 401; Series G 454–55, pp. 316–19.

27. *Teen Drinking, Smoking, and Drug Use on the Decline*

    Teen drinking has fallen steadily over the past two decades from CDC, *Health, United States, 1998*.

Teen smoking has declined modestly over the past two decades from CDC, *Health, United States, 1999*, Table 64.

28. Declining Rates of Teen Pregnancy

Teen pregnancy rates have fallen dramatically in the short and long terms from Patricia Donovan, "Falling Teen Pregnancy, Birthrates: What's behind the Declines?" *The Guttmacher Report on Public Policy*, vol. 1, no. 5 (New York: Alan Guttmacher Institute, October 1998).

The teen pregnancy rate shows generally the same pattern as the teen birth rate from Patricia Donovan, "Falling Teen Pregnancy, Birthrates: What's behind the Declines?" *The Guttmacher Report on Public Policy*, vol. 1, no. 5.

Children born to teenage mothers are likely to be less healthy than all children from Stephanie J. Ventura, *Declines in Teenage Birth Rates 1991–98*, Centers for Disease Control, October 25, 1999.

Teenage girls who have children are much more likely to drop out of school and be poor in their 20s from Robert Rector, The Heritage Foundation.

Teen birth rate has fallen in the 1990s as well, particularly second births from Barbara Vobejda, "Teens with One Baby Now Less Likely to Have Another," *Washington Post*, December 18, 1998, p. A4.

Section VI. The American Worker

Summary

Very few Americans work on the farm from *The State of Humanity*, p. 126, Figure 12-2. Americans much more productive than are workers from other developed nations from *The Economist*, August 22, 1998.

29. Workers Leave the Farm

There has been a continuous reduction in Americans working on farms over the course of the 20th century from *The State of Humanity*, Figure12-2, p. 126.

30. The Amazing Gains in Farm Productivity

The United States feeds three times as many people with fewer farmers and less farmland, *Historical Statistics of the United States*, various years, and *United States Statistical Abstract: 1998*.

Quote from Colorado farmer Bob Sakata regarding gains in farm productivity from T. R. Reid, "Feeding the Planet," *National Geographic*, October 1998, vol. 194, no. 4, p. 64.

31. The Most Productive Workers in the History of the World

Typical American workers have increased in productivity over the course of the 20th century from *Historical Statistics of the United States*, Series W-1, p. 948; Series D 683, p. 162; and *Statistical Abstract of the United States: 1998*.

Economists measure that most of the rise in productivity is a result of the increase in capital available to workers from *The State of Humanity*, p. 169, and *U.S. Statistical Abstract 99*, no. 1382.

United States far more productive than Asian and European nations from William J. Baumol and Edward N. Wolff, "Comparative U.S. Productivity Performance and the State of Manufacturing: The Latest Data," *CVStarr Newsletter*, New York University, vol. 10, 1992, pp. 1, 4.

32. The Shrinking Workweek

Lifetime hours worked on the job down 25 percent in a little over a century from Michael Cox, Federal Reserve Bank of Dallas, *Myths of Rich and Poor* (New York: Basic Books, 1999).

33. Better Work for Better Pay

Full-time worker average hourly compensation much higher today, *U.S. Statistical Abstract: 1998*, Table 867, *Historical Statistics of the United States* D 802, p. 169.

Quote from economist David Henderson regarding hourly wages and real employment compensation from "How Fares the American Worker?" *IntellectualCapital.com*, December 18, 1997.

34. The Reduction of Labor Unrest

Major work stoppages occurring far less frequently than in the 1960s from U.S. Department of Labor Statistics, Compensation and Working Conditions, Summer 1999.

The number of strikes in the peak year, 1976, far less than the amount in each year in the 1990s from Arthur Laffer, "America, America, God Shed His Grace on Thee," Laffer Associates, December 29, 1998.

Section VII. Leisure, Recreation, and Entertainment

Summary

Quote from Juliet B. Schor regarding the opinion that Americans are overworked from Juliet B. Schor, *Overworked American: The Unexpected Decline of Leisure* (New York: Basic Books, February 1993).

35. Americans Have More Leisure Time

Quote from sociologist John Robinson regarding decrease in the length of the workweek as resulting in an increase in free time for Americans, 1997.

Average American, particularly female, having large increase in free time between 1965 and 1985 from Federal Reserve Board of Dallas, *1997 Annual Report*.

Amount of free time, leisure, and vacation days increasing dramatically since the 19th century from Federal Reserve Board of Dallas, *1997 Annual Report*.

36. Consumers Can Afford More of Everything

Affordability of nearly every consumer item rising remarkably over the 20th century from Edwin S. Rubenstein, "Keeping Up with the Gateses," Hudson Institute, *American Outlook*, Summer 1998, pp. 34–35.

Quote from Michael Cox giving examples about the increase in affordability of specific items from Cox and Alm, *Myths of Rich and Poor*.

America's material standard of living far higher than that in other countries, Stanley Lebergott, in *The State of Humanity*, p. 149.

37. Getting More Fun Out of Life: Recreational Spending

Americans spending one-third less on necessities today than at turn of the 20th century from Joint Economic Committee of the U.S. Congress, *Chartbook*, 1999.

Recreation the single fastest-growing major expenditure item for Americans, *Historical Statistics of the United States*, Series G 452, pp. 316–19, and *Statistical Abstract of the United States: 1998*.

Americans spending $5 billion on sporting events today, *Historical Statistics of the United States*, Series H 886, p. 401.

38. Surviving the Heat

Heat-related mortality is going down in the United States from Patrick Michaels, *The Satanic Gases* (Washington: Cato Institute, 2000).

Americans were first introduced to cooled homes in the summer from John Tierney, "The Optimists Are Right," *New York Times Magazine*, September 29, 1996, p. 92.

Almost all American homes in warm climates are built with air conditioning from "Poor in America," *Monthly Labor Review*, May 1996, p. 8.

The number of swimming pools increasing greatly in the United States from *American Housing Survey for the United States in 1997*, and U.S. Bureau of the Census, "Housing Then and Now."

Almost all homes have refrigeration today compared with very few at the turn of the 20th century from "Poor in America," *Monthly Labor Review,* May 1996, p. 8.

39. Entertainment: Radio, Motion Pictures, and TV

Possession of radios rising steadily since the 1920s from Monthly Labor Review, May 1996.

Quote from Alan Brinkley regarding the phenomenal rise in radio sales from Gary Dempsey, "The Myth of an Emerging Information Underclass," *The Freeman*, p. 219.

Movie sales have dropped dramatically since the peak in 1930 from *Historical*

Statistics of the United States, Series H 862–877, p. 400.

Televisions and VCRs are owned by almost every household today from Nielsen Media Research, "1998 Report on Television," and Stanley Lebergott, *The American Economy: Income Wealth, and Want* (Princeton, N.J.: Princeton University Press, 1976), *Historical Statistics of the United States*, Series R 105, p. 796, and Motion Picture Association of America.

Cable TV exploding in popularity, climbing steadily since the 1950s from Nielsen Media Research, "1998 Report on Television," and Stanley Lebergott, *The American Economy*, op. cit., *Historical Statistics of the United States*, H 522, and Motion Picture Association of America.

Section VIII. Housing

40. *Home Ownership: Pursuing the American Dream*

Home ownership rate on a slow but steady rise for most of the 20th century from "Housing Vacancies and Home Ownership," U.S. Census Bureau, first quarter 1998, pp. 1–2, Table 5.

Quote from Nicholas Retsinas regarding the societal benefits of increased home ownership from "National Homeownership Surge," *Washington Times*, July 5, 1998, p. B1.

41. *Bigger, Better, Less Crowded Homes*

Homes of the late 19th century included many unsanitary conditions in tenement slums from Jacob Riis, *How the Other Half Lives* (reprinted, New York: Penguin USA, 1997).

Few Americans living in cramped housing conditions compared with conditions at the turn of the 20th century from Stanley Lebergott, *The American Economy: Income, Wealth, and Want* (Princeton, N.J.: Princeton University Press, 1976), Figure 24.2.

The number of people per housing unit progressively lessening over the course of the 20th century from ibid.

Homes bigger and better built today compared with those in the 1960s from U.S. Bureau of Census, *Construction Reports*, Series C-25, annually, 1970–88, Figure MV-4. American houses much larger than those in Japan and Russia from U.S. Department of Energy, Energy Information Administration, *Housing Characteristics 1987* (Washington: Government Printing Office, 1989), p. 25, A. S. Zaychenko, "United States-USSR: Individual Consumption," *World Affairs*, Summer 1989, p. 10, and "The Affluent Japanese Household," *Business America*, March 23, 1981, p. 10.

42. *The Modern Home Has Every Convenience*

Few homes in the early 20th century with conveniences such as running water, and in the mid-20th century few homes with luxuries such as air conditioning from Stanley Lebergott, *The American Economy*, 1976, Figure 24.2.

Almost all American homes with these amenities today from "American Housing Survey," U.S. Census Bureau, 1993 AHS-N Data Chart, Table 2-4.

43. *Electrification of the Nation*

Almost all American homes have electricity today, compared with very few at the turn of the 20th century from Stanley Lebergott, *The American Economy*, 1976, Figure 24.2.

Use of electric motors in industry beginning to explode in second decade of the 20th century from Jeremy Greenwood, *The Third Industrial Revolution* (Washington: American Enterprise Institute/AEI, 1997), p. 20.

44. *Lighting Up the Nation*

Since the turn of the 20th century, light produced by different light devices increasing more than 100-fold from *The State of Humanity*, p. 165, Figure 15.6.

Quote from economist William Nordhaus regarding the falling price of a unit of light from W. Michael Cox and Richard Alm, "The Economy at Light Speed," Federal Reserve Bank of Dallas, *1996 Annual Report*, p. 12.

Section IX. Transportation and Communications

Summary

Quote from Ben Bagdikian describing the transition from the rudimentary telegraph to the telephone from U.S. Department of Commerce, Bureau of the Census, *Historical Statistics of the United States, Colonial Times to 1970*, Tables R 9-12, R 48, R 56, and *Statistical Abstract, 1979*, Tables 971 and 973, pp. 783, 787, 788. Quote from the beginning of the 20th century showing the progression that has been made over the course of the century from "The Century," editorial from the *Daily Register*, Mobile, Alabama, January 1, 1901, p. 4, columns 2–3.

45. *The Telephone: Reach Out and Touch Someone*

Telephones, once luxury items, nearly ubiquitous today, from U.S. Census Bureau, *Statistical Abstract of the United States: 1998*, October 29, 1998, p. 573.

Phone service costs have plummeted over the past century from U.S. Census Bureau, p. 784, R 1–12.

Cost of international calls has fallen sharply since 1950 from James B. Burnham, "The Growing Impact of Global Telecommunications on the Location of Work," Center for the Study of American Business, *Contemporary Issues Series 87*, Washington University in St. Louis, October 1997, p. 2.

Telephone connections across the Atlantic and Pacific Oceans recent phenomena from "Telecommunications Survey," *The Economist*, September 13, 1997, p. 27.

46. *From Horses to Horsepower*

Quote from author E. B. White from James R. Healey, "The Car's Century," *USA Today*, Money Section, Friday, December 31, 1999, p. 1B.

Henry Ford and the discovery of cheap oil in Texas as drastically increasing the production of automobiles from *Historical Statistics of the United States*, Series Q 148, Q 152, p. 716, *Statistical Abstract of the United States: 1998*.

Real cost of automobiles has been declining from Federal Reserve Bank of Dallas, *1997 Annual Report: Time Well Spent*.

47. *Air Travel Makes the World a Smaller Place*

Air travel has grown drastically since 1960 from U.S. Travel Data Center/Travel Industry Association of America, Washington, D.C., National Travel Survey, annual, no. 429, 1985–95, p. 265.

Rapid decline in the cost of plane tickets explains the surge in air travel from Federal Reserve Bank of Dallas, *1997 Annual Report: Time Well Spent*.

Deregulation of airlines has been key in lowering airfares in the past 20 years from Brookings Institution.

48. *The Accelerating Speed of Travel*

Remarkable improvement in speed of air travel from *The State of Humanity*, pp. 166–67.

Example of travel times from New York to Boston over the course of the 20th century from D. G. Janell, *The Professional Geographer*, vol. 20, no. 1, January 1968, p. 7.

49. *The Explosion of International Travel*

Americans now traveling to foreign nations in record numbers from U.S. Travel Data Center/Travel Industry Association of America, Washington, National Travel Survey, annual, no. 429, 1985–95, p. 265.

Airline tickets to Europe much less expensive today than at the turn of the 20th century from Brookings Institution.

More than 90 percent of international travel is by commercial airline from U.S. Travel Data Center/Travel Industry Association of America, op. cit.

50. *Safer Highways and Airways*

No one killed in 1998 on a commercial airline flight from *Historical Statistics of the United States*, Series Q 628, p. 774, National Safety Council, *Accident Facts* (various years), National Highway Traffic Safety Administration (NHTSA).

Odds of a plane crash about one in 500,000 from "We Have Nothing to Fear but Fear Itself, " *Vital Stats*, Statistical Assessment Service, October 1998.

Years 1997 and 1998 the safest years ever recorded for automobiles on the basis of miles traveled from "News," U.S. Department of Transportation, Washington, NHTSA, October 27, 1998.

Increased auto safety from safer cars, much better constructed roads, improvements in people's driving, tough drunk driving laws, and better medical care from Stephen Moore, "Speed Doesn't Kill," Cato Institute Policy Analysis no. 346, May 31, 1999.

51. *Exploring the Last Frontier: Space*

Humankind has come a long way in space travel since the first liquid-fuel rocket was launched in 1926 by Dr. Robert Goddard from Edward L. Hudgins, "The Next Century of Flight," *Aviation Week & Space Technology*, March 22, 1999.

Space exploration as the birth of the age of satellite communications, *Megatrends*, op. cit. Cost of space travel expected to fall in coming decades because cost of other forms of transportation have dropped rapidly after its introduction in the 20th century from Edward Hudgins, "The Next Century of Flight," op. cit.

Section X. Invention, Innovation, and Scientific Progress

Summary

Quote from patent office bureaucrat regarding opinion that there is nothing left to invent from *Popular Science*, December 1, 1999, p. 59.

Quote from Francis Bacon saying that main goal of science is increasing human life quality with invention, Francis Bacon, *Advancement of Learning and Novum Organum* (New York: Willey, 1944), p. 339.

52. *Yankee Ingenuity: The Era of Invention*

Number of patents issued grows more than five times the pace of U.S. population in the 20th century from U.S. Patent and Trademark Office, U.S. Patent Activity, 1790–1998 (Washington: Government Printing Office, 1999).

53. *Scientists Solve the Puzzles of Our Universe*

Major inventions in the 19th century requiring far less time to become commercialized than in the 18th century from Cesare Marchetti, "Society as a Learning System," *Technological Forecast and Social Change*, vol. 18, December 1980, p. 274.

Quote from Michael Cox regarding the speed that a new product reaches a large segment of the population from W. Michael Cox and Richard Alm, "The Economy at Light Speed," Dallas Federal Reserve Bank, *1996 Annual Report*, pp. 9–10.

Section XI. The Information Age

Summary

Quote from Meadows regarding the opinion that the economy can grow only to a certain degree because it will always fall back to equilibrium from Meadows, Donella et al., *The Limits of Growth* (New York: Universe, 1972), pp. 142–43.

Founder of Apple Computer Steve Jobs scoffed at for trying to sell his invention of the personal computer in the 1970s from Robert J. Samuelson, "Puzzles of the 'New Economy,'" *Newsweek*, April 17, 2000, p. 49.

54. *The Microchip: The Greatest Invention Ever?*

Since first computer chip introduced in 1958 by Texas Instruments, semiconductor doubling in capacity and speed almost every 18 months from Howard Rheingold, "Pro & Con: The Underside of Moore's Law," *IntellectualCapital.com*, Thursday, May 20, 1999.

Microchip as the brain for many cheap consumer items as well from Cox and Alm, "The Economy at Light Speed," op. cit., p. 15.

Quote from Jeremy Atack of the National Bureau of Economic Research regarding the recent historical trend in the computational capabilities of modern computers from Jeremy Atack, *The State of Humanity*, p. 162.

Real cost of processing information and data that was once incredibly expensive quickly evaporating to nearly nothing from R. Stanley Williams, "Computing in the 21st Century: Nanocircuitry, Defect Tolerance, and Quantum Logic," *Phil. Trans. R. Soc.*, London, August 15, 1998, vol. 356, no. 1743, pp. 1783–91.

Quote from Microsoft COO Bob Herbold regarding the titanic fall in the cost of computing since the microprocessor was invented in 1971 from Bob Levy, "Microsoft and the Browser Wars: Fit to Be Tied," Cato Institute Policy Analysis no. 296, February 19, 1998, p. 33.

55. *The Personal Computer Launches the Digital Revolution*

Quotes from Thomas Watson and *Popular Mechanics* showing that the computer age was not expected by anyone in the 1940s from R. Stanley Williams, "Computing in the Twenty-First Century," *Phil. Trans. R. Soc.*, London , 1998, vol. 356, pp. 183–81.

Rapid increase in number of personal computers in existence since 1975 from Robert J. Samuelson, "Puzzles of the 'New Economy,'" *Newsweek*, April 17, 2000, p. 49.

More and more computers traded in each year, and estimate that over the next 10 years half a billion computers will be traded in for improved models from *USA Today*.

Number of households with incomes below $30,000 owing computers increasing 30 percent from 1994 to 1995 from Gary Dempsey, "The Myth of an Emerging Information Underclass," *The Freeman*, April 1998, p. 218.

56. *From the Pony Express to the Internet Generation*

At the beginning of the 1990s, only 1 million Americans having access to the Internet from Gary Dempsey, "The Myth of an Emerging Information Underclass," op. cit., April 1998, p. 217.

Number of Internet hosts growing more than 30-fold between 1989 and 1999 from Internet Domain Survey, Internet Software Consortium, www.isc.org.

Almost 20 percent of today's Internet households having incomes below $25,000 per year from Gary Dempsey, "The Myth of an Emerging Information Underclass," op. cit., p. 217.

Quote from Eric Schmidt predicting that every person will be connected to the Internet by 2007 from ibid.

Section XII. Education

Summary

Percentage of Americans graduating from college higher than percentage of Americans graduating from high school 100 years ago from 1900 to 1970, *Historical Statistics of the United States, Colonial Times to 1970*, Series H 751–765, pp. 385–86; 1980 to 1990: U.S. Bureau of the Census, 1980 Census of Population, PC 80-01-B1, 1–26; and 1990 Census of Population, CP-1-1, p. 17, Table 13, and U.S. Department of Education, National Center for Educational Statistics, *Digest of Educational Statistics, 1992*, p. 241, Table 229; and *Digest of Educational Statistics, 1995*, Table 38, p. 50.

57. *The Most Educated People in History*

Median number of years of schooling dramatically increasing for whites and blacks since 1920 as well as percentage of Americans aged 5–17 attending school from *Statistical Abstract of the United States*, various years.

Quantity of education rising dramatically across the world over the last 150 years from B. R. Mitchell, *Europeon Historical Statistics 1750–1970* (New York: Columbia University Press, 1978), Table A1, pp. 3–8; Table I1, pp. 396–400.

58. *Fewer School Dropouts*

Percentage of American adults without a high school degree dropping fivefold between 1940 and 1997 from *Digest of American Statistics*, U.S. Department of Education, 1998, p. 50.

59. *College: No Longer Just for the Elite*

About 5 percent of children born in 1920 receiving a college degree, compared with well over half today from U.S. Department of Education, National Center for Educational Statistics, *Digest of Educational Statistics 1992*, p. 171, Table 159, *Digest of Educational Statistics, 1995*, Table 38, p. 50; U.S. Department of Commerce, Bureau of the Census, *Historical Statistics of the United States, Colonial Times to 1970*, Series H 700–715, p. 383, and "School Enrollment: Social and Economic Characteristics," *Current Population Reports*, Series P-20, various issues.

College opportunities vast today for blacks compared with first half of 20th century from U.S. Department of Education, National Center for Educational Statistics, *Digest of Educational Statistics 1992*, 171, Table 159, *Digest of Educational Statistics, 1995*, Table 38, p. 50; U.S. Department of Commerce, Bureau of the Census, *Historical Statistics of the United States, Colonial Times to 1970*, Series H 700–715, p. 383, and "School Enrollment: Social and Economic Characteristics," op. cit., various issues.

Number of colleges increasing by more than 2,500 since 1900 from *Statistical Abstract of the United States*, various years.

Number of higher education degrees conferred skyrocketing since the late 1960s from U.S. Department of Education, National Center for Educational Statistics, *Digest of Educational Statistics 1992*, Table 159, p. 171, *Digest of Educational Statistics, 1995*, Table 38, p. 50; U.S. Department of Commerce, Bureau of the Census, *Historical Statistics of the United States, Colonial Times to 1970*, Series H 700–715, p. 383, and "School Enrollment: Social and Economic Characteristics," op. cit., various issues.

60. *Fighting Global Illiteracy*
In the late 20th century about 20 percent of Americans unable to read or write, compared with below 10 percent in 1950 and even less today from U.S. Census Bureau, *Historical Statistics of the United States*, Series H 664, p. 382, and *Current Population Survey*, various years.

Half of adult Americans scoring in the lowest two levels for reading and writing from Cheri Pierson Yecke, "National Testing: Blueprint for Disaster," *Intellectual Ammunition*, The Heartland Institute, vol. 7, no. 1, February/March 1998.

Global adult illiteracy falling steadily from 75 percent for those born in 1926 to 20 percent for those born in 1970 from *Comparison of Statistics on Illiteracy*, UNESCO, Office of Statistics, Paris, 1990, Figure 21, p. 23.

1988 Heritage Foundation study finding female literacy rate increasing steadily in nations with higher per capita incomes from "The Global Poverty Reduction Act," Executive Monograph, September 1988.

61. *Investing in Quality Education*
Dramatic increase in private investment in school scholarship programs during the 1990s from ibid.

Number of privately funded school choice programs rising from 1 in 1991 to more than 40 in 1998 from "The State of the States," *Policy Review*, November/December 1998, p. 9.

Number of public charter schools rising from 1 in 1991 to almost 1,200 in 1999 from "New Directory Profiles Nation's Charter Schools," *School Reform News*, June 1998, p. 7.

Since 1920, rate of Americans between ages 25 and 29 with high school degree rising from 20 to 90 percent, "Summary," Section XII.

Section XIII. Safety

Summary
More than half of Americans dreading successful cloning and technology in the 21st century from CNN/*USA Today* public opinion poll, March 1, 1997.

World Almanac: 2000 (Primedia, 1999), p. 583, naming plague as killing off "as much as half the population" of Europe between 1348 and 1350.

Best way to continue reducing risk of early death and injury is promoting economic growth and rising living standards through free market capitalism from *Progressive Environmentalism: A Pro-Human, Pro-Science, Pro-Free Enterprise Agenda for Change*, Task Force Report, National Center for Policy Analysis, Dallas.

62. *A Safer World: Fewer Fatal Accidents*
Rate of deaths from accidents falling by half since the early 1900s from National Safety Council, *Accident Safety Facts*, Chicago, annual.

Accidental death rates falling steadily for every age group from ibid.
Taking a random flight every day, on average, requiring about 20,000 years before perishing in a fatal crash from Peter Spencer, *IntellectualCapital.com*.

63. *Safety on the Job*

Sevenfold reduction in job-related deaths since 1930 from National Safety Council, *Accident Safety Facts*, Chicago, annual, and Charles Murray, *What It Means to Be a Libertarian* (New York: Broadway Books, 1997).
Rate of occupational injuries falling sharply over the past 25 years from U.S. Bureau of Labor Statistics.

64. *Natural Disasters: Living with Mother Nature*

Galveston, Texas, home of worst flood in American history from *The World Almanac: 2000*, Primedia, 1999.
Death rate from tornadoes in 20th century falling more than 10-fold from Indur Goklany, "Richer Is More Resilient," in *Earth Report 2000*, ed. Ronald Bailey (New York: McGraw Hill, 2000).

65. *The Reduced Risk of Catastrophic Events*

Quote from STATS saying that one of the most substantial risks people run is fear itself from "We Have Nothing to Fear but Fear Itself," *Vital STATS*, October 1998.
Rate of death from catastrophic accidents from Metropolitan Life Insurance Company and *Statistical Abstract of the United States*, various years.
Death from terrorist attacks from E. L. Crouch and R. Wilson, *Risk/Benefit Analysis* (Cambridge: Balinger, 1982), and Paul Slovic, "Informing and Educating the Public about Risk," *Risk Analysis*, vol. 6, no. 4, 1986, Table 1, p. 407.

66. *The Diminished Threat of Nuclear Disaster*

Number of nuclear weapons tests from U.S. Department of Energy, and Brookings Institution.
Chance of getting cancer from the radiation from a nuclear power plant from Cohen, *The State of Humanity*, p. 584.

Section XIV. Environmental Protection

Summary

To read more on public opinion about environmental issues from Julian Simon, *Hoodwinking the Nation* (New Jersey: Transaction, 1999).
Cities such as Los Angeles seeing dramatic declines in smog levels over past 25 years from Steve Hayward and Laura Jones, *Index of Environmental Indicators, 1998*, (San Francisco: Pacific Research Institute, 1998) p. 23.
Quote from William Baumol and Wallace Oates saying that the automobile is a major improvement from the messy streets and waterways of medieval and Renaissance cities from *The State of Humanity*, p. 447.

67. *Breathing Clean Air*

Quote from Kenneth Galbraith saying that economic growth outweighs pollution problems from Kenneth Galbraith, *The Affluent Society* (Boston: Houghton Mifflin, 1998).
Quote from Al Gore saying that the environmental future has been sacrificed in the pursuit of economic growth from Al Gore, *Earth in the Balance* (New York: Plume, 1993).
Lead concentrations falling by more than 90 percent since 1976 from Environmental Protection Agency, Office of Air Quality, Planning and Standards, *National Air Quality and Emissions Trends Report*, various years.
Between 1940 and 1990, air pollution emissions falling 3 percent per year relative to output from Environmental Protection Agency data as cited in Indur Goklany, *Clearing the Air* (Washington: Cato Institute, 1999), pp. 67–86.
Quote from Pacific Institute's Index of Leading Environmental Indicators saying that, in large part because of the introduction of unleaded gasoline, the 97 percent reduction in the air has generated a huge improvement in blood lead levels from "Ideas in Action: Index of Leading Environmental Indicators," *Pacific Research Institute Fact Sheet*, April 1999.

68. *Reducing Smog in Cities*

Quote from Paul Ehrlich saying that smog might kill 200,000 people in New York and Los Angeles by 1973 from Paul Ehrlich, *The Population Bomb,* 1968.

Long-term improvements being made in heavily polluted cities in the United States since the 1960s and 1970s in large part because of the 1972 Clean Air Act from Steve Hayward and Laura Jones, *Index of Environmental Indicators, 1998,* Pacific Research Institute, p. 23.

From 1985 to 1995 the number of days in the year of unhealthy air quality falling by half from ibid.

Since the 1960s, the number of "smoky" days per year falling from about 300 to 60 from U.S. Council on Environmental Quality, *Annual Report* (Washington: Government Printing Office, various years) and U.S. Environmental Protection Agency, Office of Air Quality Planning and Standards, *National Air Quality and Emissions Trends Report, 1996,* Table A-17, EPA, OAQPS, Research Triangle Park, N.C., 1997.

69. *Cleaner Lakes, Rivers, and Streams*

Over the past quarter century lakes and streams becoming much less polluted from Council on Environmental Quality (CEQ), *Annual Report,* various years.

In the 1930s and 1940s about 25 waterborne disease outbreaks per year compared with almost none today from "Watered Down Data," *Vital STATS,* November 1998, p. 2.

Percentage of water sources judged to be poor or severe by the Council on Environmental Quality falling from 30 percent in 1961 to less than 5 percent today from Council on Environmental Quality, op. cit.

Number of Americans served by wastewater treatment plants since 1960 rising from 22 to 70 percent today from U.S. Environmental Protection Agency, Office of Wastewater Management.

Industrial water pollution plummeting since 1980 from Council on Environmental Quality, op. cit.

In 1994, 86 percent of U.S. rivers and streams were usable for swimming and fishing, and 91 percent of U.S. lakes were also safe from CEQ, *Annual Report,* various years.

70. *Fewer Oil Spills*

Quote from Stan Senner regarding the Exxon Valdez accident from Traci Watson, "Wildlife Recovering from Exxon Spill," *USA Today,* Thursday, February 11, 1999, p. 3A.

Quote from Steve Hayward showing the comparison between the amount of oil-based products poured down the drain each year by American households and the amount spilled into Prince William Sound during the Exxon Valdez accident from Steve Hayward and Laura Jones, *Index of Environmental Indicators, 1998,* p. 23.

71. *The Energy Efficient Society*

Quote from the National Center for Policy Analysis saying that the amount of energy needed to produce a dollar of GNP has been steadily declining at a 1 percent rate each year since 1929 from "Progressive Environmentalism: A Pro-Human, Pro-Science, Pro-Free Enterprise Agenda for Change," Task Force Report, National Center for Policy Analysis, Dallas.

North Korea using three times as much energy to produce a dollar output than does South Korea from ibid.

Fuel efficiency of new cars rising from about 15 miles per gallon in 1940 to 21 today from *Statistical Abstract of the United States,* various years.

Amount of energy recovery through incineration skyrocketing by 800 percent between 1960 and 1990 from Steve Hayward and Laura Jones, *Index of Leading Environmental Indicators,* Pacific Research Institute, April 1998.

Section XV. Natural Resources: An Age of Abundance

Summary

World running out of energy, food, forests, and minerals from *Limits to Growth,* Club of Rome, 1972, and *Global 2000,* Carter Administration, 1980.

Quote from the Office of Technology Assessment saying that the nation has never been in better shape facing the costs of natural resources from Office of Technology Assessment, *Technology and the American Economic Transition,* Washington, 1988.

72. *The Green Revolution Proves Malthus Wrong*

Quote from British economist Thomas Malthus saying that food supplies would run out for mankind, *Essay on the Principles of Population.*

Over the past 50 years food production has grown 40 percent from Food and Agriculture Organization.

Scientists say world could feed another billion people with existing knowledge and farm capacity from *Forbes,* November 16, 1998, page 36.

73. *Minerals and Metals: The End of Scarcity*

Cost of a ton of copper about a 10th now of its cost 200 years ago from U.S. Geological Survey, *Commodity Statistics,* various years.

74. *The Age of Cheap and Abundant Energy*

Quote from President Jimmy Carter saying that all of the oil reserves in the entire world could be used up by the end of the 1980s from Christopher Byron, "Yes, There Is an Energy Crisis," *Time,* October 10, 1977, p. 62.

Oil today about five times cheaper than in 1900 from Department of Energy, *Annual Energy Review,* various years.

75. *Gaining Ground: The False Threat of Lost Land*

From 1960 to 1990 the number of acres classified as "urban land" more than doubling from Council on Environmental Quality, *Annual Report,* various years.

Rate at which land being converted to suburban development about 0.0006 percent per year from *Policy Review,* September/October 1998, p. 29.

Quote from Pacific Research Institute from Steven Hayward, Elizabeth Fowler, and Erin Schiller, *Index of Leading Environmental Indicators,* Pacific Research Institute, April 1999.

76. *More Trees and Forests*

Forest Service reporting that the United States is growing about 22 million net new cubic feet of wood a year and harvesting only 16.5 million from "The Great Forest Debate," *Reader's Digest,* November 1993, vol. 143, no. 859, p. 125.

For information documenting the improvement in the inventory of U.S. forests see Roger A. Sedjo and Marion Clawson, "Global Forests Revisted," in *The State of Humanity,* pp. 328–45.

Section XVI. Social and Cultural Indicators

Summary

United States experiencing social and cultural retrenchment from Pat Buchanan, Rush Limbaugh, and William Bennett's book, *The Index of Leading Cultural Indicators* (New York: Broadway Books, 1999).

77. *Thank You for Not Smoking: Americans Quit the Habit*

Cigarette sales falling 20 percent in past decade from U.S. Department of Agriculture Economic Research Service, *Tobacco Situation and Outlook Report,* various years.

Percentage of pregnant women who smoke down from 20 percent in 1989 to 14 percent today from *Health, United States, 1998.*

78. *Alcohol Abuse on the Wane*

Quote from James Roberts arguing that alcohol consumption generally a product of growing prosperity rather than index of social misery from *The State of Humanity,* p. 118.

Quote from Dwight B. Heath showing that only about 10 percent of drinkers suffer in any respect from drinking from *Wall Street Journal,* February 25, 1985.

Percentage of Americans who say alcohol has been a source of trouble in their families declining from more than one-third in 1950 to one-sixth today from

USA Today, December 31, 1999.
Long-term trend in fatalities due to drunk driving trending downward from Lawrence A. Greenfeld, *Alcohol and Crime: An Analysis of National Data on the Prevalence of Alcohol Involvement in Crime*, Bureau of Justice Statistics, Washington, April 5–7, 1998.

79. Volunteerism in America

Climb in personal involvement of time in serving needs of other people from Everett Carll Ladd, "Volunteering in America: The Cast Has Changed, but the Levels Are Up," *Philanthropy*, May/June 1999, pp. 24–26.

80. The Most Generous Society Ever

Charitable giving as a share of gross domestic product rising from 1.7 percent in 1960 to 2.2 percent of incomes in the 1990s from American Association of Fund-Raising Counsel Trust for Philanthropy.

81. A Symphony of Music

Percentage of Americans who listen to classical music rising from 19 percent in 1982 to 41 percent today from Douglas A. Blackmon, "Forget the Stereotype: America Is Becoming a Nation of Culture," *Wall Street Journal*, September 17, 1998, p. A1.

Quote from Tyler Cowen showing Americans have far more classical music selections to choose from than ever before from Tyler Cowen, "Is Our Culture in Decline?" *Cato Policy Report*, September/October 1998, vol. 20, no. 5, p. 1.

82. America's Cultural Resurgence

Quote from Edmund Burke describing culture as something that raises life above merely surviving from Mark L. Melcher, "Left of Nero," *Strategy Weekly*, January 7, 1998, p. 34.

Theater Communications Group in New York saying there are now more than 800 nonprofit professional theater companies in the United States compared with 60 in 1965 from Blackmon, "Forget the Stereotype."

Opera attendance in 1997 tripling the 2.5 million attendance in 1970 from "Renaissance in the Arts," *Megatrends 2000*, p. 50.

Between 1965 and 1990, museum attendance rising from 200 million to 500 million from "Renaissance in the Arts," p. 76.

Private philanthropic sector contributed more than $1 billion to the arts in 1990, up from $22 million in 1967 from ibid.

Between 1950 and 1995 the number of symphony orchestras in the United States nearly doubling from American Symphony Orchestra League.

83. A Century of Reading

Number of books sold rising by 50 percent from 1975 to 1997 from U.S. Bureau of the Census.

Average American buying twice as many books today as in 1950 and 50 percent more than in 1900 from U.S. Bureau of the Census.

Ten times as many book stores today as in 1950 from Tyler Cowen, "Is Our Culture in Decline?" *Cato Policy Report*, September/October 1998, vol. 20, no. 5, p. 1.

Section XVII. Human Achievement in Sports

84. Faster: The 4-Minute Mile and Other Milestones

Fastest recorded time in the mile less than 3:50 minutes from Gary M. Krebs, ed., *The Guiness Book of Sports Records, 1995–1996* (New York: Facts on File, 1995).

85. Female Athletes Shatter Sports Records

Twenty-five years ago top women runners crossing the tape about 30–40 minutes behind the men in the marathon, but now the female winner only about 15 minutes behind the male winner from Howard Wainer, "Sex and Sports," *Intellectual Capital.com*, November 12, 1998.

86. The Sporting, Physically Fit Society

Amount of time Americans spend on fitness and sports roughly tripling since 1965 from National Sporting Goods Association, *The Sporting Goods Market in 1996* (Mt. Prospect, Ill.: NSGA, 1996).

Percentage of Americans working out daily rising from 24 to 60 percent since 1960 from "How We've Changed," *USA Today*, December 31, 1999.

Spending by American households on personal care increasing more than six-fold since 1900 from *Statistical Abstract of the United States*, various years.

Number of golfers in the world drastically increasing since the 1960s from James P. Sterba, "Playing the Lie: Golf Is Booming—Except That It Isn't, Unless You Count TV," *Wall Street Journal*, April 13, 2000, p. A1.

Women now spending more than three times as many hours a week in sports/outdoor activities as they did in 1965 from John Robinson of the University of Maryland.

Section XVIII. The Remarkable Gains by Women

Summary

Quote from John Tierney regarding the "gap" between one group and another from John Tierney, "The Optimists Are Right," op. cit.

Quote from Gertrude Thayer in 1899 regarding the gains she hoped women would make in the 20th century from *USA Today*, December 31, 1999, p. 31A.

In 1960s and 1970s, many women wearing famous buttons reading "59 cents," said to be the amount that women earned for every dollar earned by a man from Francine D. Blau, "Trends in the Well-Being of American Women, 1970–1995," Working Paper 6206, National Bureau of Economic Research, Cambridge, Massachusetts, October 1997.

87. Liberating Women from Housework

Amount of time women chained to domestic housework tumbling in 20th century by almost half from Cox and Alm, Federal Reserve Board of Dallas, op. cit. Since 1970, a small but noticeable reallocation of housework between husbands and wives from Francine D. Blau, "Trends in the Well-Being of American Women, 1970–1995," op. cit.

Only 62 percent of husbands helping with housework in 1950; now 85 percent doing so from *USA Today*, December 31, 1999.

88. Economic Equality in the Workplace

Before 1850 women making about 40 cents for every dollar earned by men in the same professions, but that gap closing to 65 cents per dollar by 1950, and today pay nearly equal from *Journal of Economic Literature*, vol. 29, September 1991, p. 34, and *Women's Figures* (Washington: American Enterprise Institute, 1999).

Quote from Congressional Budget Office director June O'Neill saying that when earning comparisons are drawn between men and women more similar in experience and life situations, the differentials are minimal from Diana Furchtgott-Roth and Christine Stolba, *Women's Figures*, op.cit., p. xvii.

89. The Rise of the Female Entrepreneur and CEO

Between 1972 and 1997 the number of female-owned businesses increasing from 1 million to 8.5 million from Diana Furchtgott-Roth and Christine Stolba, *Women's Figures*, op. cit., p. 94.

The 8.5 million women-owned businesses employing nearly 24 million workers and generating about $3 trillion in sales from ibid.

More than 80 percent of Fortune 500 firms now having women on their boards of directors from "Women and Work Survey," *The Economist*, July 18, 1998, p. 10.

Number of female vice presidents of major companies doubling over the decade of 1985–95 from Stephan Thernstrom, Fred Siegel, and Robert Woodson Sr., "The Kerner Commission Report and the Failed Legacy of Liberal Social

Policy," The Heritage Foundation, *Heritage Lectures*, June 24, 1998, no. 619.

90. *The Educated Woman*
Today, women more likely to attend college than are men from *Women's Figures*, op. cit. In 1950 half of American female workers having a high school degree, now 90 percent having one from *Women's Figures*.

Section XIX. The Decline of Racism

Summary
Quote from the Kerner Commission in 1968 regarding the opinion that the nation is moving toward two societies separate and unequal from Stephan Thernstrom, Fred Siegel, and Robert Woodson Sr., "The Kerner Commission Report and the Failed Legacy of Liberal Social Policy," The Heritage Foundation, *Heritage Lectures*, June 24, 1998, no. 619.

91. *No More Racial Terrorism*
In late 19th century hundreds of lynchings occurring every year, but in recent decades virtually no lynchings from *Historical Statistics of the United States*, Series H 1168–1170, p. 422.

92. *Huge Economic Gains for Black Americans*
Since 1900, per capita income for black Americans increasing from below $1,500 to $9,000 from Robert Higgs, *Competition and Coercion: Blacks in the American Economy, 1865–1914* (New York: Cambridge University Press, 1977), and U.S. Bureau of the Census, *Measuring 50 Years of Economic Change* (Washington: Government Printing Office, 1998).

Poverty rate among blacks estimated at about 80 percent before the 1940s, but today at only 25 percent of blacks from "The Standard of Living of Black Americans," by Robert Higgs and Robert Margo, in *The State of Humanity*, p. 183.

In 1900 only about 25 percent of blacks owning their own home, but today nearly half of black families as homeowners from U.S. Bureau of the Census, *Measuring 50 Years of Economic Change, 1998*.

93. *Moving toward a Colorblind Society*
In 1900, black earnings relative to whites only about 15 percent from Robert Higgs and Robert Margo, "The Standard of Living of Black Americans," in *The State of Humanity*, p. 183.

Quote from Robert Higgs of the Independent Institute and Robert Margo of Vanderbilt University regarding the fact that increasing over the long run average black income much faster than average white income from ibid.

In 1967 average black woman earning 79 percent of white woman's income, but today up to 95 percent, and in 1967 black male earnings at 57 percent of those of white men, but by 1997 up to 69 percent from U.S. Bureau of the Census, op. cit.

94. *Getting Along with Each Other: Race Relations*
Quote from W. E. B. Du Bois at the turn of the 20th century predicting that United States would struggle for years to overcome its homespun system of legal apartheid from Ellis Cose, "Our New Look: The Colors of Race," *Newsweek*, January 1, 2000, p. 28.

Quote from Stephan and Abigail Thernstrom of the Manhattan Institute regarding the much higher proportion of black and white people with a "good friend" of the other race since 1975 from "We Have Overcome," *National Review*, October 13, 1997.

Level of bigotry lower in United States than in many nations supposedly racially tolerant from Times Mirror Center, "The Pulse of Europe, 1991," as printed in *American Enterprise*, November/December 1998, p. 18.

95. *Minority Gains in Health and Education*
Almost 20 percent of adult blacks earning a college degree and that percentage

still rapidly rising, U.S. Bureau of the Census.

Since 1920, median years of schooling for 25 to 29 year olds rising from 8 years to 12 from U.S. Bureau of the Census.

XX. Freedom and Democracy

Summary

At least 200 million people perishing as a consequence of brutality in the 20th century, from Freedom House, *Freedom of the World Index* (Washington: Freedom House, 1999), and "A Survey of the 20th Century," *The Economist*, September 11, 1999.

The proportion of the world's population living in freedom the highest in the history of the survey from Freedom House, *Freedom of the World Index*, and "A Survey of the 20th Century," *The Economist*, September 11, 1999.

96. *The Relentless March toward Freedom*

Quote from Stanley Engerman noting that in the late 18th century 95 percent of people either slaves or tyrants, *The State of Humanity*, pp. 171–77.

Quote from Adam Smith in 1762 estimating that slavery had been abolished in only a small part of Europe from Paul Bairoch, *Economics and World History* (Chicago: The University of Chicago Press, 1995), paperback edition.

Steady decline in slavery from 1750 through the end of the 20th century from authors' calculations based on various years of data.

In 1950 more than one-third of the world's population living under Marxist-Leninist regimes compared with 2 to 3 percent today from Freedom House, op. cit.

97. *The Diffusion of Democracy and Human Rights*

Quote from *The Economist* explaining democracy taking precedence today because people want to stop unaccountable authority from Freedom House, *Freedom of the World Index*, and "A Survey of the 20th Century," op. cit.

Democracy spreading from 12 percent of the world population to 63 percent today from Freedom House, op. cit.

Percentage of people living in nations that are free or partly free rising from 58 to 67 percent since 1981 from Freedom House, op. cit.

98. *The Expansion of Free Trade Promotes Prosperity*

Average tariff on imports falling from between 40 and 50 percent in the early part of the 19th century to 20 percent in 1900 to less than 5 percent today from Paul Bairoch, *Economics and World History,* op. cit.

Wave of protectionism in 1929 as an instigator of the great stock market crash from Jude Wanniski, *The Way the World Works* (Washington: Regnery, 1998).

Section XXI. The American People: The World's Greatest Resource

Summary

Quote from Paul Johnson noting that Americans are the first and best hope of the human race from Paul Johnson, *A History of the American People* (New York: HarperCollins, March 1999).

99. *A Nation of Immigrants: The Melting Pot Still Works*

Immigrants adding about $10 billion each year to the size of the economy from National Research Council, National Academy of Sciences, *The New Americans: Economic, Demographic, and Fiscal Effects of Immigration* (Washington: National Academy Press, 1997).

100. *The Greatest Trend of All: 270 Million Americans and Growing*

Fertility rates falling all over the world from National Geographic Society.

If every family in the United States to move to Texas, still enough room for every household to have about 5 acres of land from Population Research Institute.

Index

Human welfare
  gains for Americans, 1–2
  world trends and pursuit of
    improvement in, 1–2
Hunger
  effect of lower food costs on incidence
    of, 52
  historical incidence of, 49
  reduction in America, 196
  See also Famine
Hygiene, 46

Immigrants
  contributions to American way of
    life, 12, 261
  impact on U.S. economic growth, 262
Income
  inequality now and in the past, 21
  of median family in United States, 62
  mobility in United States, 78
  racial gap, 11, 246
  rise in noncash, 100
  See also Wages
Income per capita
  at beginning of 20th century, 8, 11
  for black Americans, 244
  Canada, Germany, and Japan, 60
  gains in developing countries, 8, 18
  increase in, 8
  as indicator of improved well-being,
    3-4
  relation to literacy, 166
Industrial sector
  air and water pollution caused by, 5
  electric power used in, 124
Information
  Internet as tool to access, 156
  potential information underclass, 154
  using a computer to process, 152
Internet, 154, 156
Inventions
  computer, 183
  diffusion rates of, 146
  in early part of 20th century, 6, 146
  modern household appliances and
    amenities, 117, 122, 232
  during 19th century, 3
  revolutionizing progress, 6–7
  See also Technology
Isaacson, Walter, 1

Jobs, Steve, 151
Johnson, D. Gale, 8
Johnson, Paul, 261
Johnson, Theodore J., 64
Jordan, Michael, 6

Kerner Commission, 241
Knowledge
  medicine, 32
  scientific, 148
Kolata, Gina, 36
Kuznets, Simon, 57

Ladd, Everett Carl, 212
Land
  concerns related to use of, 202
  forests throughout world, 204
  protected and converted, 202
Lebergott, Stanley, 52
Leisure time
  of American worker, 98
  estimated lifetime, 9, 106
  free time (1965–85), 106
  See also Entertainment
Life expectancy
  at beginning of 20th century, 4–5, 7,
    26
  for blacks, 250
  in developing countries, 26
  in free countries, 13
  improvements permitting longer, 26
  increase in, 25
  as indicator of improved well-being,
    3-4
  rise in poor countries, 4
  in Russia and China, 13
Limits to Growth (Club of Rome), 20,
    151, 195, 200
Lincoln, Abraham, 78
Lindbergh, Charles, 138
Literacy rates
  present-day illiteracy in United
    States, 10, 166
  rise in, 159
  in United States and worldwide, 166
Living standards
  changes in industrialized economies
    (1900–98), 60
  contribution of American worker's
    productivity to, 96
  current, 100
  future visions at beginning of 20th
    century, 5–6
  historically slow gains in, 2–3
  improvement in (1950s, 1960s), 100
  of poor people, 76
  preconditions for increasing, 92
  rapid gains in 20th-century, 3–4
  in United States, 57, 60, 76, 108
Lynchings, 5

McGwire, Mark, 223

290

living standard in United States
   for, 76
nutrition levels for children, 52
ownership, 76, 132
pre-1900 in America, 74
Population
   change in average height of people
      in, 54
   Malthus's forecast of growth in, 19
   reason for growth of, 3
Poverty
   as cause of death in America, 171
   decline during 20th century, 74
   in early 20th century, 6
   present-day definition, 76
   rates during Great Depression, 74
   recipe to avoid, 74
   reduction in United States, 9
   trends in income poverty in United
      States, 73
   in United States in 19th century, 8-9
Productivity
   agricultural, 92, 94, 96
   of American worker, 96
   contribution of computer to, 152
   effect of improvements in, 91
   with electrification, 124
   of European and Asian workers, 96
   of European farmer, 94
   gains in American farm, 94
   reflected in increase in real wages,
      100
   with use of electric motors, 124
Progress
   with beginning of industrial age, 3
   doomsday predictions of Club of
      Rome report, 20, 151, 195
   doomsday predictions of *Global 2000*
      report, 20, 195
   education required for, 159
   future sustainable, 23–24
   influence of freedom on, 11–16
   irreversible gains, 17
   Malthus's prediction and reversal
      related to, 19–20
Prowse, Michael, 23
Publishing trends, 220

Race relations, United States, 248
Racism
   decline in racial terrorism, 242
   decline of, 241
Radio
   as entertainment, 105, 114
   music on, 216
Reagan, Ronald, 195

Recreation and leisure
   increase in spending for, 9
   more time for, 105
Rector, Robert, 52
Regulation
   credited with economic gains, 14–15
   of drug industry, 15
   effect of heavy burden of, 15
   of energy, 195
   See also Deregulation
Retsinas, Nicholas, 118
Rickey, Branch, 241
Riis, Jacob, 120
Risks, catastrophic, 171, 176, 178
Roberts, James, 210
Robinson, Jackie, 241
Robinson, John, 106, 228
Rogers, Will, 24
Roosevelt, Franklin Delano, 261
Rubenstein, Ed, 108
Ryan, Jim, 224

Safety
   fears related to natural environment,
      176
   food safety, 49
   in modern technology, 171, 172
   occupational, 15, 174
   of transportation and travel, 140
   workplace measures for, 174
Sakata, Bob, 94
Samuelson, Robert J., 8, 82
Schmidt, Eric, 156
School enrollment
   decline in dropout rates, 162
   increases at college level, 164
   increases in, 160
   years of schooling and Americans
      enrolled, 160, 162
Schools
   declining quality of U.S. public, 166,
      168
   private investment in alternative, 168
   public charter schools, 168
   school choice programs, 168
Schor, Juliet B., 105
Scientific journals, 148
Scientists, 148
Sedjo, Roger A., 204
Semiconductor. *See* Microchip, or
   semiconductor
Sen, Amartya, 15
Siegel, Jeremy, 66
Sigerist, Henry, 7
Simon, Julian, 14, 20
Slavery, 254

Slesnick, Daniel T., 74
Smith, Adam, 3, 76, 254
Smoking, 86, 207, 208
Socialism, 12
Social trends, 19
Space
  chronology of exploration of, 142–43
  tourism industry, 142
Spencer, Peter, 172
Spending
  for books and magazines, 220
  by government in United States and Europe, 19
  for personal care, 46
  for recreation and entertainment, 9, 105
  on toys and sports equipment, 84
  in United States for scientific research, 148
Spielberg, Steven, 176
Sports
  Americans participating in, 228
  female athletes, 226
  human achievement in, 223
  track and field, 224
Stalin, Josef, 16
Statism, 15–16
Stock market, 66, 68, 70

Taxes, higher U.S., 18
Technology
  air conditioning, 112
  contributes to improved environment, 183
  contribution to mining and excavation, 198
  contribution to productivity, 91, 96
  fear of, 171
  impact on quality of life, 21
  invention of electric light bulb, 126
  motion picture, 105, 114
  radio, 105, 114
  refrigerators and freezers, 112
  safety aspects of, 171, 172
  telephone, 129, 130
  television, 105, 114
  transoceanic fiber-optic cables, 130
  See also Biotechnology
Teenagers
  incidence of drinking, smoking, and drug use, 86
  incidence of pregnancy among, 88
Telegraph, 129
Telephone
  development of use of, 130
  transition from telegraph to, 129

Television
  cable television, 114
  as entertainment, 105, 114
Thayer, Gertrude, 231
Thernstrom, Abigail, 244, 248
Thernstrom, Stephan, 244, 248
Thomas, Clarence, 242
Thomas, Lewis, 22
Tierney, John, 231
Time
  decline in number of hours of work, 98
  hours worked to buy consumer products, 108
  hours worked to earn money to buy food, 52
  trend in women's use of, 231, 232
  See also Leisure time; Recreation and leisure; Work
Tocqueville, Alexis de, 12, 212
Totalitarianism, 12, 254
Trade
  open and free, 258
  worldwide reductions in barriers to, 258
Transportation
  changes in modes of, 10
  choices among modes of, 136
  improved safety of, 140
  quality and cost of present-day, 129
  reduced costs of, 136
  See also Automobiles; Space; Travel
Travel
  air travel, 134, 136, 140
  auto, 140
  improved safety of, 140
  international, 138
  mortality rates related to, 172
  in space, 142
  speed of, 136
Trends
  air quality improvements, 184, 186
  in book publishing, 220
  in economic growth, 8
  improvement in measurable, 21
  in income poverty in United States, 73
  in quality of U.S. education, 19
  in women's use of time, 231, 232

United States
  contributions of immigrants, 12, 261
  demographic changes, 261
  economic growth (1850–1950), 60
  as economic superpower, 60
  financial wealth in, 68

293

Cato Institute

Founded in 1977, the Cato Institute is a public policy research foundation dedicated to broadening the parameters of policy debate to allow consideration of more options that are consistent with the traditional American principles of limited government, individual liberty, and peace. To that end, the Institute strives to achieve greater involvement of the intelligent, concerned lay public in questions of policy and the proper role of government.

The Institute is named for *Cato's Letters*, libertarian pamphlets that were widely read in the American Colonies in the early 18th century and played a major role in laying the philosophical foundation for the American Revolution.

Despite the achievement of the nation's Founders, today virtually no aspect of life is free from government encroachment. A pervasive intolerance for individual rights is shown by government's arbitrary intrusions into private economic transactions and its disregard for civil liberties.

To counter that trend, the Cato Institute undertakes an extensive publications program that addresses the complete spectrum of policy issues. Books, monographs, and shorter studies are commissioned to examine the federal budget, Social Security, regulation, military spending, international trade, and myriad other issues. Major policy conferences are held throughout the year, from which papers are published thrice yearly in the *Cato Journal*. The Institute also publishes the quarterly magazine *Regulation*.

In order to maintain its independence, the Cato Institute accepts no government funding. Contributions are received from foundations, corporations, and individuals, and other revenue is generated from the sale of publications. The Institute is a nonprofit, tax-exempt, educational foundation under Section 501(c)3 of the Internal Revenue Code.

Cato Institute
1000 Massachusetts Ave., N.W.
Washington, D.C. 20001